BEEHIVE DWELLINGS
OF THE HEBRIDES

BEEHIVE DWELLINGS
OF THE HEBRIDES

A PHOTOGRAPHIC RECORD

MARC CALHOUN

Registered Charity SC047866
Scottish Charity Regulator

First published in 2021 by Acair,
An Tosgan, Seaforth Road, Stornoway, Isle of Lewis, Scotland HS1 2SD

info@acairbooks.com
www.acairbooks.com

Text, photographs, and maps © Marc Calhoun unless indicated otherwise, 2021

Text and drawings attributed to Elspeth Logan © Elspeth Logan – used with permission, 2021

The rights of Marc Calhoun to be identified as the author, of this work have been asserted in accordance with Section 77 of the Copyright, Designs and Patents Act 1988.
All rights reserved.

No part of this publication may be reproduced, stored in a retrieval system nor reproduced or transmitted by any means, electronic, mechanical, photocopying or otherwise, without the prior permission of the publisher.

Cover and interior design by Joan MacRae-Smith for Acair

A CIP catalogue record for this title is available from the British Library.

Printed by Hussar Books, Poland

ISBN: 978-1-78907-077-4

Exploring the Isles of the West
Journeys to the Beehive Dwellings of the Hebrides
— A Photographic Record —

Marc Calhoun

For my wife, Shawna, who has spent many an hour dropping me off for walks to find beehive cells in remote parts of the Hebrides, and then waited patiently for me to return days later. She always worries I'll get lost, break a leg, fall off a cliff, sink in a bog, or be eaten by midges. I have been dined on by midges—they do seem to like A positive—but none of the others have happened, yet.

Contents

Acknowledgments xiii

A few words of caution..xiv

Definitions/Acronyms...xv

The Beehive Dwellings of the Hebrides 2

Section 1 – Cnoc Dubh..8

Section 2 – Southwest Lewis..13

    2.1 Journey to Aird Bheag..15

        2.1.1 Airighean Tighe Dhubhastail 16

        2.1.2 Loch an Ath Ruaidh 25

        2.1.3 Bothan Aird 39

        2.1.4 Bothan Ura 48

        2.1.5 Gearraidh Cleit Gruineabhat..52

        2.1.6 Ceann Chùisil 56

        2.1.7 Gearraidh Aineabhal 58

    2.2 Journey to Fidigidh 69

        2.2.1 Gearraidh Bheinn na Gile...71

        2.2.2 Gearraidh Uidh Phàil 75

        2.2.3 Fidigidh Iochdrach 80

        2.2.4 Both Ruadh 85

        2.2.5 Fidigidh Uachdrach 88

        2.2.6 Bothan Mileabhat 97

        2.2.7 Both Cleit na Crich 101

    2.3 Journey to Aird Mhòr 104

        2.3.1 Loch na h-Airigh 106

        2.3.2 Gearraidh na h-Airde Mhòire...109

        2.3.3 Màghannan 122

        2.3.4 Airidh a' Loch Thaine 125

2.4 Loch a' Sguair Loop 128
    2.4.1 Tom Ni Bharabhais 129
    2.4.2 Airigh a' Sguair 130
    2.4.3 Gearraidh Coire Geurad 140
    2.4.4 Gleann Marstaig 147
    2.4.5 Airigh Creagan nam Beartan 149
2.5 Bo'h Hunting in Morsgail 151
    2.5.1 Gearraidh Ascleit 152
    2.5.2 Airigh a' Chlàir Mhòir 162
    2.5.3 Both a' Chlàir Bhig 166
2.6 Return to Beinn a' Bhoth 173
    2.6.1 Beinn a' Bhoth 174
    2.6.2 Both a' Ghriosamul 177

Section 3 – Harris and North Uist 182
3.1 Bothan Sròn Smearasmal – Harris 183
3.2 Dun Charaigearaidh – North Uist 187

Section 4 – Inner Hebrides 192
4.1 Eileach an Naoimh – Garvellachs 193
4.2 Allt nam Bà – Islay 198
4.3 Port nan Urrachann – Scarba 204
4.4 Gleann Chàràdail – Eigg 207
4.5 Sgòrr nam Bàn-naomha – Canna 212

Section 5 – Remote Outliers 217
5.1 Rona – Teampull Naoimh Rònain & Fianais 217
5.2 Sùlaisgeir – A Desert Place in the Sea 228
5.3 Calum Mor's House – Hirta, St Kilda 232
5.4 Eilean Mòr – Flannan Isles 234
5.5 Eilean Fir Chrothair 244

Parting Words 248

Appendix A: Cells Unseen 250

Appendix B: Essentials for overnight beehive excursions 253

Appendix C: References 254

Index 260

Acknowledgments

My thanks to Elspeth Logan for allowing me to use previously unpublished beehive cell descriptions and plan drawings, from her 1996 work *A Study of Beehive Structures in the Uig Area of the Isle of Lewis*—one of the most significant studies of these beautiful structures since the days of Captain Thomas (1850s).

My thanks to my sister, Dia Calhoun, for her invaluable editorial comments.

My thanks to my niece, Jessie Ringlien, for her drawings of Cnoc Dubh and Beinn na Gile.

I am grateful to the Society of Antiquaries of Scotland for permission to reproduce the following images:

Section 1: Both Cnoc Dubh
Section 2.1.1: Airighean Tighe Dhubhastail
Section 2.1.2: Bothan Ath Ruaidh (5) and Bothan Aird (1)
Section 2.2.2: Fidigidh Iochdrach
Section 2.3.2: Gearraidh na h-Àirde Mhòire—three views of the 12-chambered cell
Section 2.4.2: Loch a' Sguair Cell 1
Section 2.4.2: Loch a' Sguair Cell 4
Section 2.4.3: Both Coire Geurad
Section 2.4.4: Both at Glen Marstaig
Section 3.1: Bothan Sròn Smearasmal
Section 4.5: The Altar—Canna
Section 5.4: The Three-Chambered Cell—Flannan Isles
Section 5.5: Both Eilean Fir Chrothair.

Also by Marc Calhoun

Exploring the Isles of the West, The Firth of Clyde to the Small Isles (2012), The Islands Book Trust

Exploring the Isles of the West, Skye & Tiree to the Outer Isles (2012), The Islands Book Trust

Exploring the Isles of the West website: www.marccalhoun.blogspot.com

A few words of caution

The maps included here are intended to give an overview of the various walks and site locations. Do not use them for navigation, use the listed Ordnance Survey map. Unless indicated otherwise, all maps are oriented north up.

When venturing into remote areas, in addition to a map, take a compass and know how to use it. A GPS is also invaluable—be sure to have spare batteries. Always let someone know your route, take a first aid kit (with tick extractor), and midge repellent. See Appendix B for a list of beehive-hunting essentials.

Always take a mobile phone, although there is a good chance it won't get a signal. But you may get lucky. I have been able to get a signal from atop Beinisbhal (near Kinlochresort), and the high ground above Aird Bheag.

Be sure to wear gaiters and/or rain pants. In addition to keeping you dry, they keep scratchy twigs of heather, and, more importantly, hungry ticks, from your ankles. Speaking of ticks, check for them every day. They manage to find their thirsty way into the most tender places. Also, be careful when you sit on the moorland to rest (which I do a lot). As you sit, a gap can open between shirt and pants; a gap ready made for hungry ticks to hop into. If that happens, you'll need a very good friend to get them out.

You *will* get ticks. There's no avoiding them. I once discovered a tick had latched onto me during a hike on Lewis, and had gone unnoticed for three days. A few months later I started feeling tired, sore all over, every joint seemed to ache. I thought of that tick, and Lyme disease came to mind. I had the blood test and, fortunately, it was not Lyme disease. As for the tiredness, the aches and pains… it turns out I am getting older.

Then there are Midges—they deserve a capital M. You will come to despise them, dread them, and have no qualms about resorting to chemical warfare to kill as many as you can. In the space of a minute these minuscule vermin can turn a delightful moorland campsite into the pit of Hell. The best precautions are strategic campsite placement, a good bug-net, and a bottle of strong repellent. Campsite placement involves finding a spot that has the chance of getting a steady breeze, but not too exposed such that a gale will blow the tent away. A good bug-net is one that has stretchable under-arm straps that keep your neck area protected, while still allowing you to pull the net up to take a sip of water. As for repellent, I'm a hard-core, full-strength, DEET user. It is nasty stuff, but nothing works better or lasts longer.

Please don't let these words of warning deter you from venturing out in search of beehive cells. These amazing structures are a delight to find, crawl into, and camp next to. And as you do, you will be following in the footsteps of those who, centuries ago, called these wind- and water-proof havens on the moorland, and far-flung isles, home.

Definitions/Acronyms

As shown in this example, each site has an identifier:

Airigh a' Chlàir Mhòir
Landranger Map: 13
Location: NB 12088 16043
CANMORE IDs: 352042 & 133871
Access: A859 at Bogha Glas (NB 1861 1154) – a 12 km walk

The identifier includes the site's name, associated Ordnance Survey (OS) Landranger (1:50000) map, OS grid location, CANMORE ID(s), and nearest public road.

The **location** (OS grid coordinates), in most cases, were measured using a Garmin eTrex, 12-channel GPS. I have listed the locations to the six figures reported by the GPS (indicated position to 1 square metre). That does not mean the positions are accurate to one metre. I did not record the accuracy reported by the GPS at each site, but typically it was ten to twenty metres.

How to use grid the coordinates: Example NB 12088 16043

The first two characters, NB in this example, defines the National Grid 100 km square. For the Hebrides the grid squares range from NA in the far northwest (Flannan Isles) to NR in the southwest (Islay). The outliers of Rona and Sùlaisgeir are on grid HW.

The first set of numbers in the example, **12088**, are the Eastings. The example coordinate is 12,088 metres east of the 00000 horizontal map datum. On the map's horizontal scale locate the '**12**' grid line, then go another 0.088 of a grid line east. This establishes the east/west position.

The second set of numbers in the example, **16043**, are the Northings. The example coordinate is 16,043 metres north of the 00000 vertical map datum. On the map's vertical scale locate the '**16**' grid line, then go another 0.043 of a grid line north. This establishes the north/south position. Where the horizontal and vertical positions intersect defines the location.

CANMORE IDs, where they exist, refer to the site's identification number on the CANMORE website. You can find information on the site by entering the ID number in the website search window (https://canmore.org.uk).

Access typically specifies the nearest starting point(s) for walking to the site from a public road. Unless stated otherwise, the indicated length is the one-way distance.

Acronyms

CANMORE: Online catalogue to Scotland's archeology, buildings, industrial and maritime heritage

OS: Ordnance Survey

PSAS: Proceedings of the Society of Antiquaries of Scotland (http://archaeologydataservice.ac.uk/archives/view/psas/volumes.cfm)

RCAHMS: The Royal Commission on the Ancient and Historical Monuments of Scotland

Important note on the walks: The careful reader will note that in several walks I pass very close to some beehive cell sites without visiting them. In these cases I refer the reader to another journey description where I did visit the bypassed site. The reasons I passed by these sites are that either I did not know of them at the time, I'd seen them before, I did not have the time, or, more likely, the energy to visit them.

Journeys to the Beehive Cell Dwellings of the Hebrides

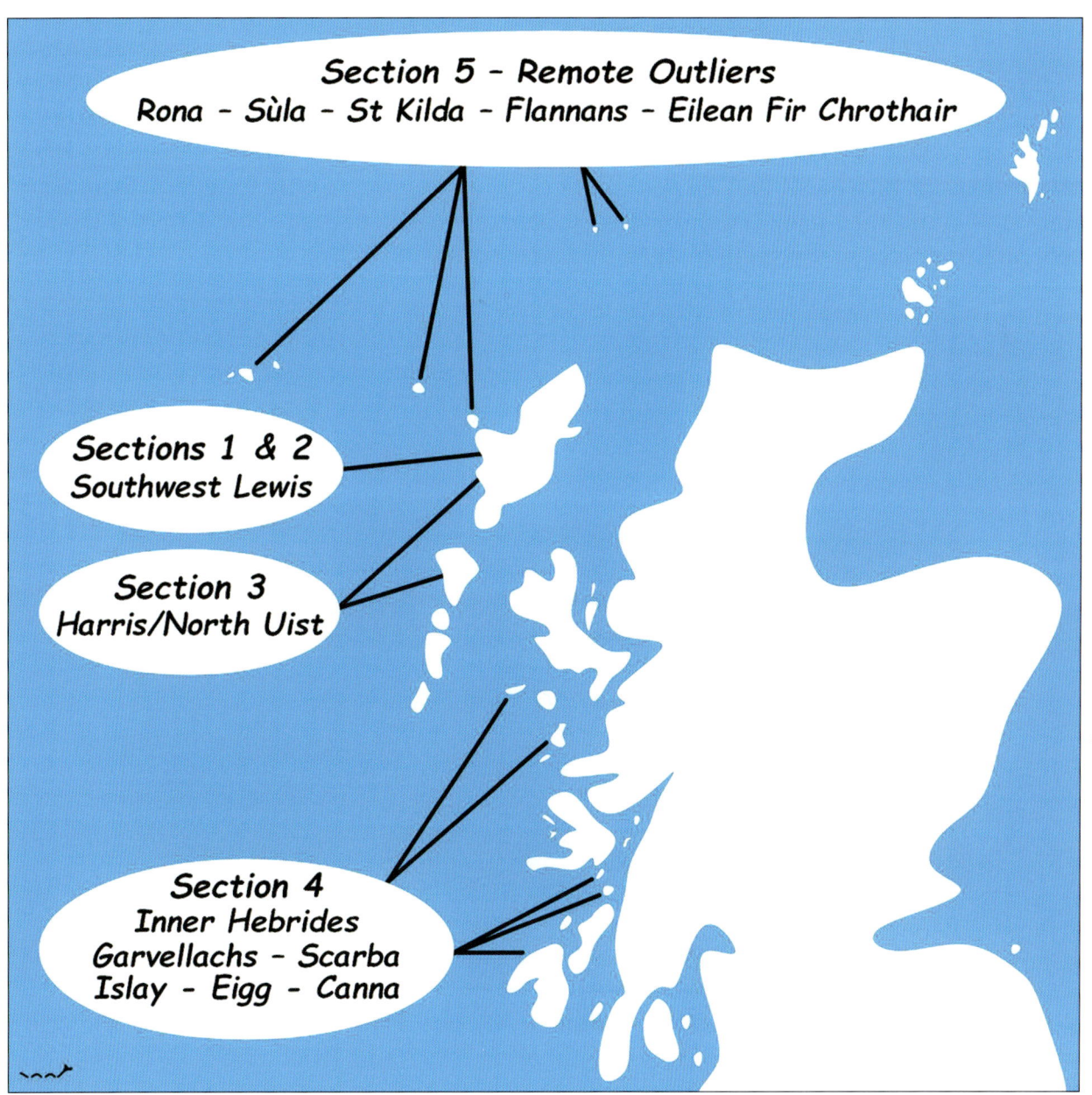

The Beehive Dwellings of the Hebrides

Beehive dwellings, with their beautiful stone-corbelled domes, are remarkable remnants of past ways of life. Ways of life that span 1200 years; from early hunter-gatherers and Celtic Christian monks, to the people of Lewis and Harris, who used them for summer shielings well into the 1800s. That some of these cells survive today is a testament to how well they were constructed, and to their remoteness; a remoteness that has fended off most vandalism, but not all. Some 'well-intentioned' vandalism occurred when, during their survey work, early researchers caused several cells to collapse.

This book recounts journeys to the beehive cells of the Hebrides. It was a visit to the cells of Skellig Michael in Ireland in 1991 that sparked my interest in beehives; a spark that gradually grew, year by year, into a blaze. A blaze I would need to keep me warm over the years while marching across rain-swept bogs in search of cells. (I exaggerate a little for effect, there were more sunny days than rainy ones). I was so touched by their elegance that I started seeking them out, from Islay in the south to Rona in the far north.

Both Cleit na Crich—Isle of Lewis

I am neither an archaeologist, nor a historian. My goal is to record journeys to the cells, and their condition, as I saw them between the years 1997 and 2019. This is by no means a comprehensive compilation of all the cells in the islands. They can be hard to find, and I have walked by several over the years without noticing them. Also, to visit all of the hundreds of shieling sites, to see which have corbelled cells, would take far more than the twenty-two years of adventures recounted here.

The Scottish Gaelic for a beehive cell is *both* (plural *bothan*), sometimes abbreviated as *bo'h*. In Ireland they are referred to as *clochán/cloghaun*, and in some cases *Torthaigh/Tory* (tower house). Many versions of corbelled cells are found in Europe; such as the Borie (France), the Barraca (Spain), the Trullo (Italy), the Girna (Malta), and the Kutja/Hiska in Slovenia. Of all these structures, the Hebridean *Both* may be the least written about. Here is the definition of a beehive from the *RCAHMS Ninth Report with Inventory of Monuments and Constructions in the Outer Hebrides* (1928):

By beehive shielings we mean the small, circular, dry-stone buildings roofed with overlapping slabs so arranged as to form what is known as a 'false arch'. As a form of construction this type of arch is archaic; it was used for roofing the cells of brochs and also for early Christian buildings. But it does not follow that the few examples which still exist are of any great antiquity. Originally the roof was protected by an outer covering of turf, the disappearance of which tends to be followed by a rapid disintegration of the main fabric. They generally stood in small clusters on the old-time airigh or summer pasture, each separate shieling being known simply as bothan or both, a hut. On the average they had an interior diameter of from 7 to 8 feet and were 7 to 8 feet high in the inside, with one or two recesses in the wall.

Regarding their ability to stay dry, this is how Fraser Darling describes their construction in *A Naturalist on Rona*:

There is one art common to the houses on Rona, the beehive shielings and the black houses of the Outer Isles, an art carried intact from the mists of antiquity. It is in the set of the flat stones of which all these buildings are made. Each stone is set highest at its inward edge, so that the slope is downward and outward. If this technique is carried through from floor to roof, it is possible to bank up the outside with turf without any fear of wet trickling to the inside.

Built to survive the centuries, built to keep out wind and rain, built as sturdy as their original inhabitants, these stone igloos are so well constructed that many have survived long after being skinned of their turf coats; be it by weather, grazing sheep, or people. Many had two doorways, that could be blocked off with wicker frames depending on the wind direction. Most had fire spots, and some an adjacent chamber for sleeping or a dairy. Quite a few had two or three-sided porches. Very few had window openings, but all had a capstone, or a rug of turf, that could be removed to allow smoke to escape, and let light in.

Beehives were in use for centuries in the Hebrides, but were only brought to the attention of the public in the 1850s and 60s. Two individuals were primarily responsible: Captain FWL Thomas (1812-1885), and Dr Arthur Mitchell (1826-1909). Captain Thomas (Royal Navy), worked on hydrographic surveys off the west coast of Lewis and Harris; and on a voyage to St Kilda in 1860, took the first known photographs of the island. His work provided opportunities for exploration ashore, and after hearing of a circular stone hut on Harris, near the head of Loch Mhiabhaig, he decided to find it. He failed on the first attempt, but found it on his second. That started his subsequent journeys to, and published descriptions of, the cells of Lewis, Harris and North Uist. Thomas's and Mitchell's reports on the cells can be found in the various Proceedings of the Society of Antiquaries of Scotland (PSAS) volumes referenced in Appendix C.

As for Dr Arthur Mitchell, in 1857, at age 31, he was appointed Deputy Commissioner in Lunacy of the Board of Lunacy for Scotland, and in 1870 became its Commissioner. His obituary states: *Dr Mitchell was an enthusiastic supporter of all views tending to rescue the insane from neglect, and to free them from needless restrictions on their happiness and liberty which had grown round them during ages of ignorance and superstition, and had been followed by acquiescence in evils supposed to be irremediable.*

Dr Mitchell also had a great interest in archeology and anthropology, and was Honorary Secretary to the Society of Antiquaries of Scotland. He became its Vice President in 1882, and in 1886 received the Order of the Companion of the Bath from Queen Victoria. In 1876 he presented his antiquarian research in a series of lectures, which were later published in *The Past in the Present* (1880). In this book, his visits to beehive cells with Captain Thomas are described in a chapter titled *The Black Houses and the Beehive Houses of the Hebrides*.

In the writings of Mitchell and Thomas, we find memorable descriptions of their encounters with people living in beehive cells, such as this from *The Past in the Present*, describing a visit to Tighe Dhubhastail in 1866 (see section 2.1.1):

We found one of these beehive houses actually tenanted, and the family happened to be at home. It consisted of three young women. It was Sunday, and they had made their toilette with care at the burn, and had put on their printed calico gowns. None of them could speak English; but they were not illiterate, for one of them was reading a Gaelic bible. They showed no alarm at our coming, but invited us into the bo'h and hospitably treated us to milk. They were courteously dignified, neither feeling nor affecting to feel embarrassment. There was no evidence of any understanding on their part that we should experience surprise at their surroundings. I do not think I ever came upon a scene which more surprised me, and I scarcely know where or how to begin my description of it.

Little research has been done in the 150 years since Thomas and Mitchell. The one exception I know of being in 1996, when Elspeth Logan, as part of her thesis work, described, and made plan drawings, of over thirty cells in the Uig area of Lewis. Her thesis, *A Study of Beehive Structures in the Uig Area of the Isle of Lewis, Taking into Account Architecturally Similar Structures Within the Western Atlantic Seaboard and Beyond,* is a remarkable look at these long-neglected survivors of times past. Elspeth has allowed me to use her drawings, and descriptions, of the cells of Uig as she saw them in the 1990s.

Were beehives originally built for monastic use, secular dwellings, or both? The cells on the Garvellachs and Rona were certainly monastic. Could some of the cells of Lewis and Harris, latterly used for summer shielings, have been recycled monastic dwellings? In Donald Macdonald's *Tales and Traditions of the Lews* there is an all-too-short chapter dedicated to beehive cells. In it, he says: *These 'boths' were used by the early hunting inhabitants, and then by a semi-pastoral people, who lived for months in them, making butter and cheese, salted for winter use, from the milk of the black Highland cows.*

There are hundreds of these cells in the west of Ireland; some possibly built as accommodation for those making the various pilgrimages in the area. One Irish pilgrimage site, Skellig Michael, stands above all, as it has a stunning collection of intact beehives. The sixth- or seventh-century monastery dramatically clings to the side of a pyramid of stone rising out of the Atlantic, ten kilometres off the coast of Kerry. It was a visit to Skellig that started my own fascination with beehives. Due to their appearance in *Star Wars*, the cells of Skellig Michael have been seen by millions.

The beehives of Skellig Michael

Of all the cells in the UK and Ireland, the most visited is a cluster of six seen by thousands of pilgrims every year in a ritual that has survived the centuries. The cells are on Station Island in Lough Derg, and are the only remnants of the island's sixth century monastery. They are built on the side of a large mound, now topped by a bell tower that marks the site of St Patrick's Purgatory; a cavern where, as one tale goes, Christ showed St Patrick the entrance to hell. But according to Henry of Saltey's *Tracatus de Purgatorio Santi Patricii* (Treatise on St Patrick's Purgatory, c.1152), it was a knight named Owen, not St Patrick, who was led on a journey through heaven and hell during his 24-hour stay in the cave.

Up until the 1700s pilgrims came to the island to spend a night in the cave. In an effort to suppress the pilgrimage the cells were knocked down in 1632; because, as DDC Pochin Mould wrote in *Irish Pilgrimages* (1955):

For the Irish Catholics Lough Derg was the outstanding symbol of their Faith and of that Faith's unbroken links with the past and with the first Irish saints. For the reformers it was the outstanding symbol of Popish superstition and as such to be ended at all costs.

The foundations of the cells were eventually restored. Referred to as the Penitential Beds, they form part of the Station Island pilgrimage today. Shaded by a large sycamore, each cell is named after a saint: Bridget, Brendan, Catherine, Columba, Molaise and Dabeoc (who may have established the monastery). The cells dedicated to Columba and Dabeoc are conjoined, similar to the cells on the Garvellach Islands of Scotland (section 4.1). The pilgrim's ritual around the cells is also described by Pochin Mould in *Irish Pilgrimages*:

At each bed (cell) the pilgrim makes a series of rounds, three times around the outside saying three Paters, three Aves and one Credo; then kneeling at the entry and repeating the same group of prayers; three times round the inside saying them again, and finally kneeling at the cross in the middle and repeating the same group of prayers yet another time. This is done at each bed in the same way, except at the conjoined beehives he goes six times round the outside saying six Paters, six Aves and one Credo.

I visited my first Hebridean cell in 1997, the massive one on Eileach an Naoimh of the Garvellachs. At the time I did not know there were other corbelled cells in the Hebrides. That ignorance came to an end a year later on a wet and blowy Harris day. I was walking from Tarbert to Ardhasaig when a hailstorm blew through. I ran to shelter in a road-side kiosk with displays of things to see in the area. One display described beehive cells, and was illustrated with a drawing of those at Clàr Beag, two kilometres from the head of Loch Reasort. Getting there requires a twelve kilometre hike, which I did the following day. At the site I found a pastoral shieling village centered around something impressive; an elegant pair of beehives, their turf-covered domes fully intact. Upon seeing these beautiful structures I became obsessed with finding more.

The Penitential Beds—the bell tower marks the site of the cave (St Patrick's Purgatory)

Seeking out these cells would become pilgrimages of a sort. If Dr. Arthur Mitchell, that beehive enthusiast and expert on lunacy in the 1880s, was watching me from a distance he might think he was seeing a lunatic. First, he'd notice me drop reverentially to my knees as I approached the cell—exhausted after hours of bog-hopping. Next, he'd watch as I bow down several times while circling the cell—to take pictures. Then the good doctor would wonder what this nut was up to as I kneel at the entrance to the cell, appearing to cross myself as I did—I'd actually be securing the camera so it would not drag on the ground. Finally, scratching his head in puzzlement, Dr. Mitchell would see me lie prostrate in front of the tiny doorway, in a seeming supplication to the saints. He would not be far off the mark here, as I would in fact be praying; praying that I stay dry and sheep-shit free, as I prepare to crawl through the inevitable muck to enter the cell.

Over time many, if not most, beehives have collapsed, and/or been robbed of their stone. It was fortunate the first remote cell I visited—Both a' Chlàir Bhig, the one on that roadside display—was beautifully intact; if it had been a ruin, I would probably not have continued this quest. Another thing I did not know at the time, was that a short distance north of Clàr Beag are the two magnificent double cells of Clàr Mòr. Twenty years would pass before I'd see them. Twenty years of beehive hunting started, and ended, in places only a kilometre apart.

What follows are the stories of journeys to nearly a hundred Hebridean cells; some by boat, most on foot, and one by car. So where should we start? An intriguing question, but an easy one. We'll start on the island of Lewis with a true icon, a cell extensively documented, knocked down, and restored. It is also the one you can drive to. We will start with Cnoc Dubh, on the road to Uig.

Section 1 – Cnoc Dubh

Landranger Map: 13
Location: NB 23195 30193
CANMORE ID: 4175
Access: 200-metre walk (on a track) from the B8011

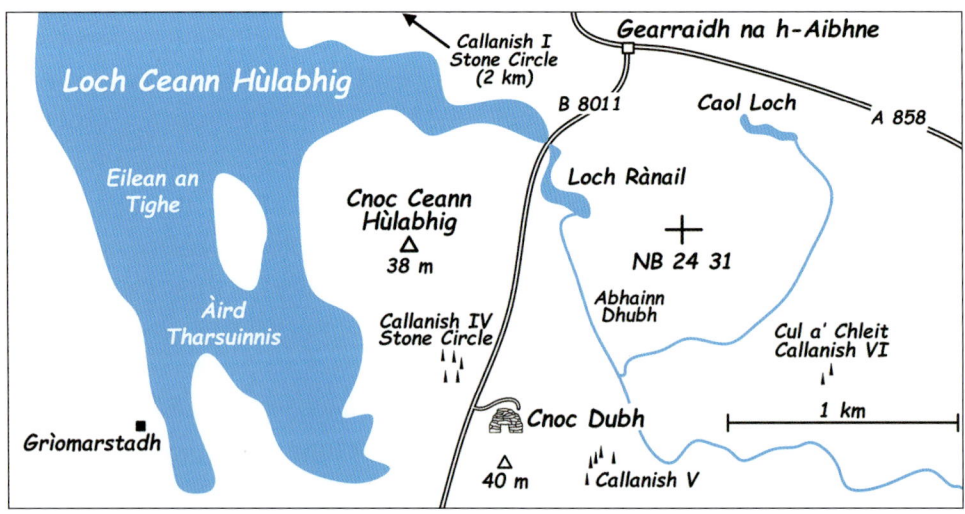

Map 1: Cnoc Dubh

Two miles southeast of the famous Calanais stone circle on the isle of Lewis is one of the most beautiful beehive cells in the Hebrides. It is also the easiest to visit, as it lies on the north side of Cnoc Dubh, a small hill next to the B8011 highway to Uig. The beehive is five meters in diameter, nearly three high, and has a feature unique among all Hebridean cells, a chimney (possibly a later addition).

Both Cnoc Dubh

*Depiction of Cnoc Dubh in the 1930s (Calanais IV on the horizon at left)
Artist Jessie Ringlien—based on a photo in The Hebrides: A Cultural Backwater*

*Both Cnoc Dubh looking west-northwest
(same perspective as the above drawing)*

Cnoc Dubh was surveyed by Captain Thomas. In his report, he says: *It is of a beehive form, about 18 feet in diameter, 9 feet high, and covered with green turf outside. There are two doors opposite to each other, higher (3 feet), and better formed than is usual. Within the chamber is dome-shaped, and is between 7- and 8-feet square on the floor. A row of stones, half a foot in height, cuts off one half of the floor for a bed. There are several small recesses in the wall to serve for cupboards. But what distinguishes this bo'h from all others, is the presence of a chimney over the fire-place. The woman who was living in it told us it was built for his shieling, by Dr Macaulay's grandfather, who was tacksman of Linshader. Dr Macaulay died a few years ago at Liverpool; and I conclude from various circumstances, that this bo'h was made about ninety years back.*

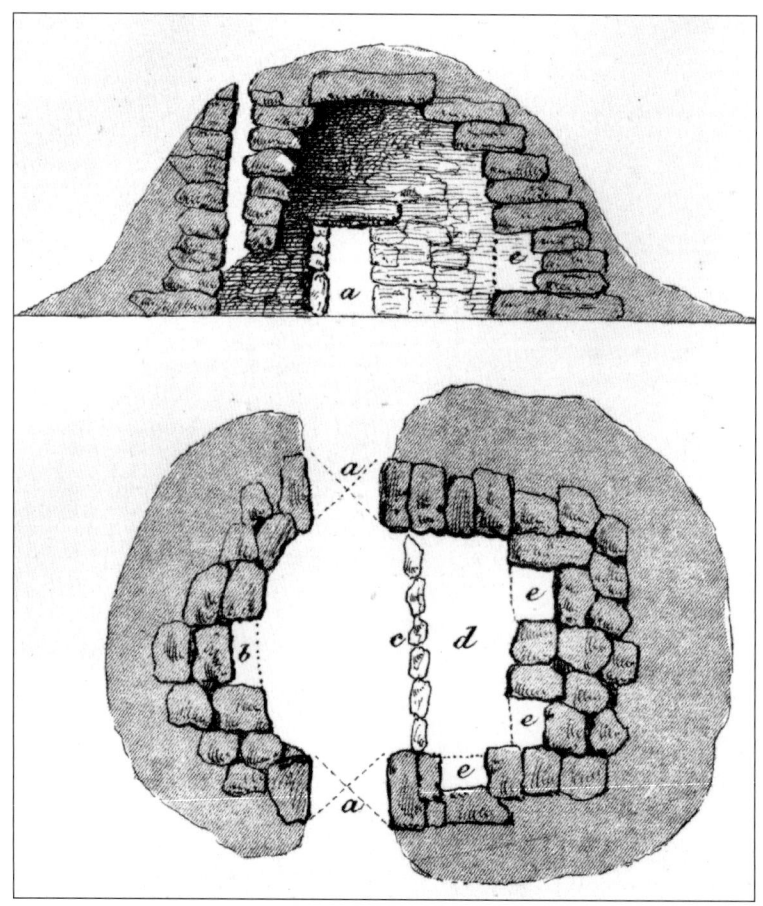

Both, Cnoc Dubh, Capt. Thomas R.N.
Proceedings of the Society of Antiquaries of Scotland, Vol. VII (1866-68)
a = doorways, b = fireplace, c = row of stones separating sleeping area,
d = bed, e = cupboards

Cnoc Dubh stood for centuries, gradually deteriorating to such a precarious state that, sometime in the mid-20th century, parents, fearing their children could get hurt playing there, knocked it down. Fortunately, enough was left to warrant, and guide, reconstruction. In the early 2000s, after much research, and armed with photos and descriptions of how the cell once looked, Seamus Crawford of Lewis restored this beautiful structure. The photographic record of the cell is astounding, hundreds exist, taken from the 1890s to the 1990s.

Top of the dome—Both Cnoc Dubh

The fireplace—Both Cnoc Dubh

Aside from the monastic cells on the Garvellachs, and Calum Mor's House on St Kilda, Cnoc Dubh is constructed of stones much larger than any other Scottish beehive I've encountered. Based on what he was told in the 1860s, Captain Thomas estimated the cell was constructed around 1780—but that date could have been a rebuild. The beehive called Calum Mor's House on St Kilda (see section 5.3) dates to at least 1600. Cnoc Dubh could be as old, if not older.

Cnoc Dubh is set in an ancient ritual landscape. The standing stones of Calanais V lie 350 metres to the southeast, near *Airidh nam Bidearan*, the shieling of the pinnacles. And if you look on the horizon in the drawing of the cell in the 1930s, you can see the stone circle of Calanais IV, which lies across the road, 300 metres to the northwest.

Cnoc Dubh (arrow) seen from the stones of Calanais IV

To visit Cnoc Dubh, park off the B8011 at NB 2308 3024, from where a track climbs the hillside to the east. An easy walk up the track leads to the cell. It is a thing of beauty. With its turf coat firmly intact, it should stand for a few more centuries.

Section 2 – Southwest Lewis

In the Uig, Ardveg, and Morsgail area of Lewis, you will find the greatest concentration of beehive cells in the Hebrides, and as late as the 1850s, twenty were still in use. The cells can be a challenge to find, as they lie in difficult terrain, far from the nearest road. That's the bad news. The good news is that the distances involved often require spending at least one night under the stars, if not two or three.

As shown on Map 2, four of the journeys (2.1, 2.2, 2.3, 2.6) start from the gate of the road to Morsgail Lodge (NB 1391 2374). The other two journeys (2.4, 2.5) cover terrain farther east, and start from the highway near Tom Ni Bharabhais (NB 1547 2516).

Walk 2.1: Journey to Aird Bheag—visits the following sites: Tighe Dhubhastail, Loch an Ath Ruaidh, Bothan Aird, Bothan Ura, Gearraidh Cleit Gruineabhat, Ceann Chùisil, Gearraidh Aineabhal

Walk 2.2: Journey to Fidigidh—visits the following sites: Gearraidh Bheinn na Gile, Fidigidh Iochdrach, Both Ruadh, Fidigidh Uachdrach, Bothan Mileabhat, Both Cleit na Crich

Walk 2.3: Journey to Aird Mhòr—visits the following sites: Loch na Airigh, Gearraidh na h-Airde Mhòire, Màghannan, Loch Tana—also revisits Gearraidh Bheinn na Gile, Loch an Ath Ruaidh, Bothan Aird

Walk 2.4: The Loch a' Sguair Loop—visits the following sites: Tom Ni Bharabhais, Airigh a' Sguair, Gearraidh Coire Geurad, Gleann Marstaig, Airigh Creagan nam Beartan

Walk 2.5: Bo'h Hunting in Morsgail—visits the following sites: Gearraidh Ascleit, Both a' Gharaidh, Airigh a' Chlàir Mhòir, Both a' Chlàir Bhig, and—also revisits Loch a' Sguair, Gearraidh Coire Geurad, Gearraidh Bheinn na Gile

Walk 2.6: Return to Beinn a' Bhoth—visits the following sites: Beinn a' Bhoth, Both a' Ghriosamul—also revisits Gearraidh Bheinn na Gile

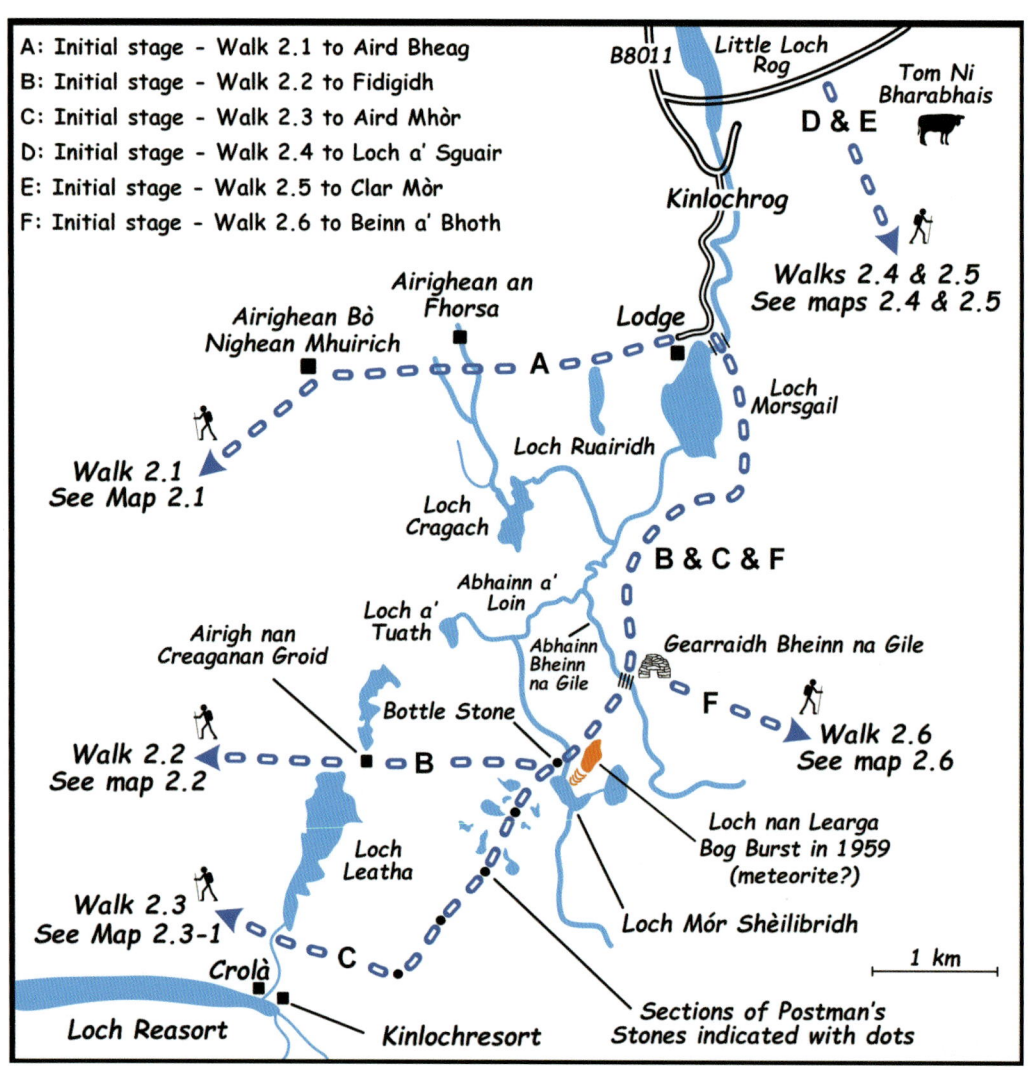

Map 2: Initial stages of Journeys 2.1, 2.2, 2.3, 2.4, 2.5 & 2.6

2.1 Journey to Aird Bheag

Sites visited: Tighe Dhubhastail, Loch an Ath Ruaidh, Bothan Aird, Bothan Ura, Gearraidh Cleit Gruineabhat, Ceann Chùisil, Gearraidh Aineabhal
Total distance: 34 km

A question I'm often asked, is "What's your favourite place in the Hebrides?" It's an easy question. The southwest corner of Lewis: the Morsgail Deer Forest, Uig, and Aird Bheag: the heart of the Hebrides. A vast mix of moorland and hills, full of wildlife, beehive cells, and perfect for solitary wanderings. Over the years I've made many hikes through this remote area, which usually means carrying a tent and sleeping bag, as the best parts are more than a day's walk. This also provides opportunities to sleep under Hebridean stars on open moorland, hilltops, or coastal cliffs, serenaded by barking deer and drumming snipe. It is not paradise by any means, for there are the midges. They can turn a beautiful summer evening into a waking nightmare. But, looking on the bright side, they keep down the crowds.

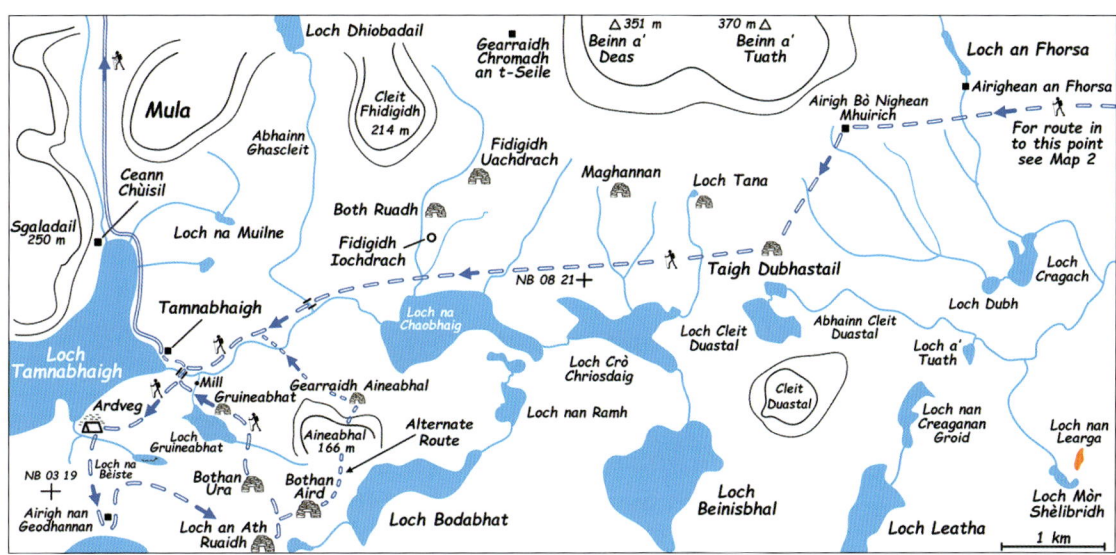

Map 2.1: *Journey to Aird Bheag*

My goal on hikes through this area is to visit the old shieling sites, some with beehive cells, where people migrated with their livestock in summer to take advantage of common grazing land. I set out for a walk in this area in the August of 2016. Hunting season was approaching, so I contacted the Estate Managers for the Morsgail and Hamnaway estates. They told me there'd be no activity on the days I'd be hiking (it's always good to check). I had planned to start on August 7, but on that day a severe windstorm blew through the Highlands and Islands; a storm that caused an oil rig to break its tow and crash ashore on nearby Dalbeag beach. On the following Monday the weather had calmed down, and so I set out on foot down the track to Morsgail Lodge.

See Map 2 for the initial route of this walk (A).

– DAY 1 –

From the track near Morsgail Lodge, I headed west onto the open moorland. Once you start across uneven grass and heather, it can take a while to get up a head of steam. After twenty minutes of huffing and puffing, I finally got into the bog-hop rhythm: like riding a bicycle, even if it's been a while, it comes back to you.

Two kilometres west I crossed Allt Loch an Fhorsa, the stream that flows down from Airighean an Fhorsa, the shieling of the waterfall (visited in walk 2.3). A half hour after that, on the gradually rising terrain at the base of Beinn Mheadhanach, I reached Airighean Bo Nighean Mhurich (CANMORE ID 133738). Here there were the ruins of five shieling huts, and a large sheep fank, but no beehives. It was a pleasant spot, with open views across the vast interior of Lewis to the distant hills of Harris.

I then headed southwest, across gradually descending terrain, to Airighean Tighe Dhubhastail. Because of a description of its inhabitants, written 150 years ago, this is one of the premier beehive sites of all.

2.1.1 Airighean Tighe Dhubhastail

Landranger Map: 13
Locations:
Tighe Dhubhastail **(1)**, Logan site 18: NB 09958 21299
Tighe Dhubhastail **(2)**, Logan site 19: NB 09970 21300
Cairn made from cell: NB 09946 21301
CANMORE ID: 71052
Access: B8011 at Kinlochrog (NB 1391 2374) – a 6 km walk

Tighe Dhubhastail (the house of Dubastal—a freebooter, so the story goes) lies in a pastoral site straddling a peaty stream. Here you'll find the ruin of a rectangular shieling, its stones covered with yellow lichen, along with two multi-celled beehives. There may have been three other beehives here, as the vague outline of two circular structures can be seen next to the shieling, and the footprint of another lies across the stream.

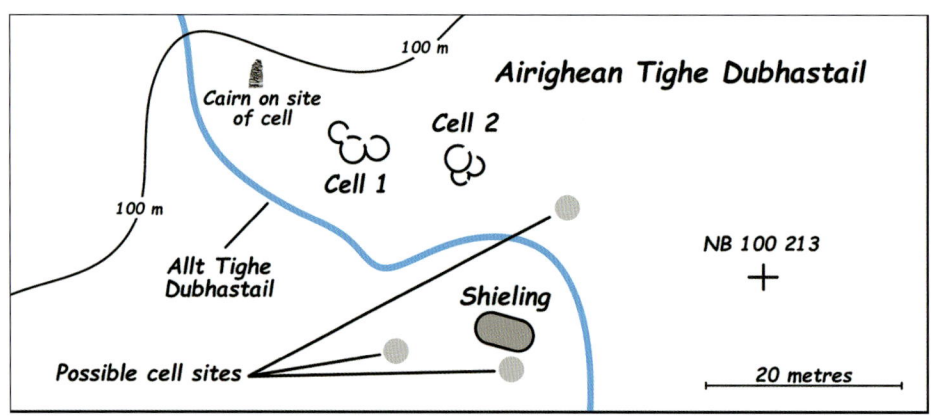

Map 2.1.1-1: Airighean Tighe Dhubhastail

I wanted to see this site because of a drawing of one of its double cells, Tighe Dhubhastail **(1),** made when it was occupied (PSAS Vol. VII). The drawing was part of a report on a visit to the site Captain Thomas and Dr Mitchell made around 1863. Here is a paraphrased version of the report:

Being Sunday-stayed at Kinlochresort, we thought to improve the occasion by visiting the shielings in the neighborhood. Along with the gamekeeper we were soon at Tighe Dhubhastail (Dubastal having been a freebooter who lived on the world at large). Here was a bothan, in which the family was at home. This was the summer pasturage of the tenants of Crolista on Loch Roag.

The bothan was double of the usual beehive shape, with the dwelling and dairy attached, and green with growing turf. A doorway, easily closed with a straw mat, led to the boudoir within. Close to the door was the fire, the smoke escaping through a hole in the dome. In the circular wall were three niches containing drying cheeses. A low interior door led from the dwelling to the dairy, which was six feet square.

The occupants were three young women, dressed in printed cotton gowns, and, being Sunday, they had finished their toilette at the burn to good purpose. Some eight of us packed into the hut while frothed milk was handed about.

Airighean Tighe Dhubhastail

Captain Thomas's sketch and plan drawing of Tighe Dhubhastail **(1)** are presented in Figure 2.1.1-1.

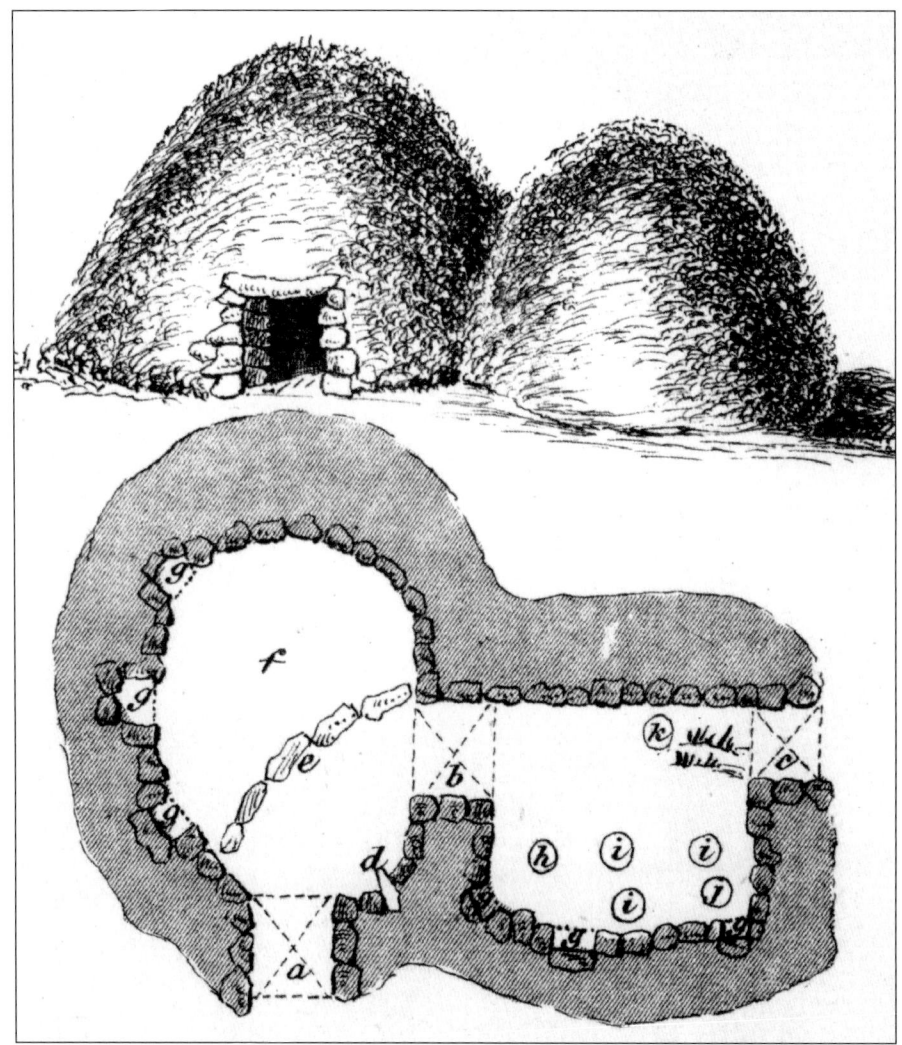

Figure 2.1.1-1: Both, Larach Tigh Dhubhastail, Capt. Thomas R.N.
a = doorway, d = firespot, e = bench stones, f = bed (hay & rushes),
k = stoup, g = cupboard, h = cream tub, I = milk/cheese tubs, j = churn
Proceedings of the Society of Antiquaries of Scotland, Vol. VII (1866-68)

Tighe Dhubhastail **(1)** has collapsed in the years since Captain Thomas visited, some of its stones taken to build the shieling hut across the stream. But the low entrance to the cell that Thomas used and the passage between its chambers are intact.

Entrance to Tighe Dhubhastail (1)

This is Elspeth Logan's description of Tighe Dhubhastail **(1)** from *A Study of the Beehive Structures in the Uig Area of the Isle of Lewis*. (Her plan drawing is presented in fig. 2.1.1-2):

Single cell beehive structure with two "annexes". In good condition of preservation, walls of main cell upstanding to height of 1.4m, walls of annexes more dilapidated. The walls are on average 1m thick and corbelling is clearly visible in the upper courses. There are three cupboards in the main cell which also has two doors, one which accesses an annex, the other annex only accessible from outside the main cell. The beehive is situated 3m east of Allt Tighe Dhubhastail in a sheltered river valley.

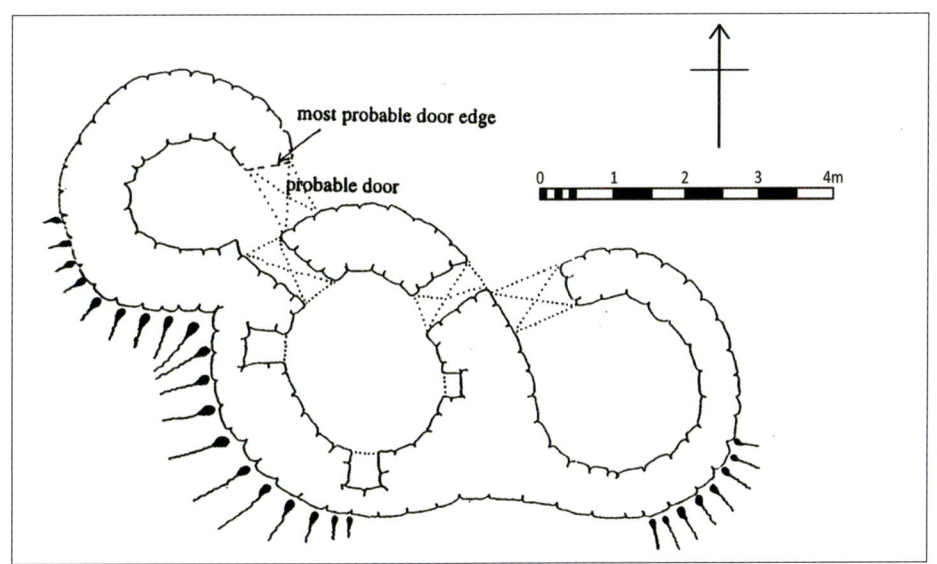

Figure 2.1.1-2: Tighe Dhubhastail (1) plan drawing (Logan site 18)

*Interior view of Tighe Dhubhastail **(1)***

Thick grass clogged the entrance, but I was able to tunnel through to crawl into the boudoir, the main dwelling chamber (unfortunately, no young women where there to greet me). The chamber, about 2.5 metres in diameter, must have been quite crowded when Captain Thomas, and seven others, sat here to enjoy some frothed milk. Another bit of grass-tunneling took me through the low passage to the dairy chamber, from where more crawling led outside via the back door.

The second beehive, Tighe Dhubhastail **(2)**, lies twelve metres to the east. Cloaked with a thick layer of turf, it is more ruinous than cell **(1)**. It has one main chamber, with two small cells built against it.

*Tighe Dhubhastail **(2)** in foreground—cell **(1)** in the middle distance*

Elspeth Logan described Tighe Dhubhastail **(2)** as a *single cell beehive with two "annexes" but these may be later additions to the structure since they are not incorporated into the masonry of the main cell, which can clearly be seen in the walling. In quite good state of preservation, height of highest point of wall to existing ground level is 0.8m. Interior overgrown and filled with rubble from collapse of walls and roof. Remains of corbelling still visible however. No cupboards visible.* (Plan drawing fig. 2.1.1-3.)

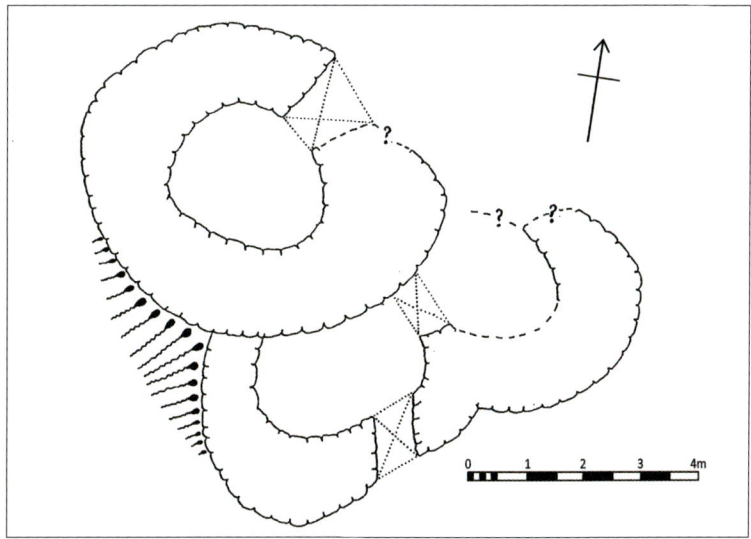

Figure 2.1.1-3: Tighe Dhubhastail (2) plan drawing (Logan site 19)

There used to be a cell at the west end of the settlement. But, sadly, someone decided to build a cairn from its stones. This is Logan's description: *There is another structure situated 6m upstream (north) of (1) and (2) which is roughly 4m by 5m. it may once have been a beehive, but the shape of the structure is now indiscernible since vandalism has occurred and the stones from the structure have been used to build a square cairn on the spot instead.*

Airighean Tighe Dhubhastail—cairn (left) made from the stones of a beehive

Before leaving the site I found the spot where the drawing of Tighe Dhubhastail **(1)**, the cell Captain Thomas entered, had been made 150 years ago. Standing there, with that old drawing in hand, and reading Captain Thomas's description of his visit, made for a special moment. Tighe Dhubhastail is an amazing place to visit, and think back on all the summers once spent by the people of Crolista in this beautiful oasis on the moorland.

Tighe Dhubhastail (1)—the chamber Captain Thomas entered at left, dairy chamber at right

Leaving Taighe Dubhastail behind, I carried on west to Màghannan. I had read of a beehive cell there, and the map showed a solitary structure at NB 0824 2127. When I reached it, I found a rectangular shieling hut, but there was no sign of a beehive. (I would later learn I'd missed the Màghannan beehive by 750 metres. It will be described during the Ardmore walk of section 2.3.)

From Màghannan, I set a course to the southwest, aiming for the footbridge over the the Abhainn Ghasacleit (NB 05405 20696). The route passed just south of the cells of Fidigidh and Both Ruadh, but having seen them before I carried on to the bridge. (See walk 2.2 for a description of those cells.) Then something extremely unusual happened. Never, in all my years of hiking in the interior of Lewis, had I ever encountered anyone. And so, when I reached the footbridge over the dark, cascading waters of Abhainn Ghasacleit, I was startled to see two young fellows out on the moor. They were not hikers—neither had a pack. They were not hunters—neither had a rifle. They appeared to just be out for a stroll in the great back of beyond.

It turned out that they were not out for a stroll. They were employed by the Tamnabhaigh estate. In the aftermath of the windstorm they had been checking that the boats kept at the moorland lochs were still there—it seemed the guests at Tamnabhaigh Lodge were in the mood for some fishing. You do not often get a chance, out in the bogs, to get local information, so I asked if they knew anything about the new owners of the neighboring Ardveg estate.

The estate, 2700 acres that includes the Ardveg and Ardmore peninsulas, had just been sold. I had fantasized about buying it when it came on the market the year before; but the lottery numbers did not match, so that dream had to be put on hold. With his tales of the MacDonalds and MacLennans, who once lived in Ardveg, Alasdair Alpin MacGregor made this remote hamlet immortal in his book *The Haunted Isles* (1933). That wonderful story inspired me to camp in the Ardveg for the first time in 2001 (see chapter 21, *Skye and Tiree to the Outer Isles*). I was fortunate to return in 2013 for the book launch of John MacDonald's *An Trusadh, Memories of Crofting in the Ardveg*; an engaging book that describes John's life growing up there.

I was told the new owners were friendly, and at home. My destination for the night was the Ardveg, so I decided to pay them a visit before setting up camp. Under the bright sun of a late summer afternoon, with a steady sea-wind keeping the midges at bay, I arrived to find three of the new owners in residence: Julie —, and two of her children. Grazing contentedly in front of the house was their horse Joe, who curiously looked on as I pitched my tent near the old Ardveg #1 blackhouse. I was then treated to supper in the new Ardveg #1, built by John MacDonald's father in 1934, a roaring coal fire warming cold toes.

The original No. 1 Ardveg

After enjoying some island hospitality—the highlights, two slices of homemade cake, and some Gaelic conversation—I stepped out into the darkness. I had forgotten to take my flashlight when I'd gone for dinner, and in the pitch blackness it took a while to find the tent. Aside from the lumpy terrain, there was one obstacle that had me worried—the stream that flows down from Loch na Bèiste (loch of the beast). But I was eventually able to hear its trickling waters and easily stepped across. (The beast referred to in place names like 'Loch na Bèiste' is typically an otter.)

A few big beasts (deer) were about, barking as I settled in, but there were no wee beasts about (midges)—paradise, indeed. I needed to get some rest, as I had a long day ahead of me. There were several sites in the area with beehives I planned to visit, before making the long walk up the track to Uig, and another campsite under Hebridean stars.

– DAY 2 –

In the morning I looked out of the tent to see what the weather was like. All I saw was a blur. Oh, I thought to myself, things sure look fuzzy, I should put on my glasses. On went the glasses, and I took another look. Uh-oh, things are still blurry. That blur was a frenzied mass of hungry, hovering midges, greedily drawn to the tent by the carbon dioxide wafting from the tent. A vast horde waiting for me to come out and play. Then I realized I'd made a tactical mistake. My bug net was in the pack, and the pack was . . . outside . . . . uh oh . . . .

What to do . . . . I was stumped. Without my usual morning infusion of caffeine it took a while to realize that there was something of use in the tent. It was a bottle of the island-hiker's best friend—no, not Scotch, though that would have taken my mind off the bugs—it was a bottle of DEET. Now there are better ways to start a day than by smearing yourself with insecticide, but that's what I had to do. Prepared for action, the next step was to retrieve the bug net. I unzipped the tent, stepped out, and started to dig through the pack to find it.

I was immediately engulfed in a cloud of thirsty, teeny-tiny bugs; my DEET-drenched hands soon coated by hundreds of midges, all squirming in their little midgy death throes. Then I noticed an itch in my scalp, the only area not drenched with poison. It was either dandruff, or a second wave of desperate midges looking for breakfast—probably both. Spurred on by my own desperation, I grabbed the bug-net and quickly put it on. With shields up, it was time to look for some beehives.

I broke camp and, leaving a cloud of hungry midges in my wake, climbed up the Allt Chonagar stream into Gleann nan Geodhannan. My first stop was the shieling site Airigh nan Geodhannan. There I came across a half dozen ruins, one that may have been a beehive, but it was too tumbled to know for certain.

Ruin at Airigh nan Geodhannan

The next destination was the settlement at the head of Loch Tealasbhaigh, a kilometre to the southeast. I continued in that direction, but was stopped dead in my tracks by a steep slope down to the sea: a 60 metre shear drop to Loch Tealasbhaigh. Even though I had to backtrack, my climb was rewarded with an expansive view across the mouth of Loch Reasort to the lone house at Cravadale.

After backtracking, I dropped down into Gleann Tealasbhaigh to see the township ruins at the head of the loch. I had read something that hinted there were beehives in the glen, but found none. But I did know where there were cells, lots of them. A zig-zag hike up the Abhainn Tealasbhaigh and a turn to the southeast led to Loch Sneathabhal. My destination was only 200 metres to the north: the beehive cluster at Loch an Ath Ruaidh.

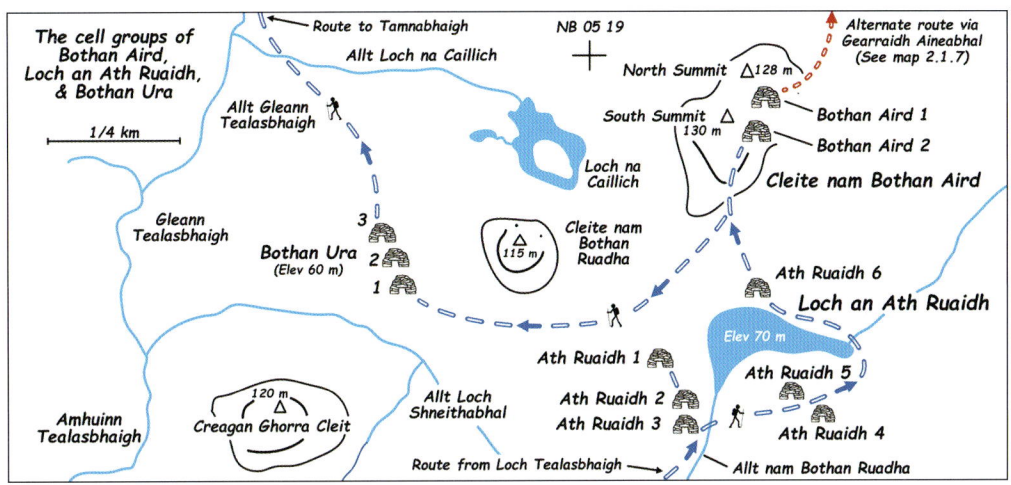

Map 2.1.1-2: Route through the cell-groups of the Ardveg

2.1.2 Loch an Ath Ruaidh

Landranger Map: 13
Locations: See below
CANMORE IDs:
133817: General reference to the site
304639: Ath Ruaidh **(6)**
Access:
B8011 at NB 0317 3133 (Uig) – a 20 km walk
B8011 at NB 1391 2374 (Kinlochrog) – a 13 km walk

A beautiful village of cells surrounds Loch an Ath Ruaidh (loch of the red-stone ford). The cells here are ruinous, but the close communal setting, in combination to the fact that they have been studied in the past, makes them a must-see. Drawings of how one of the cells, Ath Ruaidh **(5)**, looked in the 1850s is to be found in PSAS Vol. III (plate XI, figure 1). Sadly, the cells have suffered significant deterioration over the past 150 years.

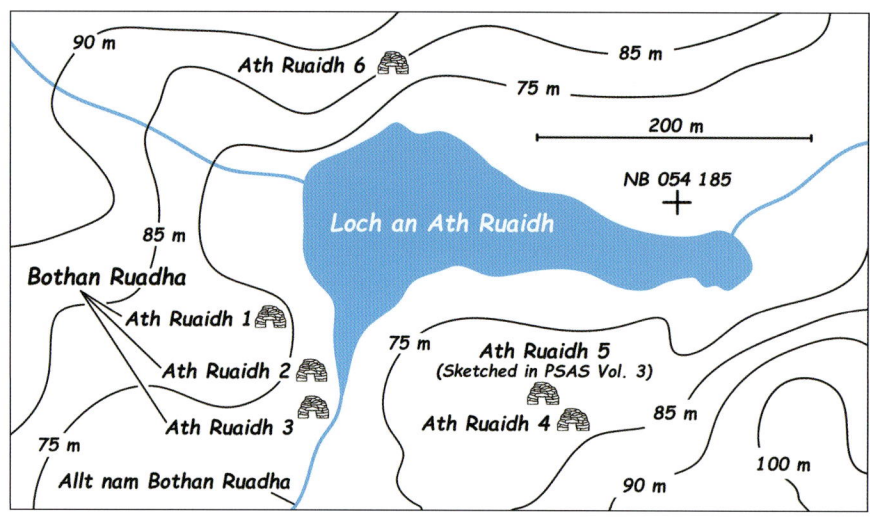

Map 2.1.2: The cells of Loch an Ath Ruaidh

Ath Ruaidh (1)

Location: NB 05174 18429
References: Logan site 20

The cells around Loch an Ath Ruaidh were surveyed by Elspeth Logan. We will let her descriptions speak for themselves, as we make a circuit around the loch. Due to its commanding view, the best place to start is the west-most cell, Ath Ruaidh **(1)**—ten metres above, and 30 metres from, the southwest side of the loch. Due to the red sandstone prevalent here, the three cells around the southwest side of the loch are marked on the 1854 OS map as Bothan Ruadha (the red bothies).

Ath Ruaidh (1) looking north to Loch an Ath Ruaidh

This is Elspeth Logan's description of Ath Ruaidh **(1)**, which is the first of three cells named Bothan Ruadha on the map of 1854: *A single cell beehive structure with two opposing doors. No cupboards visible. Situated on eastern facing slope of hill on the west side of Loch an Ath Ruaidh, overlooking the loch and sheltered from the north and west by the surrounding hills. Incorporates blocks of sandstone into its masonry, but this is not as unusual as it seems since the site is located on a sandstone outcrop.*

Figure 2.1.2-1 is Elspeth Logan's plan drawing of Ath Ruaidh **(1)**. The cell was also surveyed by Captain Thomas, and his plan drawing from the 1850s can be found in PSAS Vol. III (plate XI, fig. 4)

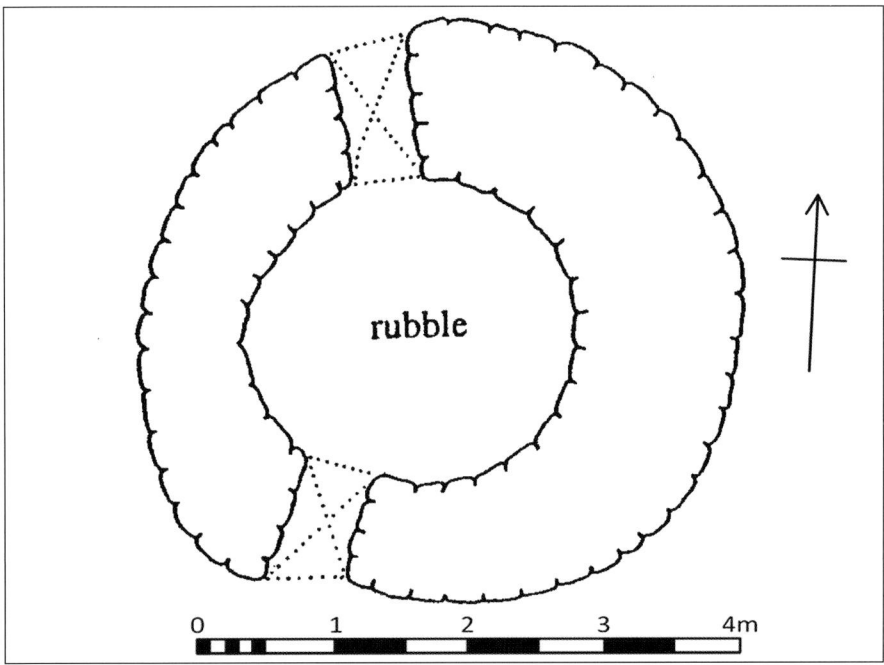

Figure 2.1.2-1: Ath Ruaidh (1) plan drawing (Logan site 20)

Ath Ruaidh (1) looking east over Loch an Ath Ruaidh–the hump of Cleit an Eoin at right

Ath Ruaidh (1) looking south to the Harris hills

Ath Ruaidh (2)

Location: NB 05204 18378
References: Logan site 21

The next cell, Ath Ruaidh **(2)**, lies sixty metres southeast of Ath Ruaidh **(1)**. The cell is so ruinous and overgrown that it is very hard to locate. I completely missed it on my first two visits to the loch. Armed with a photo from Elspeth Logan I was able to find it on a third visit in 2019.

Ath Ruaidh (2) hiding in the heather (marked by arrow)

Ath Ruaidh **(2)** is the second of the Bothan Ruadha cells. Elspeth Logan described it as a *structure built into side of hill and masonry disappearing into vegetation on hillside. Quite dilapidated in state, but 2 "cells" visible. Not possible to tell whether this was originally a beehive since the height of the walls to existing ground level is 0.5m, so no corbelling would be visible in wall courses of this height. The structure is well sheltered by the hill to its west and is approx. 5m from Allt nam Bothan Ruadha, the burn which runs south from Loch an Ath Ruaidh.* (Plan drawing fig. 2.1.2-2.)

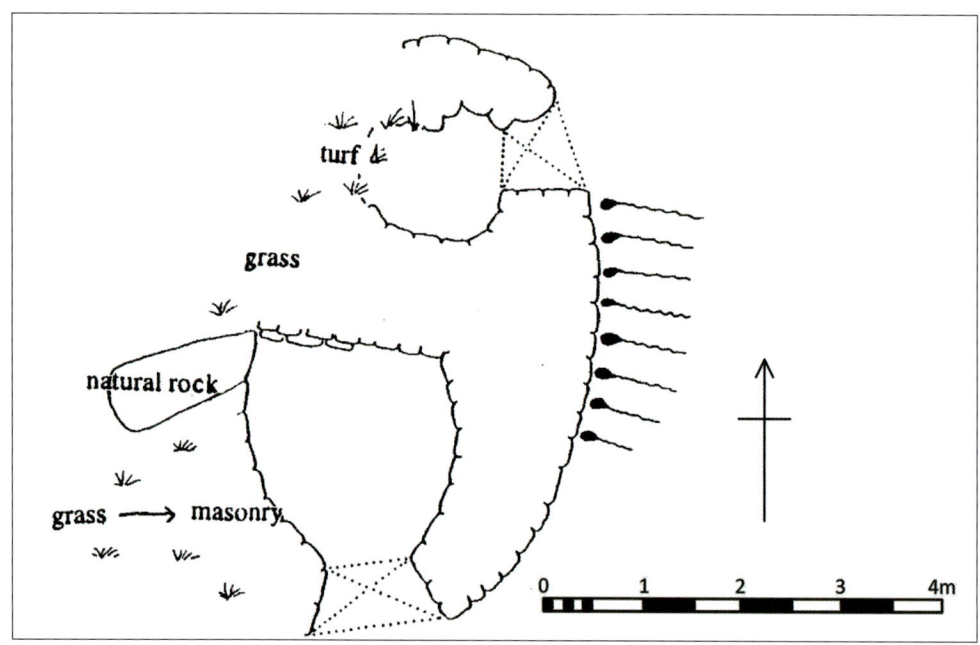

Figure 2.1.2-2: Ath Ruaidh (2) plan drawing (Logan site 21)

Ath Ruaidh (3)

Location: NB 05204 18370
References: Logan site 25

The next cell, Ath Ruaidh **(3)**, lies ten metres south of Ath Ruaidh **(2)**, near where the stream Allt nam Bothan Ruadha exits the south end of the loch.

Ath Ruaidh (3) seen from above

This is Elspeth Logan's description and plan drawing (fig. 2.1.2-3) of Ath Ruaidh **(3)**, the third of the three cells named *Bothan Ruadha* on the OS map: *Single cell beehive structure with walls standing to height of approx. 0.4m to present ground level. Natural rock outcrop utilised to form one and a half sides of beehive and there is still some masonry on top of one of the outcrops as well. Interior filled with rubble from roof collapse. 2 doors and one cupboard visible. Situated in lee of 2 hills, 10m south of site 21 and overlooking Loch Shneithabhal 5m distant from Allt nam Bothan Ruadha.*

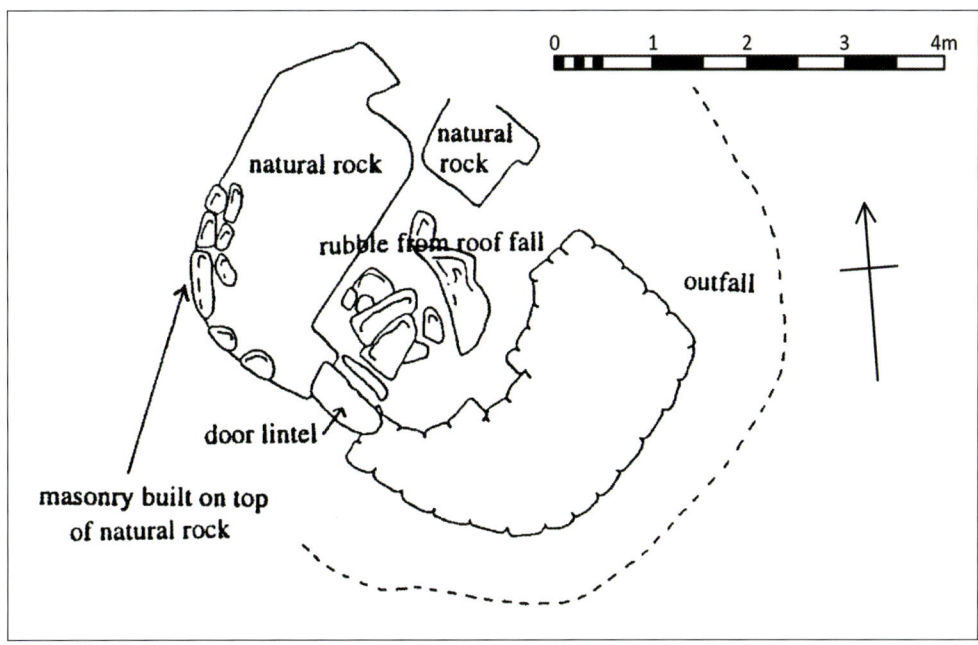

*Figure 2.1.2-3: Ath Ruaidh **(3)** plan drawing (Logan site 25)*

*Ath Ruaidh **(3)** seen from the east*

Ath Ruaidh (4)

Location: NB 05344 18352
References: Logan site 23

Ath Ruaidh **(4)** lies 100 metres from, and twenty metres above, the southeast shore of the loch. There are two cells here, Ath Ruaidh **(4)** is the east-most of the pair.

*Ath Ruaidh **(4)** looking northwest–Ath Ruaidh **(5)** in the distance*

This is Elspeth Logan's description and plan drawing (figure 2.1.2-4) of Ath Ruaidh **(4)**: *A Single cell beehive with annex. One door leads into annex, and annex itself is double entranced.*

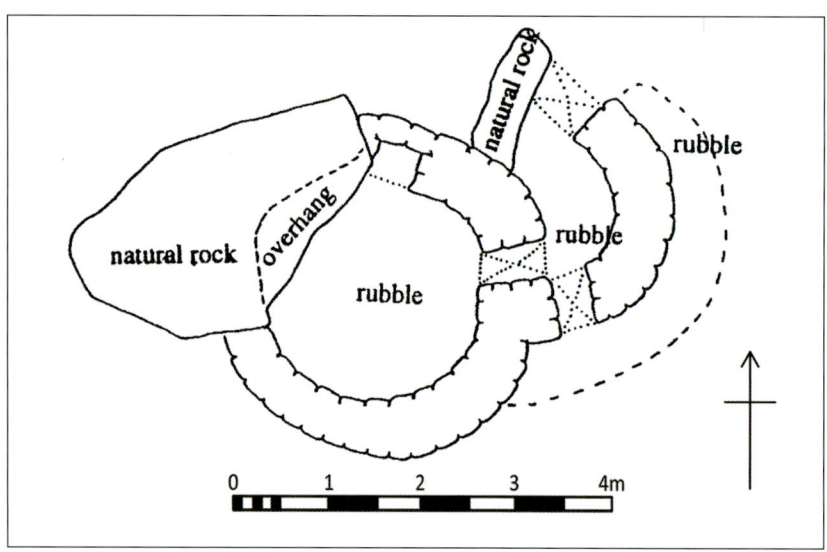

Two cupboards visible. Highest point of wall to existing ground level is 0.8m. Interior filled with stones from roof collapse. Overhang on natural rock outcrop used for east side of beehive structure. Situated in a fairly sheltered position on the SE side of the loch.

Ath Ruaidh (4)—rubble that was once the dome

Ath Ruaidh (4) looking south

Ath Ruaidh (5)

Location: NB 05329 18372
References: Logan site 24

Ath Ruaidh **(5)** lies twenty-five metres northwest of Ath Ruaidh **(4)**. It, too, is ruinous, but thanks to Captain Thomas we know how it looked in the 1800s.

Ath Ruaidh (5)—the rubble-filled interior

Elspeth Logan described Ath Ruaidh **(5)** as *a single cell beehive structure in fairly ruinous condition. Interior indistinct due to collapse of roof. Two natural outcrops of rock have been utilised in construction. One door but possibly two doors at one time since there is a section where a small wall approx. 0.65m thick has been built across what may have been the second entrance. Alternatively, this may be a large cupboard. Situated on the SE side of the loch in a fairly sheltered position.* (Plan drawing fig. 2.1.2-5.)

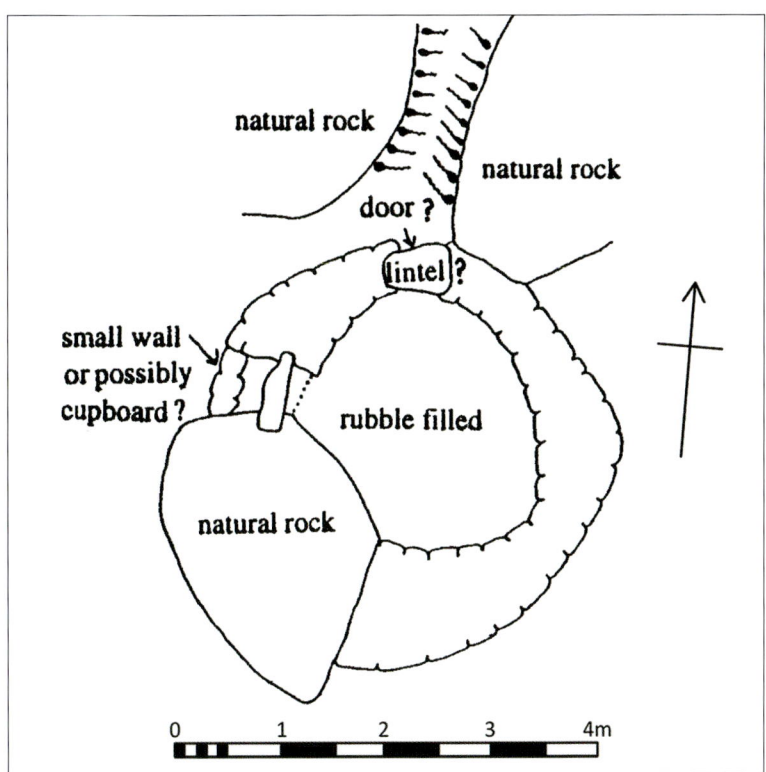

Figure 2.1.2-5: Ath Ruaidh (5) plan drawing (Logan site 24)

Ath Ruaidh (5) looking northwest

Ath Ruaidh **(5)** was surveyed by Captain Thomas and his sketch is presented in figure 2.1.2-6. It was this drawing that first spurred my interest to visit Loch an Ath Ruaidh. Sadly, it no longer looks like it did a century and a half ago. It appears as if the big boulder it was built against shifted at some point causing a total collapse.

*Figure 2.1.2-6: Both, Loch an Ath Ruaidh, Capt. Thomas R.N.   Ath Ruaidh **(5)***
Proceedings of the Society of Antiquaries of Scotland, Vol. III (1857-60)

*Ath Ruaidh **(5)** from same perspective as the 1850s sketch*

From Ath Ruaidh **(5)**, make your way around the east end of the loch, then head 250 metres west to reach the final cell at Loch an Ath Ruaidh.

Ath Ruaidh (6)

Location: NB 05246 18556
CANMORE ID: 304639
References: Logan site 22

Ath Ruaidh **(6)** lies on the hillside 30 metres north of the northernmost point of the loch. It is placed in a spectacular position, with a clear view over the entire loch. Of all the cells here it is the best preserved.

Ath Ruaidh (6) looking south over Loch an Ath Ruaidh—Loch Sneathabhal in the distance

Ath Ruaidh (6) looking southeast to the Harris hills

Elspeth Logan described Ath Ruaidh **(6)** as a *single cell beehive with one door and two visible cupboards. Collapse of masonry on east side. Interior filled with stones from collapse of roof rendering a cross section impossible to undertake without moving any of the stones. Situated on a small hillock on the north side of the loch.* (Plan drawing fig. 2.1.2-7.)

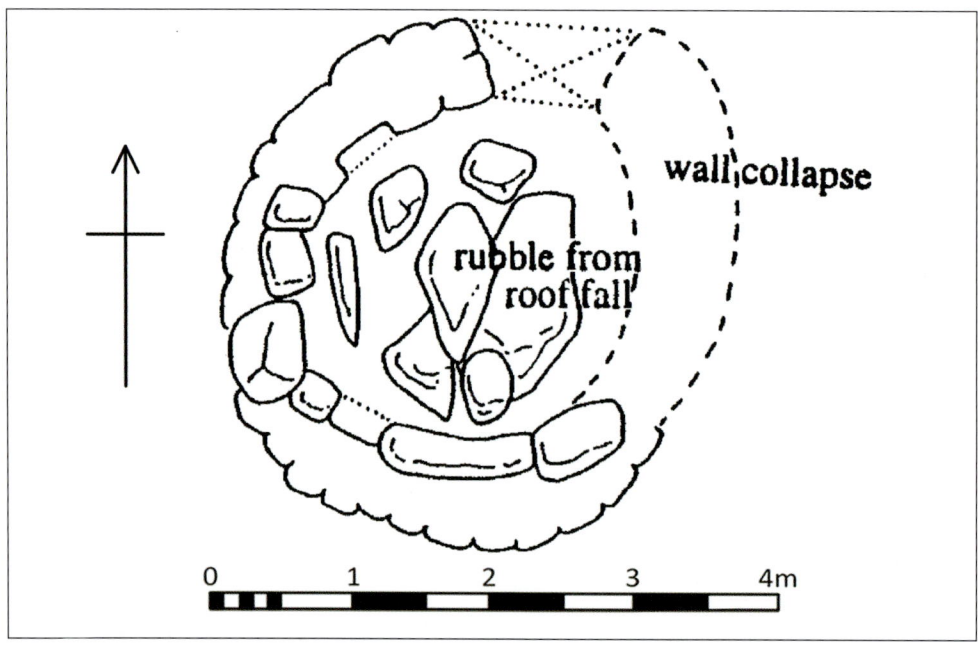

*Figure 2.1.2-7: Ath Ruaidh **(6)** plan drawing (Logan site 22)*

*Ath Ruaidh **(6)** looking east*

It was hard to leave the stunning village of cells surrounding Loch an Ath Ruaidh. It left an indelible memory, one that, in two years' time would compel me to camp here for two summer nights (see section 2.3). But there is a beehive site just as memorable and, luckily for the bog-weary bo'h hunter, only a ten-minute climb away. From the north end of Loch an Ath Ruaidh I continued north up the rocky terrain. Near the summit of Cleit na Bothan Aird, 250 metres from the loch, stood the elegant cells of Bothan Aird—the high bothies.

2.1.3 Bothan Aird

Landranger Map: 13 (also refer to Map 2.1.1-2)
Locations:
Bothan Aird **(1)**: NB 05283 18842
Bothan Aird **(2)**: NB 05281 18820
CANMORE IDs: 133816 & 304575
Access:
B8011 at NB 0317 3133 – a 20 km walk
B8011 at NB 1391 2374 – a 13 km walk

The cells of Bothan Aird lie near the summit of Cleit nam Bothan Aird: thirteen hard kilometres from the nearest road. All I initially knew about the location was what DDC Pochin Mould had to say in *West Over Sea*, in that they lay *'high up on Cleit nam Bothan Ard between Lochs Bodavat and Grunavat.'* When I first visited Cleit nam Bothan Ard, it took a while to find the site, because the cells blend so well into the terrain. So much so, that on that first visit I missed one of them, the northmost cell—Bothan Aird **(1)**.

The double cell—Bothan Aird (2)

The structures here are a single cell, Bothan Aird **(1)**, and twenty-two metres south, a double cell, Bothan Aird **(2)**. The south half of Bothan Aird **(2)** is the most intact cell in the area, only its half-moon capstone is missing, and inside are four stone cupboards. If you crawl into the cell you'll discover that the residents had a bird's-eye view over Loch Bodabhat. The north half of the cell, which makes use of a natural cleft in the rock for a cupboard, has mostly collapsed.

This is Elspeth Logan's description and plan drawing (figure 2.1.3-1) of Bothan Aird **(2)**:
The best-preserved beehive structure in whole of survey area. In excellent condition. Built into side of small crag, facing east and making use of the natural rock outcrops in the construction with great skill. Still has some turf covering on the outside. Situated round the corner from site 26 [Bothan Aird (1)] overlooking Loch Bhodabhat and the Harris hills. Walls standing to what must be their original height at 1.6m since there are only a few stones missing from the roof and most of the masonry is intact.

The structure consists of a main cell, which the single doorway leads into. There is a natural form of the rock in situ at the back of the cell which may have been used as a convenient storage space. To the right of the main cell is a line of paving which delineates a smaller cell, the roof of which is considerably lower than that of the main cell (see cross-section) and which is also collapsing. A small abraded sherd of pottery was discovered at floor level in this part of the both. There also exists an upper level at the very back of the beehive which is approx. 0.5m higher than floor level, accessible through the smaller part of the structure where the roof is collapsing. This upper level incorporates a natural crevice in the rock as a cupboard.

There are two other unidentifiable structures, or parts of walls in the vicinity of these two beehives. They are covered in vegetation and the remains of walls stand to a height of approx. 0.5m. Although roughly circular to oval in form, they were discounted from an accurate survey since their condition suggests that their walls did not originally stand much higher and they do not have the appearance of dilapidated beehive structures. They may be storage pens or some similar structure.

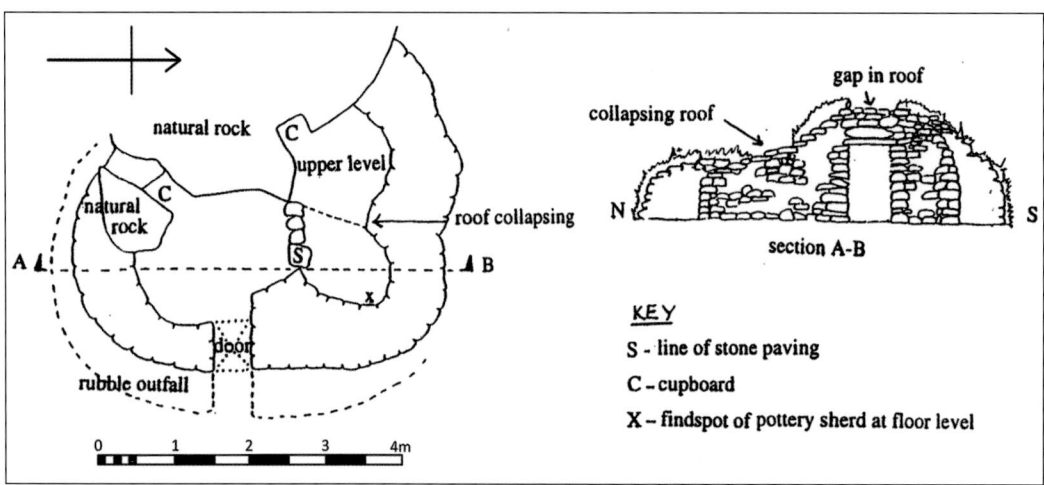

Figure 2.1.3-1: Bothan Aird **(2)** plan drawing and cross section (Logan site 27)

Bothan Aird **(2)** was also surveyed by Captain Thomas in the 1850s. His plan and cross-section drawings can be found in the PSAS volume referenced in Appendix C.

*The view to Loch Bodabhat from inside Bothan Aird **(2)***

*Bothan Aird **(2)**: The collapsed cell in foreground—dome of the intact chamber behind*

*Bothan Aird **(2)** (foreground)—Bothan Aird **(1)** marked by arrow*

*The smokehole—Bothan Aird **(2)***

Bothan Aird (2) from the east

The other cell here, Bothan Aird **(1)**, lies hidden around the corner of an outcropping of rock. Its walls stand to over half its original height, and the cell-dwellers had a great view west to Loch na Caillich with its large island. On a clear day they could see all the way to Scarp and the sparkling waters of the Atlantic.

Loch na Caillich seen from Bothan Aird (1)—Scarp in the distance

Bothan Aird (1) looking southeast—Loch Reasort and Direscal in the distance

Bothan Aird (1) looking northeast

Elspeth Logan described Bothan Aird **(1)** as a *single cell beehive in good condition. Height of wall to present ground level is 1.25m. five cupboards visible and two entrances which are very long in depth, (SW door is 1.2m long and NW door is 0.9m in length.) Despite collapse of roof, corbelling still visible. Situated very close to the base of a 4m high rock outcrop near the summit of Cleite nam Bothan Ard (the hill behind Loch an Ath Ruaidh), overlooking Loch na Caillich. Sheltered from the south, but completely exposed to winds from the north as it is situated in such a high place. (Plan drawing fig. 2.1.3-2.)*

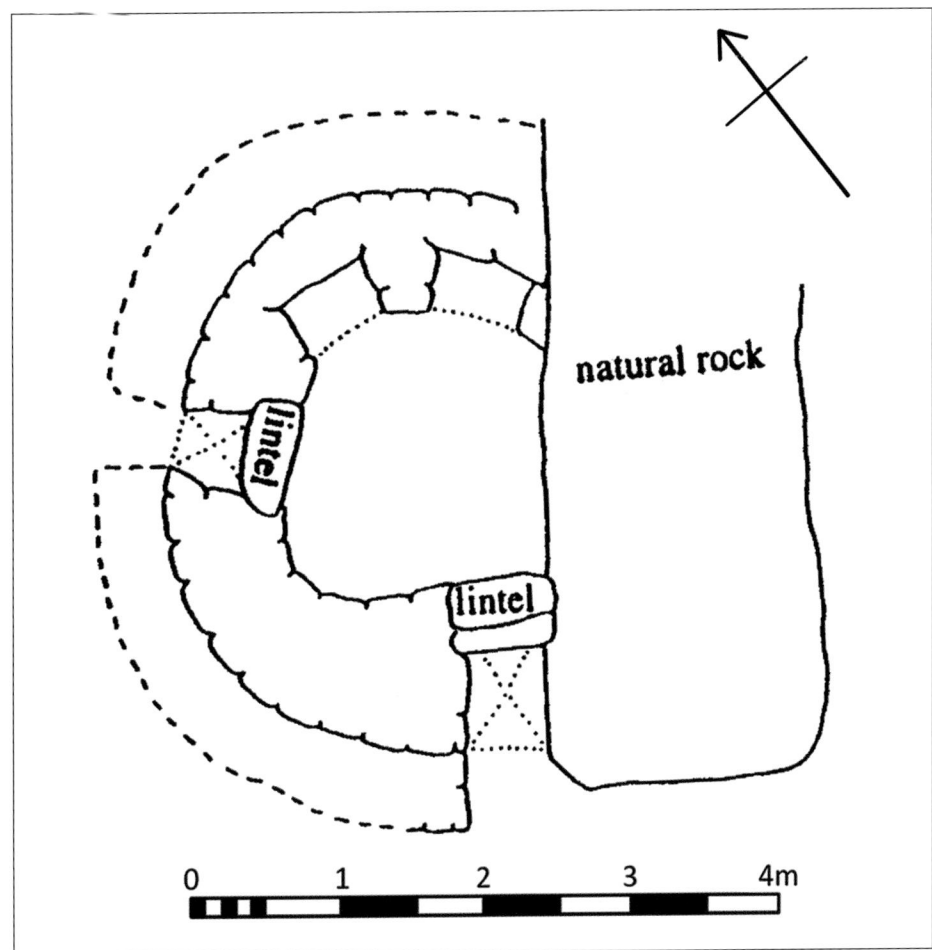

Figure 2.1.3-2: Bothan Aird (1) plan drawing (Logan site 26)

Bothan Aird **(1)** was also surveyed by Captain Thomas in the 1850s, when the dome was completely intact. His sketch drawing is presented in figure 2.1.3-3. It is interesting that the background terrain and sky depicted in the drawing are completely wrong, as the cell is built below a large rocky knoll.

Figure 2.1.3-3: Both an Aird, Capt. Thomas R.N. Bothan Aird (1)
Proceedings of the Society of Antiquaries of Scotland, Vol. III (1857-60)

Bothan Aird (1) seen from the same perspective as Captain Thomas's drawing

Bothan Aird (1) showing the interior—Bothan Aird (2) in the distance (left)

The Bothan Aird cells are beautiful structures, some of the best preserved in the Ardveg area. Their location is also interesting. At an elevation of 130 metres, they are the highest cells in the Ardveg, and so cleverly hidden you have to be looking really closely to notice them. Like many cells, when their turf covering was intact they would have been invisible, except to those who knew they were here.

Note: A walk to Bothan Aird is quite an undertaking. A day-trip on foot would be a challenge. It is a forty kilometre round-trip walk via the Uig track, or a twenty-six kilometre round-trip from Morsgail. That's why I chose to visit as part of a multi-day trek. There is only one relatively easy way, and that is to get to Tamnabhaigh by sea. If you ever have the opportunity to be put ashore there, be sure to make the following five kilometre round-trip walk to the high bothies of Bothan Aird.

Note: Another option for this walk is to skip Bothan Ura (2.1.4) and Gearraidh Cleit Gruineabhat (2.1.5)—which are quite ruinous, but still interesting—and proceed a kilometre north from Bothan Aird to Gearraidh Aineabhal. One of the beehives at Aineabhal is magnificent, nearly 100% intact. The route via Aineabhal is described in section 2.1.7.

Loop walk from Tamnabhaigh: Cross the footbridge over the Abhainn Tamnabhaigh, then follow the stony path that climbs to the southeast. The path gradually peters out as it climbs to the south above the stream Allt a' Chas Bhraighe. Continue to where the stream flows from Loch Gruineabhat, cross the outflow, and carry on along the northeast shore of the loch. A third of the way down the loch you will pass the ruins of the Gruineabhat cells (section 2.1.5). From the east end of the loch follow the Feadan Gruineabhat to the east; passing along the way a few WWI telegraph poles on the verge of toppling over. As soon as Loch Bodabhat comes into view turn right to climb Cleit nam Bothan Aird. The beehives lie near the summit.

* * *

The next beehive site lies 700 metres west of Bothan Aird. After dropping down the hill to the west, go past the south tip of Loch na Caillich, then head around a knoll to the grassy slopes above Allt Loch Sneathabhal. Nestled here on a gently sloping ledge of terrain, you will find the three cells of Bothan Ura.

2.1.4 Bothan Ura

Landranger Map: 13 (also see Map 2.1.1-2)
Locations:
Both Ura **(1)**: NB 04647 18640; Both Ura **(2)**: NB 04636 18660; Both Ura **(3)**: NB 04618 18670
CANMORE ID: 133812
Access:
B8011 (near Abhainn Dearg Distillery) at NB 0317 3133 – a 20 km walk
B8011 (near Morsgail Lodge) at NB 1391 2374 – a 13 km walk

Bothan Ura, the new bothies, are an isolated group of cells on the sloping hillside west of Loch na Caillich. One of the cells, Both Ura **(1)**, was described by Captain Thomas when its walls still stood nearly two metres high. A plan drawing was made at the time (PSAS Vol. III, Plate XIII, Fig. 7). The structures have deteriorated greatly since Thomas saw them. Additionally, in the intervening 150-plus years, the bog has risen significantly around the cells, and their walls are now only slightly above ground. According to DDC Pochin Mould's *West Over Sea*, two of the cells had porches when she visited some fifty years ago, but today only Both Ura **(1)** shows signs of a porch.

Bothan Ura **(1)**

This is Elspeth Logan's description and plan drawing (figure 2.1.4-1) of Bothan Ura **(1)**: *Structure very difficult to survey due to roof collapse and rise of surrounding bog which leaves height of door to present ground level at 0.2m. Rushes and vegetation almost completely cover the structure. Single cell with possible annex or "porch" to NW, but very indistinct. Two doors and one cupboard visible. There is a bench type construction opposite the presumed door. Situated on a plateau 50m above glen which Allt Loch Shneithabhal runs through and in the lee of a very steep hill. Surrounding ground is still boggy and situation is similar to Norwegian saetrs.*

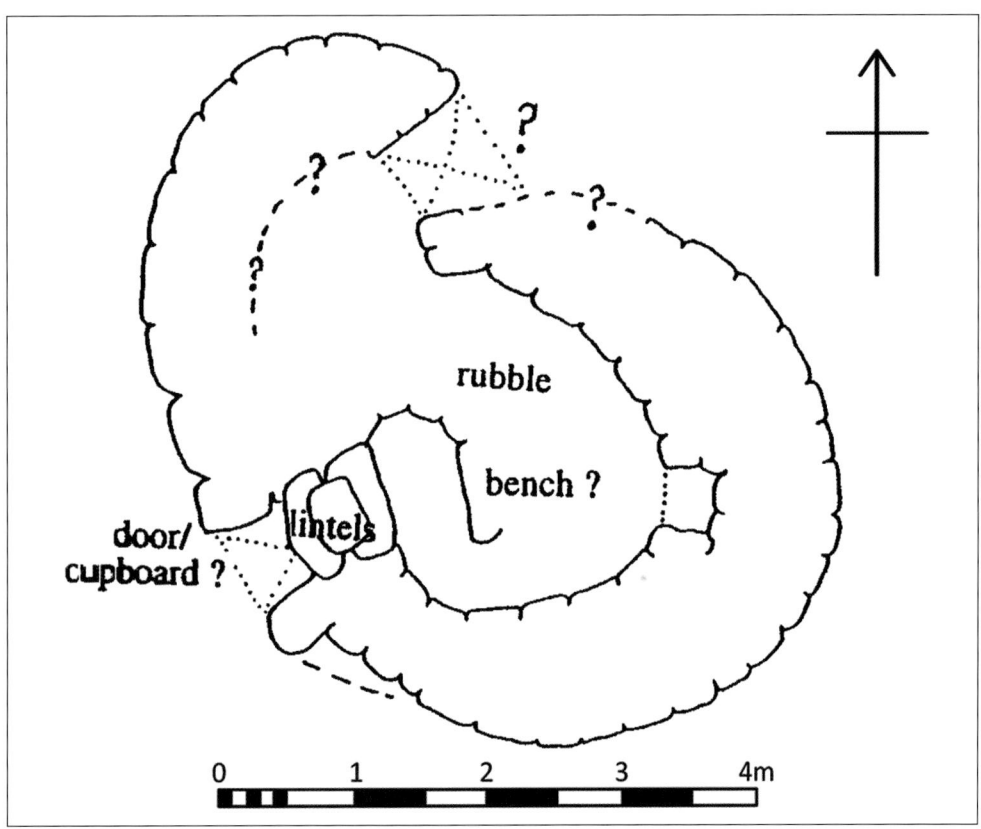

Figure 2.1.4-1: Bothan Ura (1) plan Drawing (Logan site 28)

Bothan Ura **(2)** lies twenty metres northwest of **(1)**. Elspeth Logan described is as a *structure very difficult to survey with any clarity since the surrounding bog has risen and consumed most of the masonry to the extent that no doorway or door lintels can be observed. Roof collapse has also rendered the interior of the structure difficult to determine. Presumed "porch" area, or annex due to bulge of masonry, in the grass on the north side. Dimensions of remains are of average beehive size and is circular in form. Excavation necessary to determine anything else about the architecture. Situated on the same plateau as site 28* [Bothan Ura **(1)**]. *These two structures provide an indication of the speed of growth of surrounding bog since they were in a better state of preservation when surveyed by Thomas.* (Logan plan drawing fig. 2.1.4-2.)

*Bothan Ura **(2)** looking south to Bothan Ura **(1)***

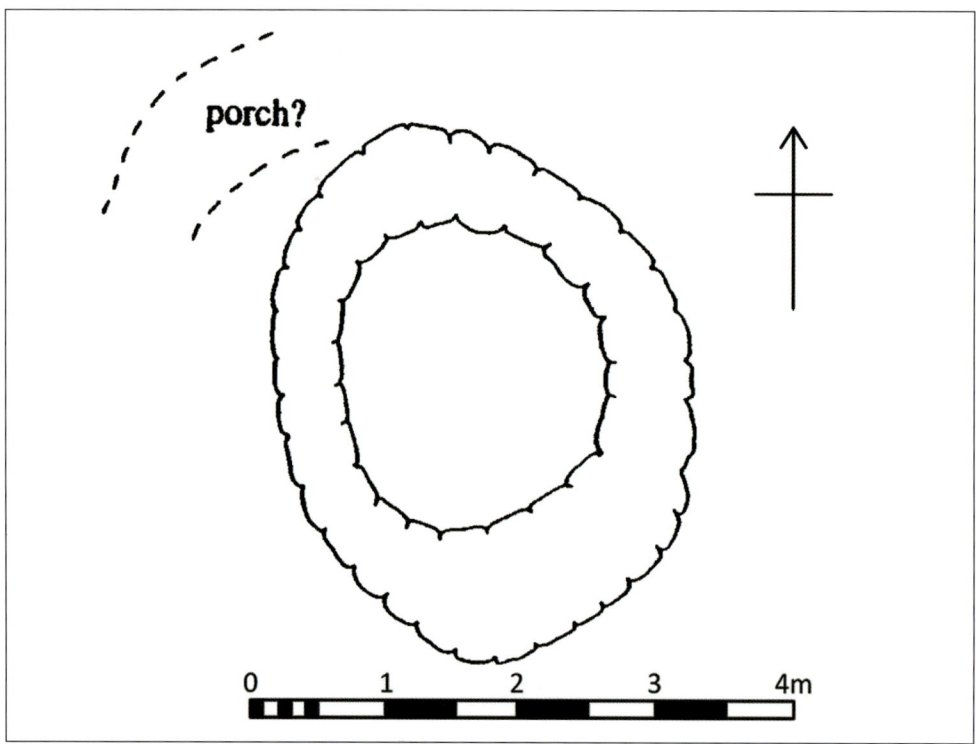

*Figure 2.1.4-2: Bothan Ura **(2)** plan drawing (Logan site 29)*

Bothan Ura **(3)** lies forty metres northwest of **(2)**. Not much remains, and it was not surveyed by Logan. The circular foundation is similar in size to the other two cells, but as there is no sign of corbelling it may have been a pen.

The scant remains of Bothan Ura (3)

The next beehive site lies a kilometre north of Bothan Ura. I headed in that direction to round the western slopes of Cleit Dubh. On reaching the east tip of Loch Gruineabhat, I veered up its northern shore. After passing a few precariously leaning WWI telegraph poles, another minute of walking led to the three cells of Gearraidh Cleit Gruineabhat.

2.1.5 Gearraidh Cleit Gruineabhat

Landranger Map: 13
Location: Gruineabhat **(1)**: NB 04424 19770; Gruineabhat **(2)**: NB 04436 19782; Gruineabhat **(3)**: NB 04476 19761; Norse Mill: NB 04271 19922
CANMORE ID: 133819
Access: B8011 at NB 0317 3133 – a 19 km walk

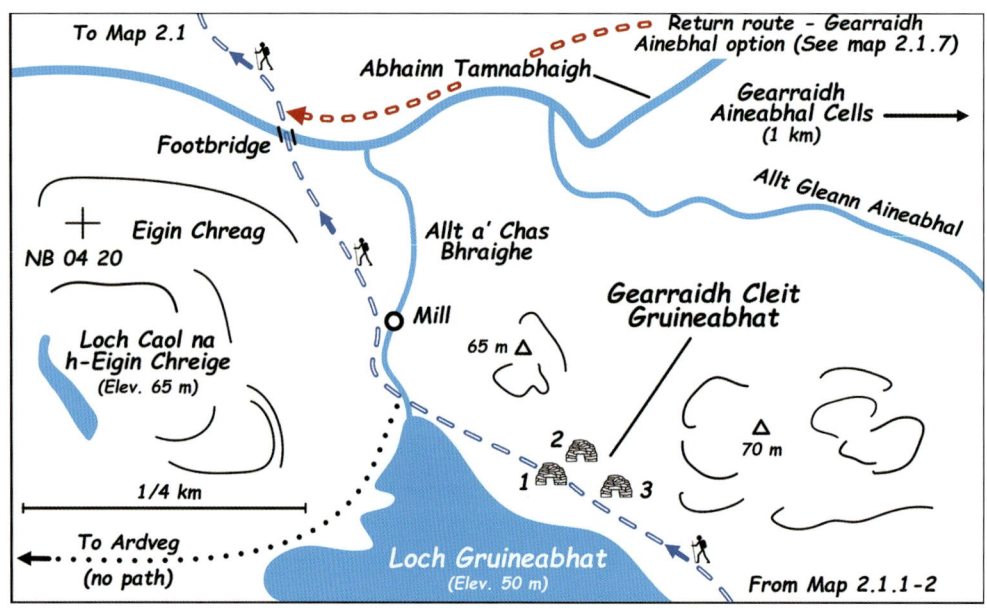

Map 2.1.5: Gearraidh Cleit Gruineabhat

Although the cells of Gearraidh Cleit Gruineabhat are ruinous, they are a worthwhile stop on any walk in the area. They are also an interesting detour if you are paying a visit to the nearby blackhouse village of Ardveg, or the Norse mill on Allt a' Chas Bhraighe. Unfortunately, due to bad weather, the site was not surveyed by Elspeth Logan in the 1990s. The first beehive I came to when approaching from the southeast was Gruineabhat (**3**). It is a totally collapsed cell nearly three metres in diameter with only one discernible doorway facing the southeast.

Gruineabhat (3)—looking to the NW with the SE facing doorway at centre

Gruineabhat **(2)** lies forty-five metres northwest of cell **(3)**. Portions of its walls stand a metre high and it is three metres in diameter. So many of its stones are missing it's hard to tell where the doorway(s) were.

Gruineabhat (2) seen from the east

Gruineabhat (2) seen from the west

Gruineabhat **(1)** lies fifteen metres southwest of cell **(2)**. It, too, is now a jumble of stones with a circular base of 2.5 metres.

Looking south from Gruineabhat (1)—WWI telegraph pole in the distance

From Gruineabhat I continued north by following the Allt a' Chas Bhraighe, which flows north out of Loch Gruineabhat. One-hundred metres downstream I came to the corn mill, last used in the 1890s. If you make the effort to look inside you'll see that the millstones are still there.

Mill on Allt a' Chas Bhraighe

Leaving the mill I continued down to the Tamnabhaigh River, crossed the footbridge, then followed the track along the shore of Loch Tamnabhaigh. At the head of the loch, just before starting up the long and winding road to Ardroil, I made a short detour to see a group of cells on the west bank of the Amhuinn Cheann Chùisil.

2.1.6 Ceann Chùisil

Landranger Map: 13
Location: NB 0339 2137
CANMORE ID: 278110
Access: B8011 at NB 0317 3133 – a 12 km walk

The Ceann Chùisil shielings are an easy detour from the track up to Ardroil. Just where it starts to climb into the hills (at NB 03445 21416), head west down to the Amhainn Cheann Chùisil and cross the stream. Ten metres up the hillside you will come to a series of three double cells that span a distance of thirty metres. Although the cells are quite dilapidated, the site is worth a visit. There is a lot of history here, and many of the stones from the cells were robbed to build the Ceann Chùisil township, 100 metres away on the other side of the stream. If the track to Ardroil had been here 150 years ago, people might still be living here.

The heather and grass were thick, but I could still make out the circular bases of the three double cells. They look similar to the western double cell at Airigh Chlàir Mhòir (section 2.5.2), in that there appears to have been a passageway between the cells of each pair.

The three double cells at Ceann Chùisil

Looking north over Ceann Chùisil

After leaving Ceann Chùisil I had planned to call my wife when I reached the public road at Ardroil, twelve kilometres up the track. She would then drive over to get me from our cottage in Valtos. But I had made a serious mistake: I'd not checked if there was mobile phone coverage in the area. When I reached the road above the white sands of Uig around 8 pm, I powered up the phone only to discover there was no signal. I'd told my wife if she did not hear from me it meant I had decided to spend another night under the stars. But I was sore from a full day of bog-hopping and the climb up the track. A soak in a tub and a beer, sounded better than another night in the tent. There was nothing to do but start walking to Valtos and hope that the phone would eventually get a signal, or that I could hitch a ride.

After ten minutes of walking I passed the Abhainn Dearg distillery. Unfortunately, it was closed—I'd get no refreshment there. I briefly considered breaking and entering—a dram, or for that matter, a whole bottle, would have hit the spot. Twenty minutes later I passed Ardroil Beach, which would have been a great place to camp. In hindsight, I should have done that, but the thought of a bath and a beer kept me going. Only two cars had passed so far; the drivers must have been tourists, as they didn't stop when I stuck my thumb out. Having covered over thirty kilometres, my legs were giving out. So, when I reached the road that comes up from Loch Stacsabhat, I walked south until I found a field that looked like a good campsite. I could go no farther, and quickly found a spot to pitch the tent on the open moorland.

Up at 6 am, a half-hour walk took me to the Uig shop. I was hoping to use their land-line phone, but they were closed. More walking led past the Uig Community Centre (closed), and a phone box (no coins). Then I headed into the mouth of Glen Valtos, the largest glacial meltwater channel in the Outer Hebrides.

I was now five kilometres from Valtos, where my wife was snugly asleep. Still no phone signal and, because it was early, no cars on the road. What I didn't know at the time was that an environmental disaster was in the making. An oil rig had broken its tow-rope and was grounded on Dalbeg Beach, twenty kilometres to the northwest. That disaster saved me. Someone was on the road early, driving to Dalbeg to help out. I saw him approach from behind, stuck out my thumb, and he gave me a lift to the Valtos turnoff. (Thanks Ian!)

Afoot again, a look at the phone showed no service—Uig may be the largest mobile-phone desert in Scotland. There was nothing to do but keep walking. Forty-five minutes later, and a hundred metres from home, the phone finally got a signal. I called my wife to tell her I was almost there, and she met me on the road with a cold carton of Ribena. A drink never tasted so good. Lesson learned: don't assume you'll get a phone signal when hiking in the islands, even in populated areas.

2.1.7 Gearraidh Aineabhal

Landranger Map: 13
Access: B8011 at NB 0317 3133 – a 20 km walk

This section describes a visit to the beehives of Gearraidh Aineabhal from Bothan Aird (section 2.1.3). This is a good option to get to the Tamnabhaigh track instead of visiting Bothan Ura (2.1.4) and Gearraidh Cleit Gruineabhat (2.1.5).

From Bothan Aird descend north to cross the Feadan Ghrunabhat stream, and then climb north across the saddle between the two summits of Aineabhal. From the top of the pass (elev 150 m) descend to the northwest where, 200 metres further on, at an elevation of 65 metres, you will find Gearraidh a' Stigh Aineabhal, the first of the three shieling sites of Gearraidh Aineabhal.

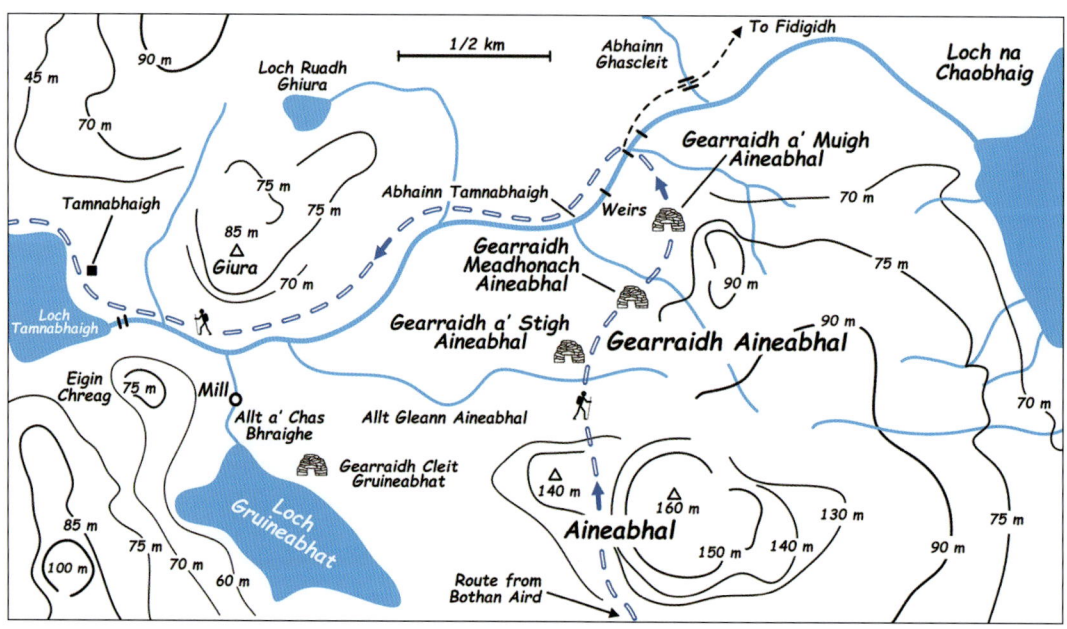

Map 2.1.7: Gearraidh Aineabhal

Gearraidh a' Stigh Aineabhal (Inner Aineabhal)

Locations:
Gearraidh a' Stigh Aineabhal **(1)**: NB 05122 20038
Gearraidh a' Stigh Aineabhal **(2)**: NB 05125 20012
CANMORE ID: 71055

Gearraidh a' Stigh Aineabhal sits at an elevation of 65 metres on the hillside that slopes gradually down to the Abhainn Tamnabhaigh. There are two ruined cells, Gearraidh a' Stigh Aineabhal **(1)** & **(2)**. The western cell of the pair, Cell **(1)**, has a southeast facing doorway and one visible cupboard.

Gearraidh a' Stigh Aineabhal (1)

Gearraidh a' Stigh Aineabhal (1) and the western shoulder of Aineabhal

Gearraidh a' Stigh Aineabhal **(2)** lies 30 metres north of Cell **(1)**. It is in slightly better shape, and the doorway openings to the northeast and southeast are still in place. The cell-dwellers had a view to Loch Tamnabhaigh, a kilometre to the west.

Gearraidh a' Stigh Aineabhal (2)

Looking west over Gearraidh a' Stigh Aineabhal (2) to Loch Tamnabhaigh

From Gearraidh a' Stigh Aineabhal head 200 metres northeast to where you will find the second of the Aineabhal sites: Gearraidh Meadhonach Aineabhal. One of the cells here is a stunner that has managed to survive the centuries intact.

Gearraidh Meadhonach Aineabhal (Middle Aineabhal)

Location: NB 05258 20169
CANMORE ID: 71054

At Gearraidh Meadhonach Aineabhal you'll find two adjacent, but not interconnected, beehives. Both of them nearly three metres in diameter. The eastern cell of the pair, Cell **(2)**, is nearly 100% intact, and the western cell **(1)** is 40% intact. The walls of Cell **(1)** stand a metre high, with a west-facing doorway.

Looking northeast: Cell (1) at left, Cell (2) at right

Interior view—Gearraidh Meadhonach Aineabhal (1)

Gearraidh Meadhonach Aineabhal **(2)** is beautiful. It is almost completely intact, with west and northeast facing doorways. The west door is larger, and easier to enter. Once inside you'll discover a window opening facing to the east, a large cupboard at ground level, and two cupboards halfway up the wall. The presence of a window is extremely unusual, something I've only seen in two other cells (Both a' Ghriosamul and St Ronan's Cell).

Front view—Gearraidh Meadhonach Aineabhal (2)

Loch Tamnabhaigh seen from inside Gearraidh Meadhonach Aineabhal (2)

Cupboards and window—Gearraidh Meadhonach Aineabhal (2)

Gearraidh Meadhonach Aineabhal (2) left—Cell (1) foreground

From Gearraidh Meadhonach Aineabhal head 170 metres to the northeast to where you'll find the third of the Aineabhal sites: Gearraidh a' Muigh Aineabhal.

Looking to Loch Tamnabhaigh from Gearraidh Meadhonach Aineabhal

Gearraidh a' Muigh Aineabhal (Outer Aineabhal)

Locations:
Gearraidh a' Muigh Aineabhal **(1)**: NB 05351 20309
Gearraidh a' Muigh Aineabhal **(2)**: NB 05338 20306
CANMORE ID: 71053

There are three structures marked on the map here, but I was only able to find two. The eastern cell, Gearraidh a' Muigh Aineabhal **(1)**, is only 10% intact; 2.5 metres in diameter, with walls a half metre high. One door opening is visible, which faces to the north.

Looking northwest—Gearraidh a' Muigh Aineabhal (1) at left—Cell (2) at right

Gearraidh a' Muigh Aineabhal (1) — looking west to Loch Tamnabhaigh

Gearraidh a' Muigh Aineabhal (1)

The second cell, Gearraidh a' Muigh Aineabhal **(2)**, is 50% intact, although when viewed from the front it appears fully intact. It is 2.5 metres in diameter with doorways that face northwest and southwest.

*Gearraidh a' Muigh Aineabhal **(2)**—looking north*

*Interior view—Gearraidh a' Muigh Aineabhal **(2)***

Front view—Gearraidh a' Muigh Aineabhal (2)

From Gearraidh a' Muigh Aineabhal head downhill (always my favourite direction) to the Tamnabhaigh River, aiming for the weir at NB 05188 20460. You should be able to ford the river here. But if the crossing does not look safe, you'll have to head west along the south bank of the river to the footbridge at Tamnabhaigh (1.2 km west). If you can cross the river, follow the fisherman's path west to Tamnabhaigh, then continue the journey as described in section 2.1.6.

Note: Optionally, if you are feeling adventuresome, and have the time and energy, you could carry on to the northeast to visit Fidigidh (section 2.2).

2.2 Journey to Fidigidh

Sites visited: Gearraidh Bheinn na Gile, Fidigidh Iochdrach, Both Ruadh, Fidigidh Uachdrach, Bothan Mileabhat, Both Cleit na Crich
Total distance: 25 km

In reading what little I could find about beehive cells, there were three remote sites that sounded especially interesting: Both Ruadh, Fidigidh Uachdrach and Fidigidh Iochdrach (Upper and Lower Fidigidh), once used as shielings by the people of Brenish. The Fidigidh, a river in the Lewis interior, flows south into Loch na Craobhaig, two kilometres northeast of Tamnabhaigh. A cluster of beehives at Fidigidh are depicted in an intriguing drawing in Volume III of the *Proceedings of the Society of Antiquaries of Scotland*.

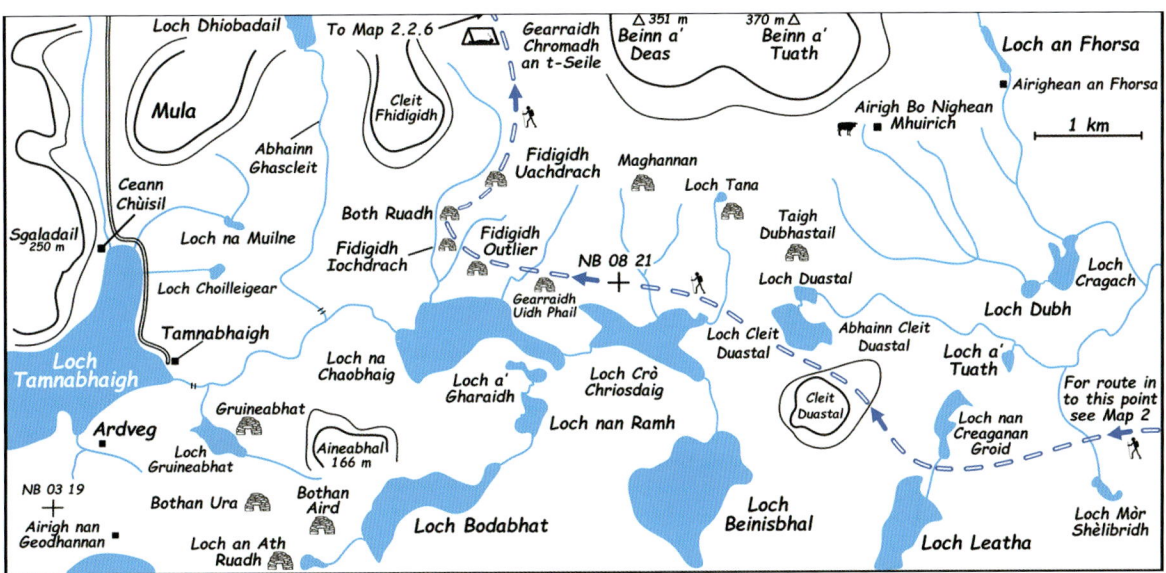

Map 2.2: Journey to Fidigidh

Figure 2.2-1: Fidigidh Iochdrach, H. Sharbau & Capt. Thomas R.N.
Proceedings of the Society of Antiquaries of Scotland, Vol. III (1857-60)

There is no easy way to Fidigidh; a walk from the west means hiking the track from Ardroil over Bealach Raonasgail to Ceann Chùisil, and then a cross-country trek to the east, for a one-way distance of about fifteen kilometres. A thirty-kilometer round-trip in one day, over difficult Hebridean terrain, is just at the limit of my capability, and I tried to do this in the summer of 2013. The first ten kilometres were along the track to Tamnabhaigh, which I left south of a hill called Mula. From there, I headed east across the open countryside.

Then the heavens opened up; a cold, rain-soaked north wind and the occasional sleet storm. It was slow going, then disaster struck. Hidden from sight on the walk across the moorland lurked an impassable obstacle—the Abhainn Ghascleit. A rainstorm the night before had transformed the stream into a wide torrent of foaming, black, peaty water. There was no safe way across, and Fidigidh lay a mere kilometre away. There is a foot-bridge over the stream, but it lay two kilometres to the south. Using it would add four difficult kilometres to the walk. That would mean hiking back in the dark—something I did not want to do. I had to turn back. As I retraced my steps to Uig I promised to try again someday by coming in from the east.

Two years after that failure I did just that: a through-hike from Morsgail to Fidigidh, then up the west side of Loch Gruineabhat to Loch Rog. The distance would be twenty-five kilometres. A possibility for a day hike, but since there was so much to see I took a tent and made it a two-day trek.

See Map 2 for the initial route of this walk (B).

The hike started by walking the private track from Kinlochrog to Loch Morsgail. From there I headed down the east side of the loch to follow one of the boggy quad-bike tracks that lead south to the Gearraidh Beinn na Gile beehives.

2.2.1 Gearraidh Bheinn na Gile

Landranger Map: 13
Location: NB 13130 20060
CANMORE ID: 4078
Access: Kinlochrog, just off the B8011 at NB 1391 2374 – a 5 km walk

As they are only a relatively short, level walk from the road, the beehives of Beinn na Gile are possibly the most visited in the Western Isles. They lie just where a quad-bike track crosses a bridge of old telegraph poles over the Abhainn Bheinn na Gile, 1.6 kilometres south of Loch Morsgail. In WWI, a telegraph line was laid from Morsgail to Kinlochresort, and west to Tamnabhaigh. After the war it was abandoned. When I first visited Beinn na Gile, in the year 2000, a few of the telegraph poles were still standing near here. But they have disappeared since then, some used to build the bridge.

The three cells at Beinn na Gile

The three cells of Beinn na Gile, last inhabited in 1885, are each nearly three metres in diameter. The complete triple-cell complex spans a distance of over ten metres. As is often the case with multiple beehives, one is intact and the domes are partially missing from the others. This makes me wonder if over the years the stones from the topless cells were taken to repair the intact cell.

Intact central cell—Beinn na Gile

In EC Curwen's *Hebrides: A Cultural backwater* (1938), there is a drawing, dated 1937, by an artist with the initials RG, of a model of these cells showing them intact. At that time the model was in the Pitt Rivers Museum in Oxford, 800 kilometres from Gearraidh Beinn na Gile. Someday I hope to see if they still have it. The illustration of figure 2.2.1-1 is based on that drawing.

Figure 2.2.1-1: Beinn na Gile when all three cells were intact
Artist Jessie Ringlien—based on a sketch in Hebrides: A Cultural backwater

Gearraidh Bheinn na Gile—Then and Now

On my first visit to Beinn na Gile, some twenty years ago, there was a dead sheep rotting away inside the larger central cell, so I did not enter. On this visit the sheep was now just a dusty memory, and I crawled in to see the beautifully constructed dome from the inside.

Smokehole of the central cell

Leaving Beinn na Gile behind, I crossed the telegraph-pole bridge, then carried on south for another kilometre to find one of the postman's stones that lead the way across the bogs to Kinlochresort. Fidigidh lay due west, but I followed the stones south for a short distance, as I wanted to pay a visit to my favourite postman's stone.

This particular stone is my favourite because on a walk in the summer of 2012, I noticed the top of a bottle sticking out of the turf next to it. It was an old, mostly empty bottle of Robert Watson brand whisky. I had read that Malcolm Macaskill of Luachair, who'd set up the postman's stones, had stashed a bottle at one of them to quench his thirst when he passed by. I cannot say for certain this was Malcolm's bottle, but it could be. I was happy to see the bottle still there. I pulled it from the turf to take a photo, then tucked it carefully back in.

The Bottle Stone

From the bottle-stone I turned west to start marching across the open moorland, zig-zagging as needed to detour around evil-looking stretches of bog. The next way-point on my

Shielings at Loch Leatha

route to Fidigidh was the shieling of Allt nan Creaganan Groid, on the isthmus between Loch Leatha and Loch nan Creagan Groid (CANMORE ID 133862). Although circular, the structures were too tumbled to tell if they had been beehives.

Then I turned northwest to traverse the shoulder of Cleit Dubastal. I was carrying my old OS Pathfinder maps (1:25000)—oh how I wish they still made this series, as they are small and easy to use in the field. Cleit Dubastal is at the corner of map 80, and after figuring out which was the next to use, I carried on to the shore of Loch Crò Criosdaig. Seven hours after setting out, I had finally reached the heart of beehive country. I was approaching Fidigidh, one of the most imposing galaxies of cells anywhere.

2.2.2 Gearraidh Uidh Phàil

Landranger Map: 13
Locations:
Gearraidh Uidh Phail **(1)** Logan site 11: NB 07552 20837
Gearraidh Uidh Phail **(2)** Logan site 10: NB 07556 20845
CANMORE ID: 133711
Access: B8011 at NB 0317 3133 (Uig) – a 15 km walk
B8011 at NB 1391 2374 (Kinlochrog) – a 9 km

When approaching Fidigidh from the east you traverse the north shore of Loch Crò Chriosdaig. It is an interesting name, one that the OS Name book of 1852 (Vol. 98, p.50) translates as 'loch of the Christian woman's hut'. But a direct translation would seem to be 'loch of the Christian enclosure'. In either case, the name implies there was a monastic settlement in the area. Perhaps it was our next stop, 250 metres farther on, the isolated cells of Gearraidh Uidh Phàil.

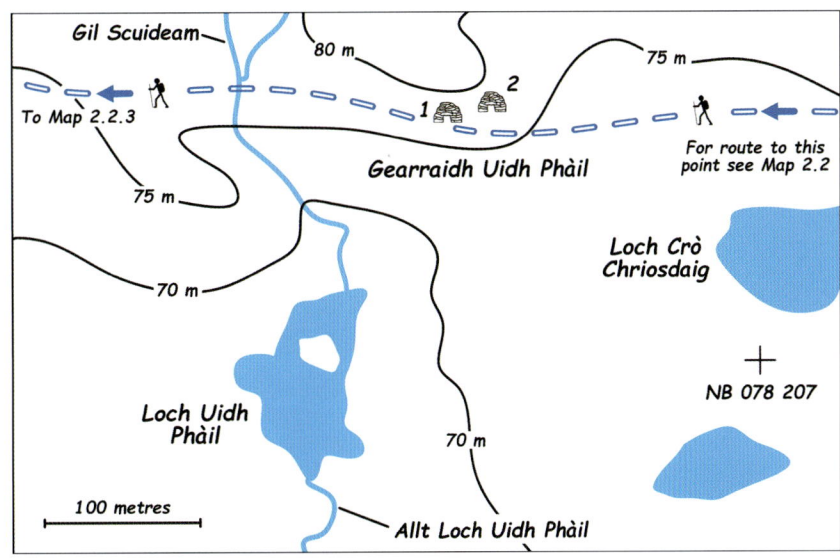

Map 2.2.2: Gearraidh Uidh Phàil

The eastmost cell, Gearraidh Uidh Phàil **(2)**, lies 140 metres northeast of Loch Uidh Phail. It is in a ruinous state, but its location overlooking Loch Uidh Phàil is alluring, and if you are looking for a place to camp it would be perfect. This is Elspeth's description and plan drawing (fig. 2.2.2-1) of Gearraidh Uidh Phàil **(2)**: *Roughly circular structure situated to the east of* **(1)**. *Also very ruinous, interior filled with rubble and much of the masonry collapsed. Very overgrown and difficult to survey with much precision. Possible "porch" with entrance in SE. One cupboard visible.*

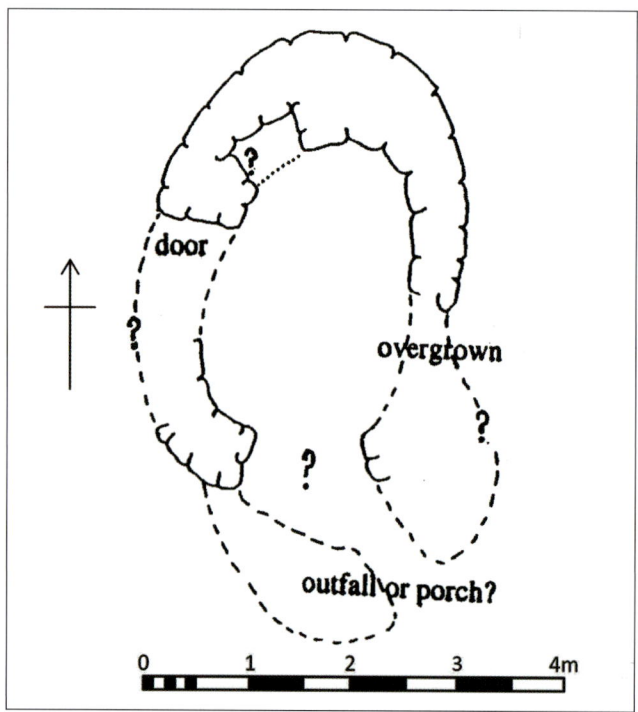

*Figure 2.2.2-1: Gearraidh Uidh Phàil **(2)** plan drawing (Logan site 11)*

*Gearraidh Uidh Phàil **(2)**—Loch Uidh Phàil in the distance*

Gearraidh Uidh Phàil (2)—Gearraidh Uidh Phàil (1) in the background (left of outcrop)

Gearraidh Uidh Phàil **(1)** lies ten metres to the southwest. Stashed in a cleft of rock next to it is a load of intact sea-shells, something Elspeth Logan commented on in 1996.

Gearraidh Uidh Phàil (1)

This is Elspeth Logan's description and plan drawing (fig. 2.2.2-2) of Gearraidh Uidh Phàil **(1):**

Condition of remains extremely dilapidated (marked as ruins on O.S map published in 1854.) Dimensions of structure approx. 2.1m (N-S) by 2 m (E-W). Walls roughly 0.7 m wide. Vegetation covered and rubble in the interior. Situated on sloping ground in lee of rocky outcrop which would afford it shelter from northerly winds. The site lies between Loch na Craobhaig and Loch Cro Criosdaig and approx. 100m north of Loch Uidh Phail. Original form of structure indeterminable. Built under slight overhang, and utilising surrounding natural rock outcrops as walls wherever possible.

A cache of shells (mussels, winkles and limpets) was found in a crevice in the rock face. Since the shells are not smashed this would indicate that they were not brought to the site by birds (since birds have to smash shells to get the food out) and this, coupled with the sheer size of the cache, indicates human consumption. The nearest sea loch where such molluscs can be found is Loch Resort 3.5 km to the south and at roughly the same distance is Loch Thamnabhaidh to the west.

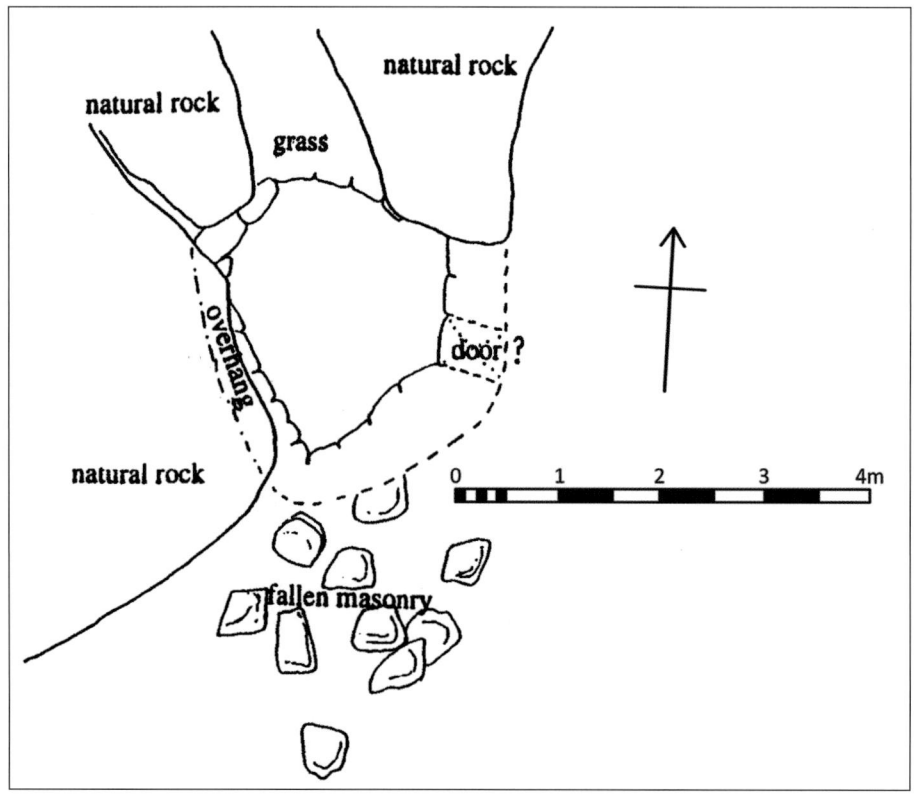

Figure 2.2.2-2: Gearraidh Uidh Phàil (1) plan drawing (Logan site 10)

Gearraidh Uidh Phàil (1)

From Gearraidh Uidh Phàil carry on a kilometre to the northwest where you will encounter the first of the Fidigidh cells.

2.2.3 Fidigidh Iochdrach

Landranger Map: 13
Location: Between NB 0647 2144 and NB 0643 2117
CANMORE ID: 133691
Access: B8011 at NB 0317 3133 (Uig) – a 14 km walk
B8011 at NB 1391 2374 (Kinlochrog) – a 10 km walk

Halfway west along the north side of Loch na Craobhaig there is an outstanding beehive at NB 06580 21011 (identified as 'Fidigidh Outlier' on map 2.2.3). The cell has over a dozen cupboards (storage niches), more than any cell I've seen.

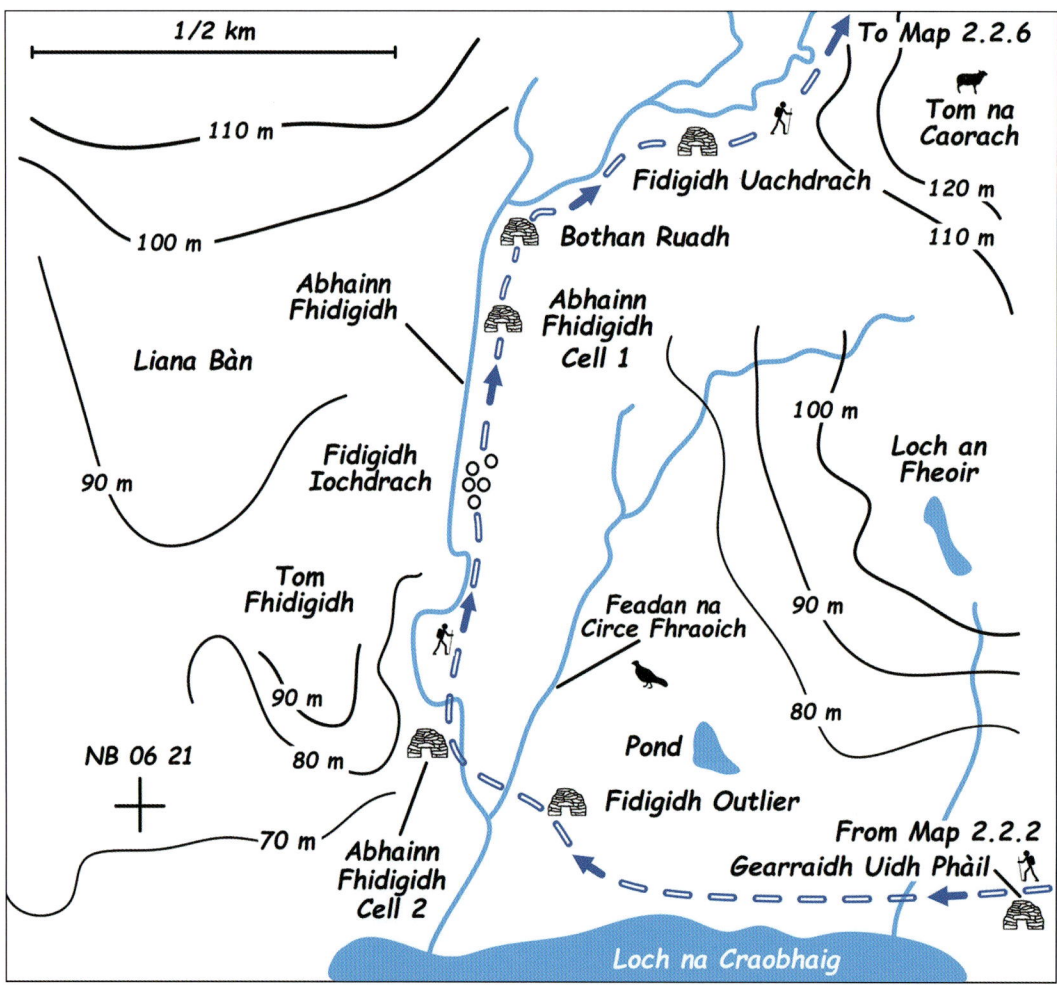

Map 2.2.3: Route through Fidigidh

Fidigidh Outlier

The multiple cupboards of the outlier—Loch na Craobhaig in the distance

Fifty metres to the west I crossed the low waters of Feadan na Circe Fhraoich, the stream of the heather-hen (grouse). Then it was time to turn northwest, aiming for the Abhainn Fhidigidh at NB 06424 21138. The river makes a 90-degree turn here, and a shieling hut lies on the north side of the bend. On the south side is the possible ruin of a beehive (identified as 'Abhainn Fhidigidh Cell 2' on map 2.2.3). Elspeth Logan described is as a *circular feature situated on the south side of the burn 4.7m from the water and opposite an airidh on the other side. One doorway, which faces almost due west. Height of wall to present ground level is 0.4m. The remains are covered in vegetation, and it is therefore difficult to determine the original form of the structure.* (Plan drawing fig. 2.2.3-1.)

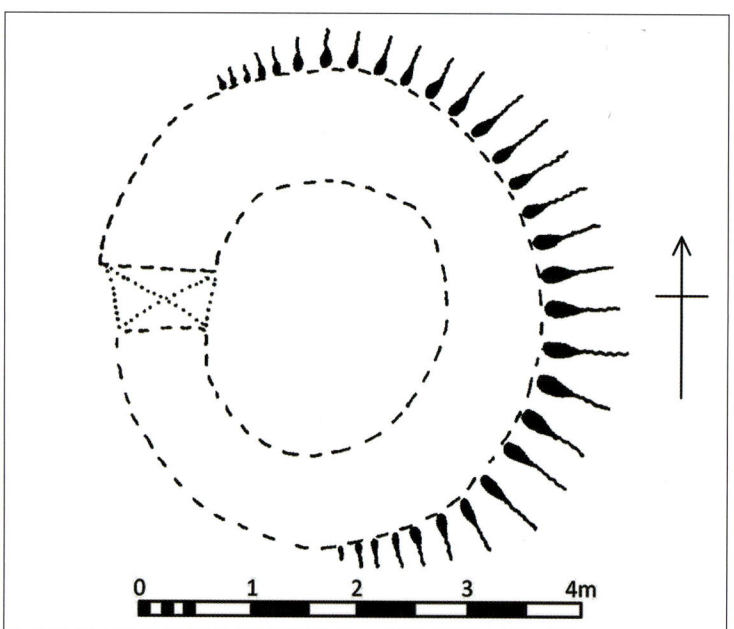

*Figure 2.2.3-1: Abhainn Fhidigidh Cell **(2)** plan drawing (Logan site 14)*

*Turf-grown foundation of Abhainn Fhidigidh Cell **(2)***

Three hundred metres north of the river-bend I came to the main settlement of Fidigidh Iochdrach (Lower Fidigidh). There are at least a half-dozen ruins here. Some might have been beehives at one time, but it's hard to tell, as most of their stones have been plundered. Captain Thomas visited these shielings when they were occupied. Accompanying him was Henry Sharbau, who made a drawing of the cells (see figure 2.2-1). Sharbau would later become chief draughtsman of the Royal Geographical Society. What follows is a paraphrased version of Capt. Thomas's report from the 1850s:

We strolled up the burn of Fidigidh till we came to twenty dwellings scattered along the banks of the burn; groups of cows, with their attendants, spread about. We selected a good position for sketching, and very soon a boy, probably the only one in the settlement who could speak English, was sent to us with the offer of milk. His stock of English was not good, and he could only speak of the group of huts as the city. Shortly a damsel brought us a bowl of milk.

Most of the cells of the 'city' Sharbau sketched are in ruins. I thought I found the spot where he made the drawing, but it was hard to tell for certain. That uncertainty was due to the sad state of the dwellings, and the fact that there is no nearby hilly terrain as depicted in the drawing. It may be the drawing was mislabeled, and was of Fidigidh Uachdrach (Upper Fidigidh) a half kilometre north. Once there I planned to see if the drawing matched its structures.

From Lower Fidigidh I headed north along the Abhainn Fidigidh where, a hundred metres north, I came across a beautiful cell at NB 06488 21562. (Identified as 'Abhainn Fhidigidh Cell 1' on map 2.2.3). Its foundation walls were a metre high, and some corbelling was visible. Its dome has collapsed, the stones probably used to build the now-dilapidated shieling hut five metres west. This cell was surveyed by Elspeth Logan, and she described it as follows (also see fig. 2.2.3-2):

Beehive situated on the east side of the burn 10m from the water and 17m to the south of a 3m high bluff. Both Ruadh visible to the north and the structures at Fhidigidh Iochdrach to the south, (which were not included in this survey since the remains were all rectangular in form suggesting that they are shieling types and not beehive structures.) Walls standing to height of 1m and corbelling visible despite collapse of roof. Cross-section pointless to undertake due to amounts of rubble in the interior of the structure. Appears to have a porch on the eastern side although its overgrown condition and the collapse of its walls rendered it difficult to survey and discern exact layout. Main cell has two doors, one leading into the "porch", which itself has a further two entrances. There are four cupboards visible.

Remains of broken iron pot of 20th century date found inside main cell. Of type used at the turn of the century over open fires. Indicates use of structure at some point in time as domestic/habitational. (Oval shieling structure in dilapidated condition lies 2.3m to the beehive's WNW. Contemporaneity between the two structures is impossible to tell.)

A hundred metres farther north I came to Both Ruadh, one of the most impressive beehive cells in the Western Isles.

Abhainn Fhidigidh Cell (1)

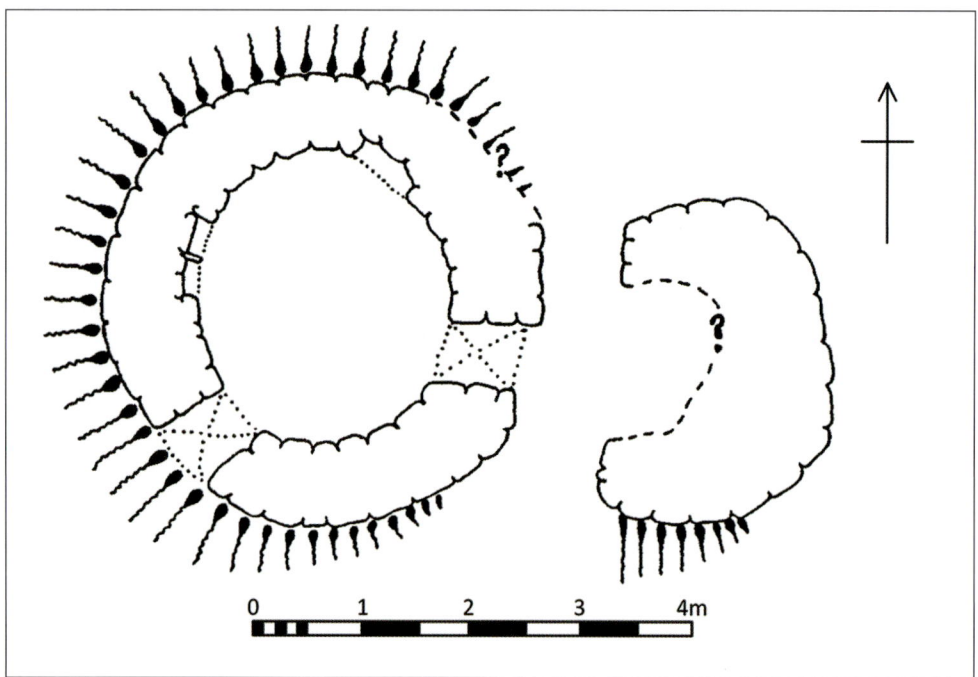

Figure 2.2.3-2: Abhainn Fhidigidh cell (1) plan drawing (Logan site 6)

2.2.4 Both Ruadh

Landranger Map: 13
Location: NB 06519 21772
CANMORE ID: 133690
Access: B8011 at NB 0317 3133 (Uig) – a 13 km walk
B8011 at NB 1391 2374 (Kinlochrog) – a 10 km walk

For years I thought of Both Ruadh as the Inaccessible Beehive, lying as it does thirteen kilometres from the nearest road. And the distance isn't the only challenge, getting there also involves 500 metres of total elevation gain. I have already recounted an earlier failed attempt to get to this area, when I had come in from the west, and was stopped by the rain-swollen waters of the Abhainn Ghascleit (section 2.2). Two years had passed since that miserable failure. And so it was a marvelous feeling to finally stand in front of this cell, which I'd first learned of when I read DDC Pochin Mould's *West Over Sea* in 1995.

The cell is massive, its survival aided by a relatively intact turf covering. Seeing the cell from the side the dome appears completely intact, but when you step inside you'll see that the top courses of the dome have fallen. Once inside you will find a couple of wooden planks that appear to be makeshift benches. But they are not benches. They had been inserted in the dome at some point in an effort to stabilise it, but have since fallen down.

Side view of Both Ruadh—the hill Cleit Fidigidh in the distance

The turf skin extends to the top of the dome—Both Ruadh

This is Elspeth Logan's description and plan drawing (fig. 2.2.4-1) of Both Ruadh: *Single cell beehive structure with two doors and nine cupboards. In good condition. Still has turf covering most of the walls. The hole in the top of the roof has quite recently been covered with planks and turf to help protect the structure. Situated 18m from Abhainn Fhidigidh, on a rise gently sloping down towards the water. Height of wall to present ground level is 1.63m, but 15 cm of organic deposit on the floor in the interior at the northeast end.*

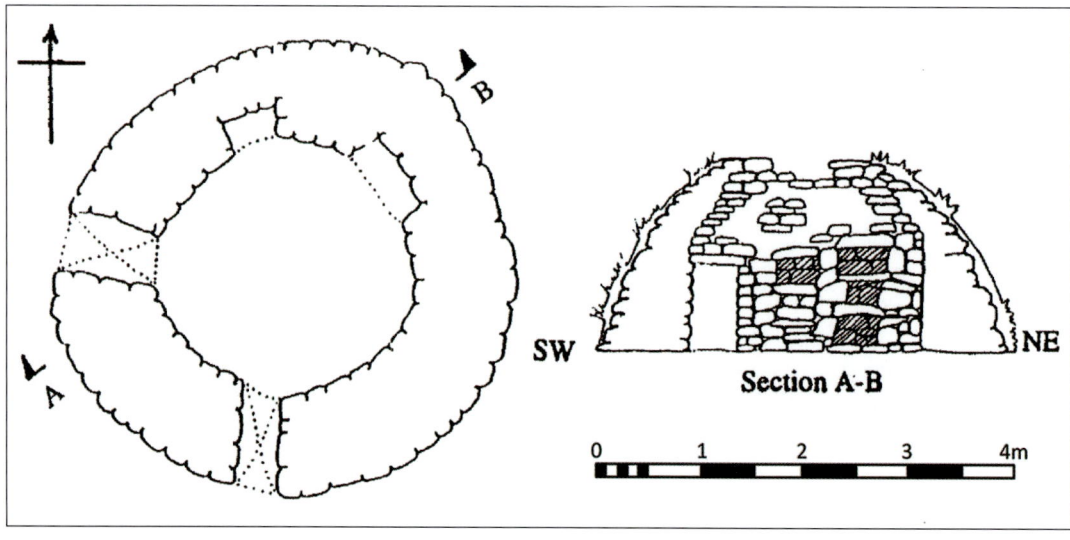

Figure 2.2.4-1: Both Ruadh plan drawing and cross section (Logan site 2)

Looking down into the cell—planks once used to stabilise the dome can be seen

Front view—Both Ruadh

Both Ruadh is an imposing structure. If you are not intent on seeing every beehive cell on Lewis, be sure to visit this one. Another reason to see it is that just 250 metres north is Fidigidh Uachdrach; one of the best cell-clusters anywhere, and our next stop.

2.2.5 Fidigidh Uachdrach

Landranger Map: 13
Locations:
Abhainn Fhidigidh **(1)**, Logan site 3: NB 06642 21830
Fidigidh Uachdrach **(1)**, Logan site 4: NB 06750 21915
Fidigidh Uachdrach **(2)**, Logan site 5: NB 06762 21907
Fidigidh Uachdrach **(3)**, Logan site 7: NB 06865 21924
Fidigidh Uachdrach **(4)**, Logan site 8: Unable to locate
Large shieling (possibly modified beehive): NB 06774 21922
CANMORE ID: 133710
Access:
B8011 at NB 0317 3133 (Uig) – a 14 km walk
B8011 at NB 1391 2374 (Kinlochrog) – a 10 km walk

Fidigidh Uachdrach (Upper Fidigidh) was an active shieling site until WWII. Along with a large rectangular shieling that maybe a modified beehive, there are two cells in good condition, one half tumbled, and two with only their circular bases in place.

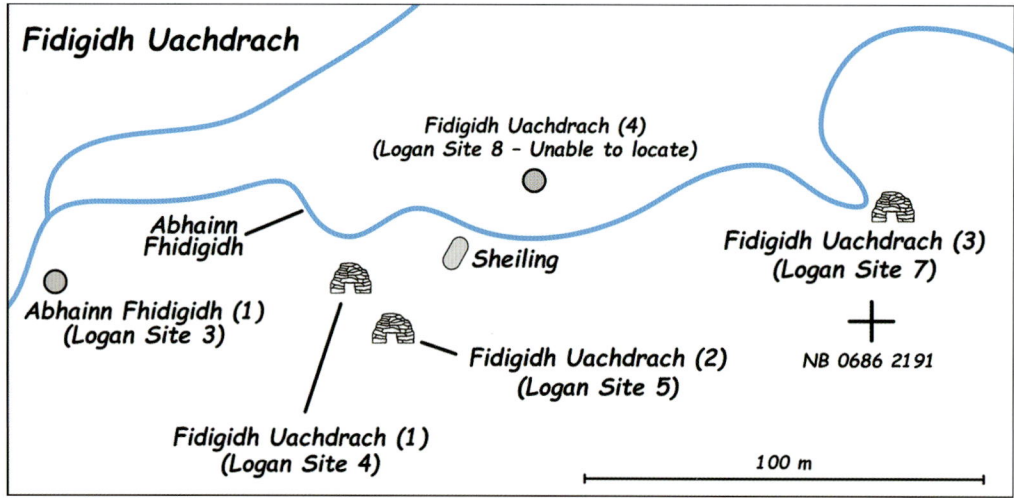

Map 2.2.5: Fidigidh Uachdrach

The first cell you come to when approaching from the west, Abhainn Fhidigidh **(1)**, is ruinous. It has one door, and what's left of its walls, barely a metre high, show slight signs of corbelling. Elspeth Logan described it as a *single cell structure situated 3.2m east of the burn on top of a small cliff 2m high. Height of highest remains of wall to present ground level approx. 0.9m. Very overgrown. Most easily determinable width of wall was at the doorway, 70cm. No cupboards visible. Slight corbelling in south corner, suggesting that the structure may once have been a beehive since this is their main architectural characteristic, but it is also of similar proportions to any roughly constructed shelter for sheep.* (See plan drawing figure 2.2.5-1.)

Abhainn Fhidigidh (1) looking east

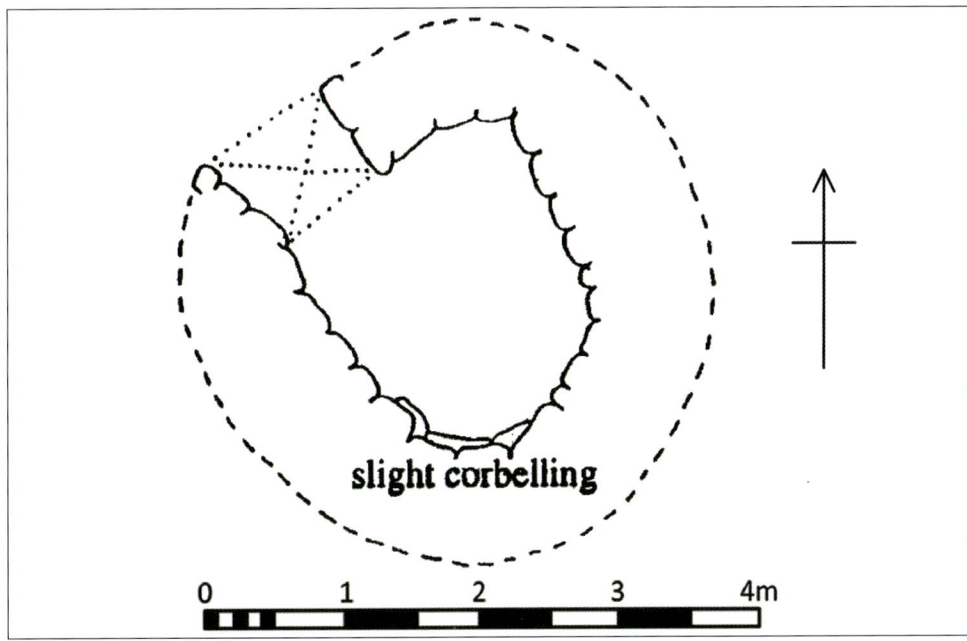

Fig. 2.2.5-1: Abhainn Fidigidh (1) plan drawing (Logan site 3)

The next cell you come to from the west, Fidigidh Uachdrach **(1)**, is 35% intact, its walls nearly a metre high. This is Elspeth Logan's description and plan drawing (fig. 2.2.5-2): *Fairly complete single cell beehive structure. Rubble filled due to roof collapse. Two cupboards visible, but possibly more below roof fall. Walls upstanding to approx. 0.95m. There are two opposing doors. Situated 2m east of Abhainn Fhidigidh and 10.6m west of structure 2* [Fidigidh Uachdrach **(2)**].

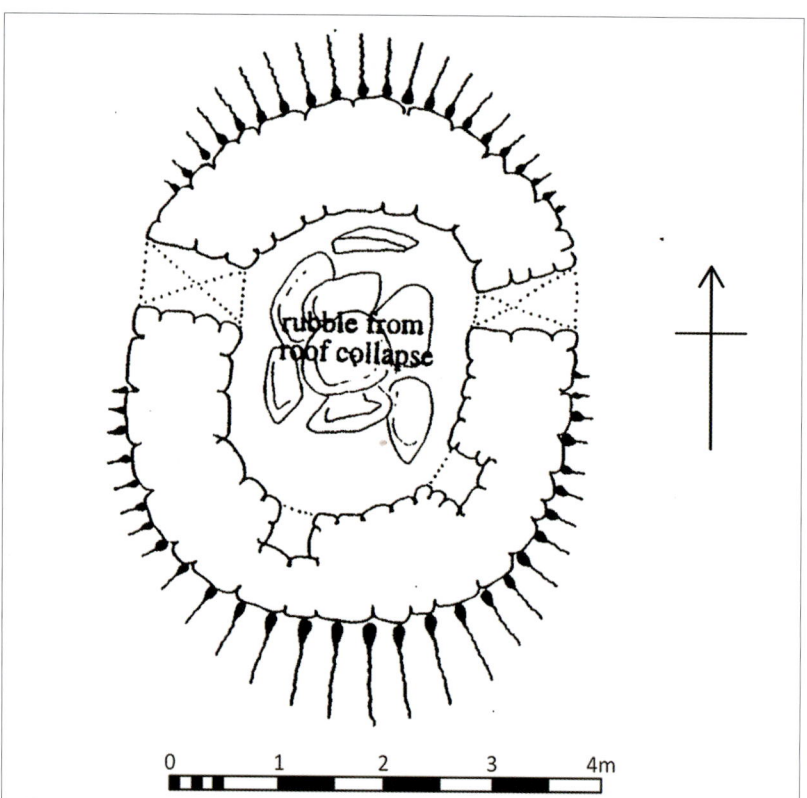

Fig. 2.2.5-2: Fidigidh Uachdrach (1) plan drawing: (Logan site 4)

Fidigidh Uachdrach (1)

The highlight of Upper Fidigidh is cell **(2)**, which lies 10 metres southeast of **(1)**. It is absolutely beautiful—completely intact except for a few missing capstones. It has two doors, and inside there are four cupboards. If not for the soggy, moss-grown floor, it would be a good candidate to spend the night in.

Caption: Fidigidh Uachdrach **(2)** (Logan site 5)

Elspeth Logan described Fidigidh Uachdrach **(2)** as an *almost complete beehive structure, with two doors and four cupboards which are built almost at floor level. Topmost capstones of roof missing, leaving gap 1.38m x 0.8m. Height from highest point to existing floor level, 1.95m.* (Plan drawing fig. 2.2.5-3.)

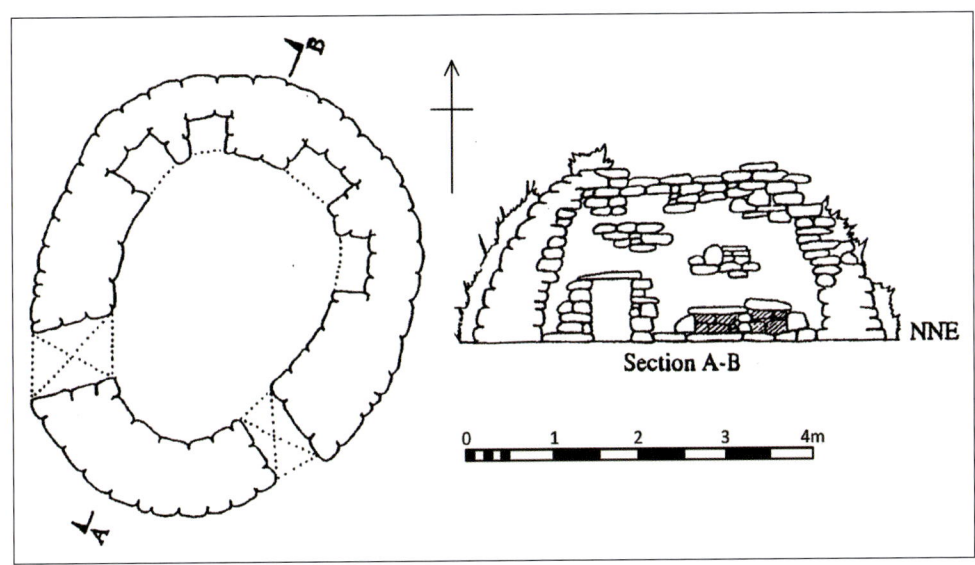

Caption: Figure 2.2.5-3: Fidigidh Uachdrach **(2)** plan drawing (Logan site 5)

Caption: Fidigidh Uachdrach **(2)**—shieling hut (possibly a modified beehive) in the distance

Leaving the cell cluster behind, I made my way 100 metres east to a sharp bend in the Abhainn Fidigidh. Just above the stream sat Fidigidh Uachdrach **(3)**, a 50% intact beehive. Its walls stand 1.5m high, and the interior is filled with slabs fallen from the dome. Elspeth Logan described it as a *fairly complete beehive with 2 doors and 4 cupboards visible. Situated 3m NE of Abhainn Fhidigidh. Walls of structure upstanding to height of 1.4m from present ground level. Rubble in interior from collapse of roof, rendering original ground level indeterminable and a cross section pointless. The masonry is fairly unstable and is without a covering of turf except for a portion on the NW side.* (See plan drawing 2.2.5-4.)

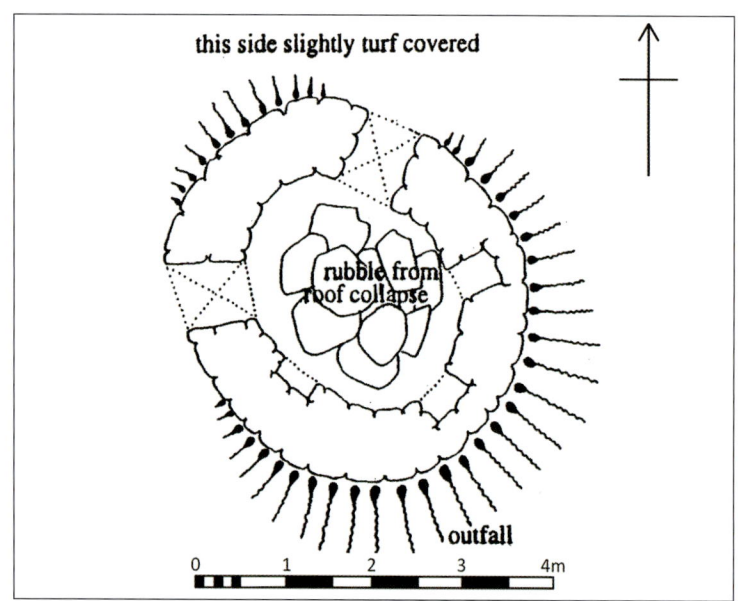

Caption: Figure 2.2.5-4: Fidigidh Uachdrach **(3)** plan drawing (Logan site 7)

Caption: Fidigidh Uachdrach **(3)**—the cell at river's bend

Caption: Fidigidh Uachdrach **(3)**—interior view

Fidigidh Uachdrach (3)—looking west to Tamnasbhal

The most unusual structure here is a shieling hut that is a drastically remodeled beehive. The original cell was massive, and said to have held eleven people. On a subsequent visit to the site, in 2019, the winds were gusting heavily from the south, so for shelter I pitched the tent inside the shieling.

A one-night shieling

As I'd done in Lower Fidigidh, I tried to compare Sharbau's 1850s drawing to the site; but again, neither the terrain in the background, nor the arrangement of structures, matched the drawing. I could only conclude the drawing is not mislabeled. It is probably of Lower Fidigidh, and Sharbau must have filled in the background hills from a faulty memory. I believe the same was done in the drawing of Bothan Aird **(1)**, as that cell is built against a rocky knoll, which is not reflected in the drawing (see section 2.1.3).

The walk to Fidigidh Uachdrach had covered twelve kilometers. I was tempted to spend the night, but I'd told my wife I'd be at the road near Carisiadar by 2 pm the following day. As there were still twelve kilometers of unknown territory to cross, I needed to make more progress before settling down for the night.

Under cloudy skies, watched by curious deer, I followed the east bank of the Abhainn Fidigidh past several shielings, then forded the stream to head up the glen between the hills of Kirabhal and Mula Chaolartan. The OS map shows a large cluster of shielings west of the ridge of Lurga Kirabhal. Thinking it might have beehives and be a good place to camp, I made my way there.

What I found was a large shieling site once used by the people of Crowlista—but no beehives. High on a windswept knoll, just east, lay more shielings that had been cannibalized to make a large sheep fank (NB 07070 24526) that looked like it had not been used in years. It was not an appealing place to camp, so I carried on north, intending to cross the stream that flows out of Loch nan Uidhean.

It was not a stream. It was a substantial river, Abhainn an Easa Dhuibh (the river of the black falls). I could not cross, so there was nothing to do but follow it east. A kilometre on I came to the waterfall that gave the river its name, Easa Dubh, the black falls, cascading down a series of dark, slick rocks. Near the waterfall is Gearraidh an Easa Dhuibh (NB 0783 2528); shielings once used by the people of Enaclete, five kilometres to the northeast. There were no beehives, the only structure a large rectangular hut.

I eventually found a place to ford the river, and around 9 pm, just when the pack seemed to be getting heavier, came to Gearraidh Chromadh an t-Seile. It was an inviting site, a dilapidated shieling hut nestled in a sharp bend of a stream. It was only ten kilometers from the road—the time had come to set up camp.

Several deer stood on the hillside above, watching with interest, as I pitched the tent, occasionally barking into the twilight—the deer, not me. Dinner was a tuna sandwich that had been squashed flat in the pack, and a bag of smoky bacon crisps, all washed down with a can of Export. Beer never tastes better than after you've lugged it for twelve hours across difficult terrain.

Gearraidh Chromadh an t-Seile

I was afoot the following morning by 8 am. Under gray and rainy skies, I made my way north to find a viewpoint over Loch Gruneabhat—refer to Map 2.2.6. Below me was Rubha Dubh (Black Point), a low-lying peninsula jutting into the loch. I decided there was time to look for something there that I'd read of long ago in Daphne Pochin Mould's classic *West Over Sea*. In chapter 14, she recounts a story that links Black Point to the death of Angus, one of the sons of Somerled, the Lord of the Isles. To abridge the tale:

The people of Uig were being plagued by the Norse, with no help from their chief, Angus, the son of Somerled. And so they nominated another chief who insisted on being formally inaugurated on the 'foot-print' coronation stone in Rodel Church. To do that, the people of Uig decided to steal the stone and carry it back to Uig. Angus found out and pursued them by sailing north to Mealasta. There was a battle, and Angus and his three sons were killed.

In *West Over Sea*, Daphne Pochin Mould mentions she was told there are four mounds on the Black Point of Loch Gruineabhat, mounds that mark the graves of Angus and his sons. Although it was just an old story (Angus and his sons were killed fighting the Norse in 1210), I still wanted to see the mounds of Black Point. Fortunately, the point, which is almost an island, is small. I walked every square metre of it, but the only mounds were natural humps of peaty turf. There was no sign of anything man-made. It was disappointing, and the ragged, feral sheep on the point thought I was trying to catch them.

Although Black Point had been a bust, my next stop was not. I climbed northwest from Loch Gruineabhat for a kilometre, and on rounding the side of a hill came to the perfectly preserved beehive of Bothan Mileabhat.

Note: A year after making this walk I learned of another Black Point in Loch Gruineabhat. It lies on the other side of the loch, 1.5 kilometers southeast of where I'd searched. Its name is Aird Dubh Mhic Shomhairle Bhàin, the black point of the fair-haired son of Somhairle. A very remote place that I will have to visit someday.

2.2.6 Bothan Mileabhat

Landranger Map: 13
Location: NB 07770 28044
CANMORE ID: 132202
Access: B8011 near Carisiadar at NB 0946 3343 – a 7 km walk

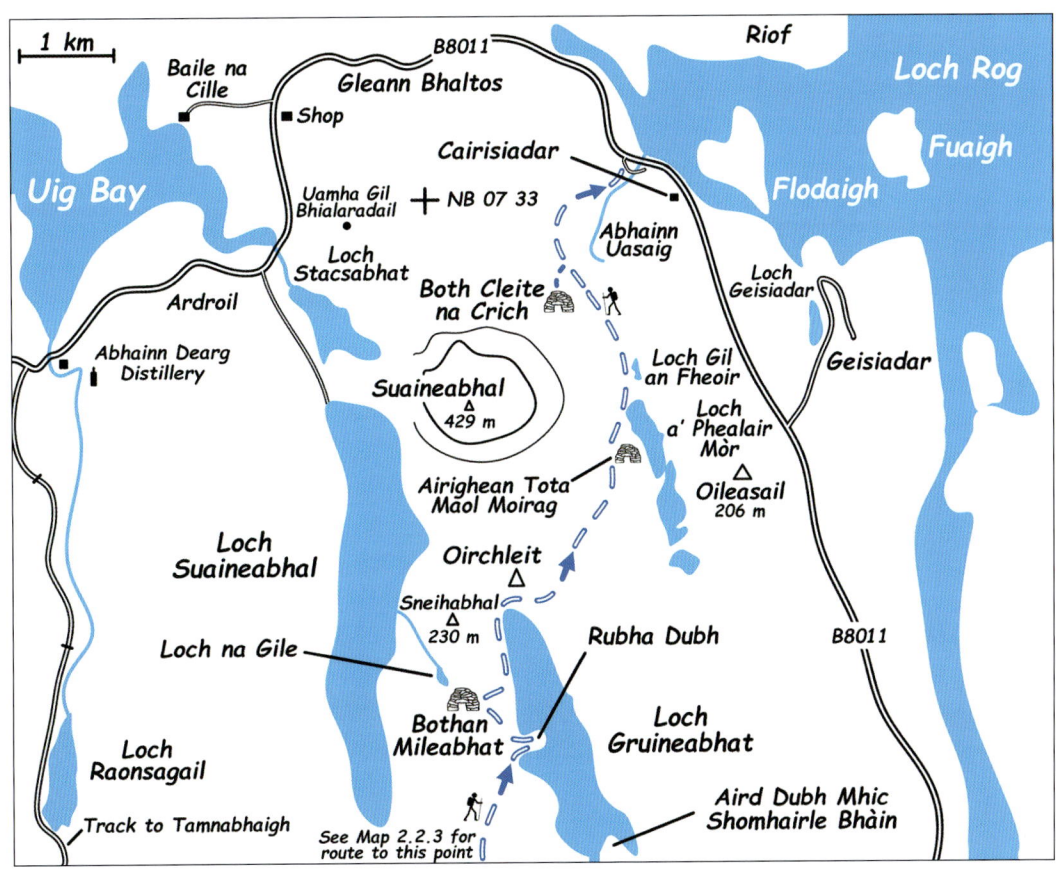

Map 2.2.6: Bothan Mileabhat & Both Cleit na Crich

Bothan Mileabhat lies 450 metres west of Loch Gruineabhat, halfway between it and tiny Loch na Gile. The cell's main doorway is quite elegant. Its invitingly angled stones and prominent eyebrow lintel make you want to crawl inside. From the outside it appears to be a stable structure, but after crawling through the tiny entrance you'll see the sun shining (or the clouds looming) through myriad openings in the dome. It wouldn't take much disturbance for the whole thing to come tumbling down.

Once inside, you will see that its capstone is still in place, and that there is a blocked up second entrance. A short distance west of the cell lie the tumbled ruins of what was either another cell or an animal enclosure, and there are several shieling ruins nearby.

Approaching Bothan Mileabhat from the east

Bothan Mileabhat—front view

Bothan Mileabhat—the intact dome

Bothan Mileabhat—side view

Direct route: You do not need to make a two-day hike, like I did, to see Bothan Mileabhat. It is one of the easiest to reach of the intact cells, lying as it does only seven kilometres from the road near Carisiadar (a series of posts marks part of the way). The directions are as follows:

Starting from the B8011 at Carisiadar (NB 09457 33426), follow the side-road for 100 metres south to reach a track that initially follows the Abhainn Uasaig. Carry on for a kilometre to where the track forks, then follow the left fork until it ends near NB 0879 3261. From there, head cross-country for a kilometre and a half to Loch Gil an Fheoir. From this small loch head southwest past the northwest tip of Loch a' Phealair Mòr to the north end of Loch Gruineabhat (NB 0819 2892). A kilometer down the west side of the loch turn west to reach the beehive. Visiting Bothan Mileabhat can also be part of an all-day outing that includes a climb to the cairn-crowned summit of Suaineabhal (429 m).

From Bothan Mileabhat, I returned east to the hillside above Loch Gruineabhat, and then turned north to follow a series of posts that mark the route to the cell if you come in from Carisiadar. Once around the north end of Loch Gruineabhat I headed northwest to Loch a' Phealair Mòr, where I came upon Airighean Tota Maol Moirag. There are a half-dozen ruined shielings there, including one that was definitely a beehive partially embedded in the hillside at NB 09306 30513. Its walls still stood a metre high, and the doorway lintel was still in place.

From the cell I climbed the narrow pass between the hills of Suainabhal and Ainebhal (see note). Then a course to the north led to the start of a rocky peat track at NB 08786 32619, which in turn led to the highway. I was on time, and saw my wife sitting in the car with a big smile on her face. I gave her a big kiss, and she gave me a cold beer in return.

Beehive ruin near Loch a' Phealair Mòr

Important note: Just after you exit the pass between Suainabhal and Ainebhal, near NB 093 320, you should make a slight detour. Seven-hundred metres to the west lies the beautiful beehive of Cleit na Crich, set high in an isolated position overlooking Loch Rog. I was not aware of the cell when I made the walk described above, but I returned two years later to find it (see section 2.2.7). Don't make the same mistake. It is worth the detour.

2.2.7 Both Cleit na Crich

Landranger Map: 13
Location: NB 08653 31956
CANMORE ID: None
Access: B8011 near Carisiadar at NB 0946 3343 – a 2 km walk

Both Cleit na Crich (cell of the remote rocky eminence), lies at an altitude of 130 metres, approximately halfway between Carisiadar and the summit of Suaineabhal. Built behind a rock outcrop, it is completely invisible from below. When I was looking for it in 2018, I almost gave up the search. I had made my way to the location coordinates in the Uig Historical Society records (NB 088 320), which is at the centre of a small, boggy glen.

There were no structures to be seen, but before giving up, I took a close look at the 1:25000 map. As I did, I noticed a tiny square on the map, a structure of some sort, 150 metres farther west, so I headed that way. On rounding a small ridge, the cell came into view. Its doorway is topped by a large lintel, and at first sight the cell seems 100% intact. But after climbing to the top of an adjacent knoll, you'll see that the upper levels of the dome have collapsed.

Both Cleit na Crich

The cell may have been monastic, as it is hidden, far from other structures, and cultivatable land. The nearest shieling site is Gearraidh Theurabridh, 400 metres to the north, where you will find four tumbled cells, two that have been modified into larger shieling huts. Alternately, with its high vantage point, Both na Crich could have been a lookout station to monitor for any unwanted arrivals by sea.

Once inside the cell you will discover several cupboards at ground level, and on the ground are slabs that have fallen from the dome. The cell dweller here, be they monk or exhilarated hiker, are blessed with an expansive, open-sky view out over Loch Rog. A walk to Both Cleit na Crich makes for a memorable day out, or as the destination for a brilliant night under the stars.

Both Cleit na Crich—looking northeast to Loch Rog

Top view—Both Cleit na Crich

Inside Both Cleit na Crich

Both Cleit na Crich

2.3 Journey to Aird Mhòr

Sites visited: Bothan Loch na Airigh, Gearraidh na h-Àirde Mhòire, Loch an Ath Ruaidh, Bothan Aird, Both Ruadh, Both Màghannan, Airidh a' Loch Thaine
Total distance: 36 km

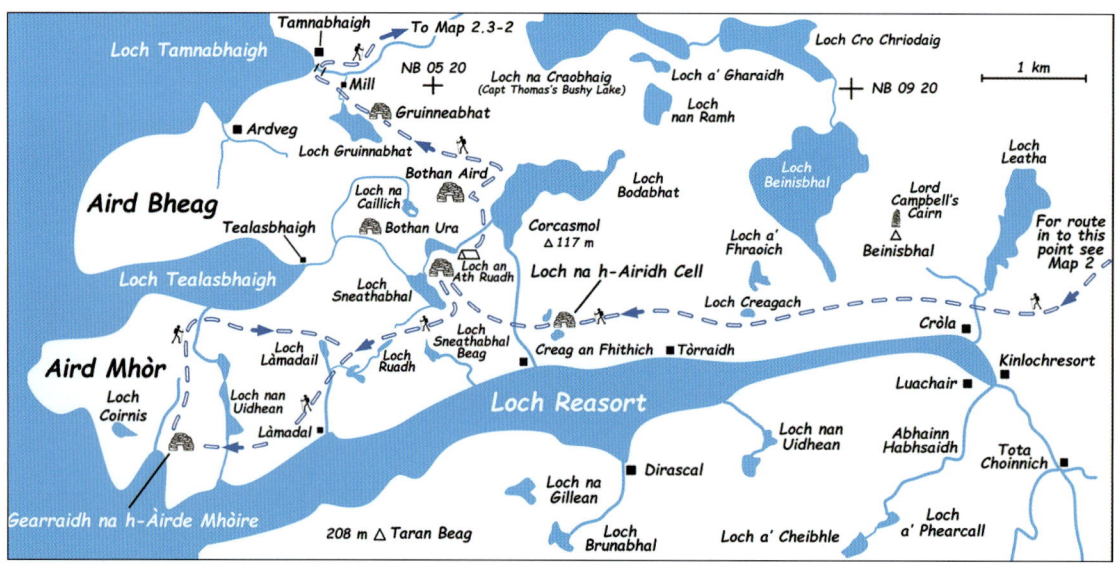

Map 2.3-1: Journey to Aird Mhòr

See Map 2 for the initial route of this walk (C).

It was noon when my wife dropped me off at the gate to Morsgail Lodge. I had ventured out this way many times in the past twenty years; this would turn out to be the hardest, but most rewarding, time of all. The purpose? (If you have to ask, you haven't been paying attention.) The purpose was to take photos of the many beehives in the area, especially the multi-chambered cells at Gearraidh na h-Airde Mhòire, one of the most remote places on Lewis. On my only previous visit, in 2000, I had to ration my film, and had not photographed all the cells I'd seen.

The first kilometre was easy, down the tarmac track that winds along the Kinlochrog River. Just before Morsgail Lodge a footbridge takes you to the east side of the river, and from there you are on mostly pathless terrain. I say mostly, because here and there bits of quad-bike tracks are apparent. But there are several, going off in different directions, so you have to know where you are going.

My first destination was the Beinn na Gile beehive three kilometres to the south, a triple cell in relatively good shape (see walk 2.2). Next to the cells a bridge of old telegraph-poles crosses the Abhainn Beinn na Gile. I crossed the bridge, and then carried on south, looking forward to visiting my favourite Postman's Stone.

The Postman's Stones, which guide you through the miasma of bog between Morsgail and Kinlochresort, were put in place by Malcolm Macaskill, the postman who once served

Kinlochresort. One of the stones is my favourite because during a walk in 2012 I found a whisky bottle buried in the turf below it. Malcolm is said to have stashed a bottle at one of the stones to refresh himself on the long walk across the moorland, and I'd like to think the bottle was his. I'd visited the bottle-stone again in 2015 (see section 2.2.1). Two years had passed and I was looking forward to seeing it again.

When I came to the bottle-stone I eagerly shoved my hand into the turf. There was nothing. I dug deeper. Still nothing. Someone had taken the bottle. It was my fault. I'd written about the bottle on-line, including a picture, but I'd never disclosed its exact location. Someone must have used the photo to locate the stone and take the bottle. I hope they are taking care of it. In hindsight, I should have taken the bottle when I found it and given it to the Uig Museum.

Greatly disappointed, I continued south, following more of the stones through the daunting peat hags for two kilometres. Just before Kinlochresort I turned west. My plan was to make it as far as Gearraidh na h-Àirde Mhòire at the mouth of Loch Reasort, eight kilometres to the west. A hike I'd last made in the year 2000.

A section of the Postman's Stones

Seventeen years had passed, and there I was hoping to repeat that feat at age 60. (I made that hike in 2000 with Diana Smith, as recounted in Chapter 20 of *Skye & Tiree to the Outer Isles*). On reaching the southern slopes of Beinisbhal I stopped to take some long-distance photos of Murdo MacDonald's house at Cròla, a beautiful oasis on the shore of Loch Reasort.

The temperature was on the rise. I had grand plans to photograph three of the old settlements on the shore of Loch Reasort. But on reaching the highlands above Tòrraidh, the first of the three, my weary legs decided otherwise. No way, in the heat, could I drop 100 metres to the shore and climb back up, so I continued west, trying (not very successfully) to stay at the 100-metre contour. After Tòrraidh I came to the high ground above Crow Cliffs (Creag an Fhithich). There were no crows, but a golden eagle made an impressive fly-by.

At a random spot on a ridge I took a break (I take a lot of breaks). As I sat on a boulder to catch my breath I noticed a large cairn. No. Not a cairn—a beehive cell! I'd stumbled upon a site not recorded by Historic Scotland; one I'd only learned of a few months earlier while browsing through photos on the Geograph UK website (a great resource for armchair exploring). Completely by accident I'd stumbled upon the beehive cell of Loch na h-Airigh (shieling loch).

2.3.1 Loch na h-Airigh

Landranger Map: 13
Location: NB 06575 17805
CANMORE ID: None
Access: B8011 at NB 1391 2374 (Kinlochrog) – a 12 km walk

Both Loch na h-Airigh sits in a prominent position, on a ridge at an elevation of 70 metres, 130 metres northeast of Loch na h-Airigh. Outside its entrance is a large, walled forecourt, which may once have been a porch or another cell. The bell-shaped cell is narrow, with room for one person at most. The floor is a jumble of fallen stones, and it's difficult to safely enter.

Unlike many cells, this one proudly stands out in the open; no attempt made at concealment. So it has great views west to the hill Taran Mor and the mouth of Loch Reasort. Directly across the loch is the abandoned settlement of Direscal. (See chapter 23, *Skye & Tiree to the Outer Isles* for a description of Direscal.)

Both Loch na h-Airigh—Loch Reasort and Direscal in the distance

Both Loch na h-Airigh—porch/annex in the foreground

A look at the watch showed it to be 7 pm. I was still hoping to reach Gearraidh na h-Àirde Mhòire, and camp next to the twelve-chambered beehive, three kilometers farther west—but that's as the gannet flies. It was probably more like six kilometres of ups and downs over difficult terrain. I was beat, and had to accept the fact I could not make it that far in the heat. It was time for Plan B.

Plan A had been to camp at Gearraidh na h-Àirde Mhòire and then revisit the cluster of cells around Loch an Ath Ruaidh. *So why not...*, I said to myself, *Why not head directly to Loch an Ath Ruaidh to spend the night? It's only an HSJ away.* (A hop, skip, and jump, 1.125 kilometers in the metric system.) *Then, in the morning, carry on to Gearraidh na h-Àirde Mhòire. Easy-peasy.*

And so, the weary hiker, talking to himself, carried on. It finally started to cool down when, at 8 pm, he hiked over Cleit an Eoin (Bird Ridge) to reach Loch an Ath Ruaidh. After passing several beehives on the high ground above the loch, he found a campsite in the soft, tall, inviting grass bordering its east end. With the tent pitched, a comfortable rock was found to sit on and have supper—two breakfast bars washed down by a warm can of beer. He burped, crawled into the tent, and slept solidly for ten hours.

Loch an Ath Ruaidh

— DAY 2 —

I was up at 8 am. Fortunately there was a slight wind, so the tent was not immersed in a swarm of thirsty midges. The first task was to take photos of the cells around Loch an Ath Ruaidh. I had visited them in the past, but this village of cells is one of my favorite places. So are the cells of Bothan Aird, 250 metres north, which I ventured up to see again.

Back at camp I decided to leave the tent pitched on what was the perfect loch-side campsite. I would make an out and back walk to Gearraidh na h-Àirde Mhòire to see its multi-chambered cells, then return to spend another night at Loch an Ath Ruaidh. The day was heating up fast as I refilled my jug, added a little apple juice for sweetness, then followed the stream down to Loch Sneathabhal. After rounding the north end of the loch, a bit of climbing up the tussocky hillside led to narrow Loch Ruadh. There are dozens of 'Ruadh' place-names out here; the word is Gaelic for the colour red, and usually a reference to red sandstone, or in some cases red deer.

From Loch Ruadh a steep descent along its tumbling stream led to Loch a Chas Bhraighe Ruaidh. There I was confronted with yet another ridge to climb, but only after traversing the upper reaches of Gleann Làmadail. Far below, on the shore of Loch Reasort, lay the remains of Làmadal, another settlement on Loch Reasort I'd planned to see. But in the heat I needed to save my energy. Làmadal would have to wait for next time.

A soft breeze kept the midges at bay, but not the big, blood-thirsty clegs (what is called a horsefly at home). As I hiked on in the heat I fantasised about taking my shirt off or rolling up my sleeves. But if I did the clegs would have a feast. The climb led to the south tip of Loch nan Uidhean, after that there was only one more little glen to cross, one more not-so little ridge to climb.

On reaching the western shoulder of Beinn a' Charnain my destination finally came into view. Remembering how seventeen years before Diana Smith and I had hiked here in one day, I felt my age. I was exhausted from the previous day's trek and the current day's five kilometres. What lay in front of me made it worthwhile. It was time to see some amazing ruins.

2.3.2 Gearraidh na h-Airde Mhòire

Landranger Map: 13
Locations:
Linear Quad Cell: NB 02565 16579 (Logan site 32), PSAS Vol. III, Plate XIV, Figs.1 and 2
Quad Cell: NB 02536 16580 (Logan site 31), PSAS Vol. III, Plate XIV, Fig.3
Double Cell: NB 02549 16551 (Logan site 30), PSAS Vol. III, Plate XIV, Fig. 4
12-Chambered Cell: NB 02453 16561 (Logan site 33), PSAS Vol. III, Plates XV & XVI
CANMORE ID: 75066
Access: B8011 (near Abhainn Dearg Distillery) at NB 0317 3133 – 20 km walk
B8011 near Kinlochrog at NB 1391 2374 – 16 km walk

Although the cells of Gearraidh na h-Àirde Mhòire are not intact, it is one of the most stunning set of beehive ruins in the Western Isles. Seton Gordon had this to say about it in *Afoot in the Hebrides*:

...here are the ruins of a cluster of very old dwellings built of stone. Little remains of these dwellings, which are smaller than summer shielings, and may have been used by the Picts in the ancient past.

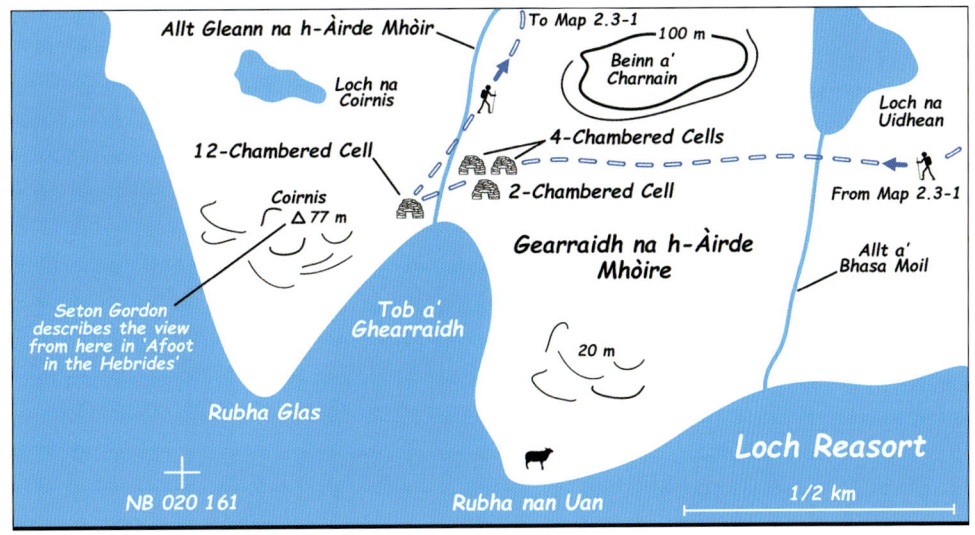

Map 2.3.2: Gearraidh na h-Àirde Mhòire

I don't agree that little remains, for there are some substantial, and beautiful, remains. Used by the people of Carinish as shielings as late as 1823, three of the structures lie on the hillside east of Allt Gleann na h-Àirde Mhòire, the stream that flows through the site. The cells are set close together; and as you approach from the east the first you encounter is a four chambered cell, which is actually a linear set of two cells, each with a porch, set back to back. Of all the ruins, it is in the best condition.

This is Elspeth Logan's description and plan drawing (fig. 2.3.2-1) of the linear four-chambered cell:

Two double celled structures built back to back, or a quadruple celled structure which has a distinct break between the buildings in the middle. One section of wall appears particularly thin being one stone width only and does not fit in with the corbelled design, which may mean that this part of the wall could be a later renovation of some sort. Height of highest part of wall to existing ground level is 0.9m. Situated on the summit of the same hillock as sites 30 and 31, overlooking the sea inlet and across Loch Resort to Harris. The three structures are surrounded by greener vegetation than is usual, indicating the presence of animals around the beehives. Immediately north of this twin double celled structure are several large stones which appear to be delineating a small area. Possible garden or animal pen?

Linear four-chambered structure at Gearraidh na h-Àirde Mhòire (Logan site 32)

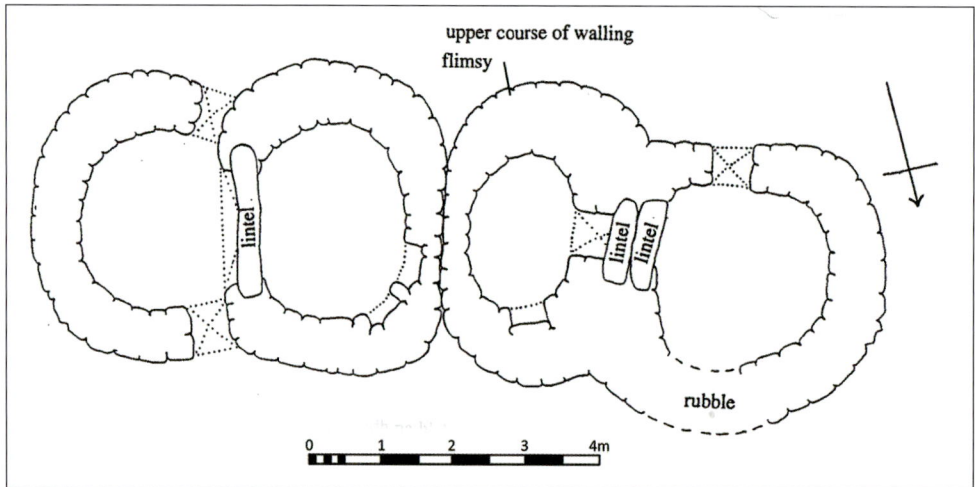

Figure 2.3.2-1: Linear four-chambered structure plan drawing (Logan site 32)

Thirty metres to the west lies another quad-cell, this one making use of natural rock for part of its foundation. DDC Pochin Mould, in *West Over Sea*, says that this one *consists of a main central chamber with a churn room opening off it and a second beehive to serve as a dairy built alongside. The main chamber has a porch outside the door.*

This complex cell was described by Elspeth Logan (also see fig. 2.3.2-2) as a *structure with four cells, three large ones and 1 smaller cell. Two cupboards visible. Highest part of wall to present ground level is 1.05m. Natural rock outcrop utilised where possible. Structure fairly dilapidated since masonry either collapsed and/or covered in vegetation. Built on sloping ground on the same northerly facing hillock as site 30. Collapse of roof made interior difficult to survey. Indistinct lines of masonry in vicinity of complex may have been walled gardens or pens of some sort.*

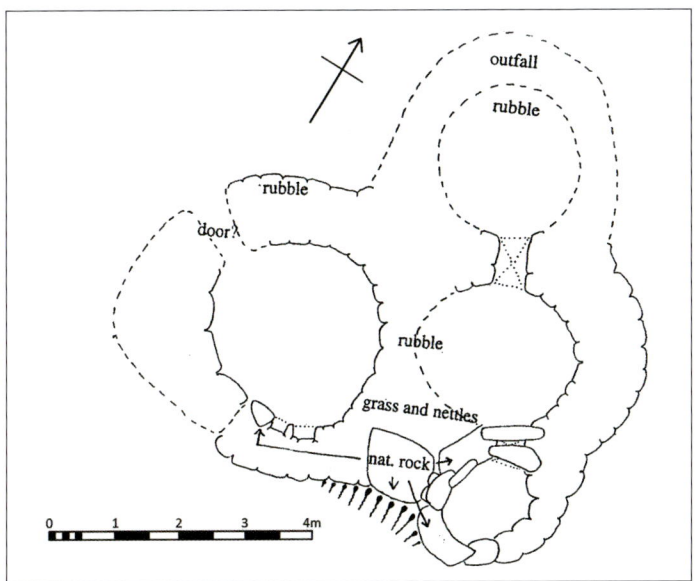

Figure 2.3.2-2: Western four-chambered cell plan drawing (Logan site 31)

The western four-chambered cell

Linteled entrance to the western four-chambered cell

Eighteen metres southeast of the four-chambered cell lies a double cell (a single with a large porch). This structure was described by Elspeth Logan (also see fig. 2.3.2-3) as a *single cell beehive with annex/porch, which single door leads into. The annex has a double entrance. One cupboard visible. Natural rock outcrop incorporated into masonry. Highest point of wall to present ground level is 0.93m. Interior filled with nettles and rubble from collapse of roof. Annex even more indistinct due to roof collapse, nettles and outwards fall of wall which itself is due to the construction of the beehive on a steep slope. The main cell was built on a flatter area and is therefore not in so ruinous a condition. Situated on northerly facing hillock on quite steep ground.*

The double cell

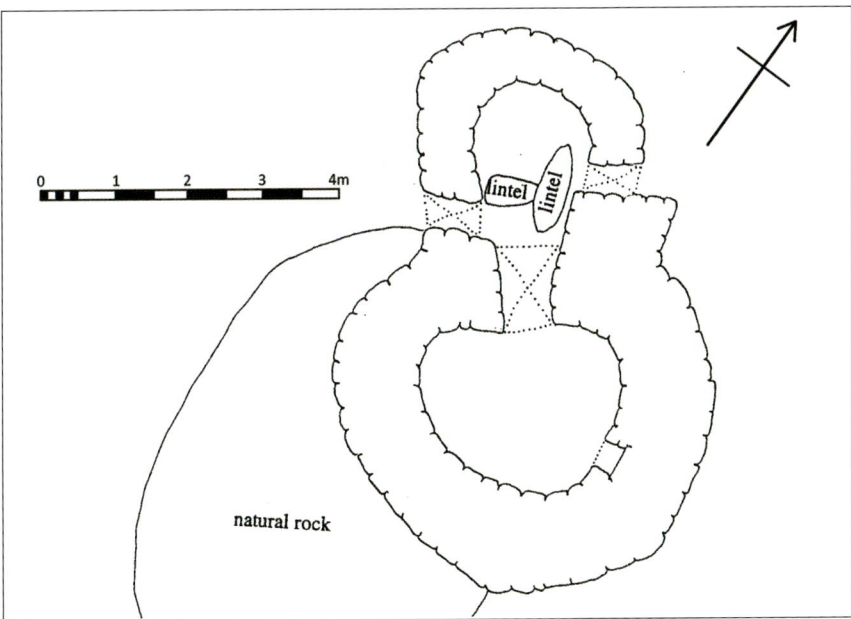

Figure 2.3.2-3: Double cell plan drawing (Logan site 30)

Looking across the mouth of Loch Reasort from the double cell

After seeing the three stunning structures east of Allt Gleann na h-Àirde Mhòire, I walked a hundred metres west to cross the stream. Before me lay something fantastic. Just above the beach lies a jumble of stones arranged in a roughly circular outline, ten metres in diameter. Within the circle, cluttered with colorful flotsam and rampant nettles, lay several circular compartments. It was the 12-chambered beehive, last occupied in 1820.

This unique and complex structure consists of a dozen cells linked together into a sort of prehistoric apartment building. It is not known whether it dates to pre-Christian times, was a

Celtic Christian settlement, or an old shieling village. This fascinating relic is described in detail in Pochin Mould's *West Over Sea*, and this is how Captain Thomas described it:

Twelve individual huts all built touching each other, with doors and passages from one to the other. The diameter of this gigantic both is 46 feet, and is nearly circular in plan. The height of the doors and passages are about 2□ feet; and under the smokehole (farlos) in two of the chambers, the height was 6□ feet. There are three distinct suites of chambers, perhaps dwellings, originally of three families. The chambers are scarcely larger than any other bothan, the size of the stones employed limiting the area they will safely cover. Two of the chambers were still roofed, but in a very ruinous condition, and both fell in just after my people, who had been digging into the floor of the chambers, had left.

This is Elspeth Logan's extensive description (for cell numbering refer to fig. 2.3.2-4):

Complex with twelve cells situated very close to the boulder beach and only 5m above the normal high tide line. In the shelter of a steep rise of hill to the west. In very bad state of preservation, due to collapse of walls, but mainly due to its close proximity to the beach where rubbish from the sea (logs, driftwood, buoys, rusty bombs, shoes, rope, refuse and seaweed) has been thrown up onto the complex, with the bigger logs dislodging masonry. The site has suffered much sea damage, which indicates that the site is now well below the highest-level spring tide line and may therefore have been built at a time when the sea level was much lower, indicating considerable antiquity for the site.

Site was very difficult to survey since much of the masonry has been damaged by high tides, covered in rubbish and is also being swallowed by nettles and other vegetation. It is also the remotest site in the survey area to reach by foot and is more accessible with a boat, although there is no decent landing spot.

Cells 4, 5, 6 and 12 were the most badly eroded by the sea and some parts of the dry stone walling are now indistinguishable from the beach boulders, which extend right up to the structure. Cell 9 differs from the rest in that it is rectangular and has a raised platform of stone slabs to the left of its entrance. Very few cupboards were visible in the complex, indicating significant deterioration from Thomas's visit in the 1850s. There is a need for a sea wall to prevent further erosion since this site is unique in the survey area, unique in Lewis and as far as I am aware it is unique in Scotland.

The site is situated in a small glen through which runs Allt Gleann na h' Airde Mhor, a freshwater burn, and is sheltered on three sides by hills and on the fourth side across the sea inlet are the sea cliffs on the Harris side of Loch Resort. The surrounding land is covered in lazy beds, but there is no reason to suggest contemporaneity, since such "feannanagan" were a 19th century invention (when population pressure forced people to cultivate every inch of the land using the most economic methods. Lazy beds are however an older tradition, and therefore cannot be used to date anything.)

Further east along the beach is a roughly circular patch approx. 2m x 2m where the boulders have been removed from the beach. There is the outline of a wall 0.4m high on one side, and on the opposite side the boulders have fallen into the space cleared. There is a similar feature further west along the beach whose outline is just discernible. Perhaps these features were created to collect the water from the burn that may have run into it creating a freshwater pool on the beach just above the high tide line.

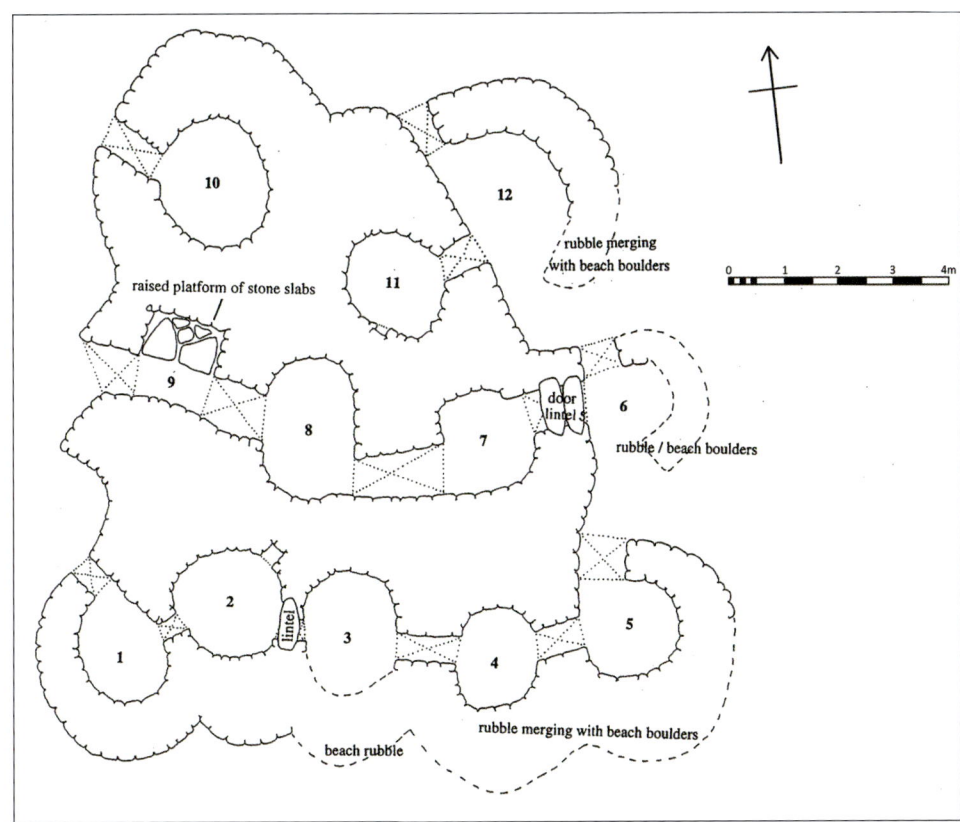

Figure 2.3.2-4: Gearraidh na h-Àirde Mhòire 12-chambered cell plan drawing (Logan site 33)

What's left of the 12-chambered cell

Looking east over the nettle-cloaked stones of the 12-chambered cell (2017)

The 12-chambered cell in the year 2000

The 12-chambered structure was also surveyed by Captain Thomas in the 1850s. His plan drawings are presented in figures 2.3.2-5 and -6.

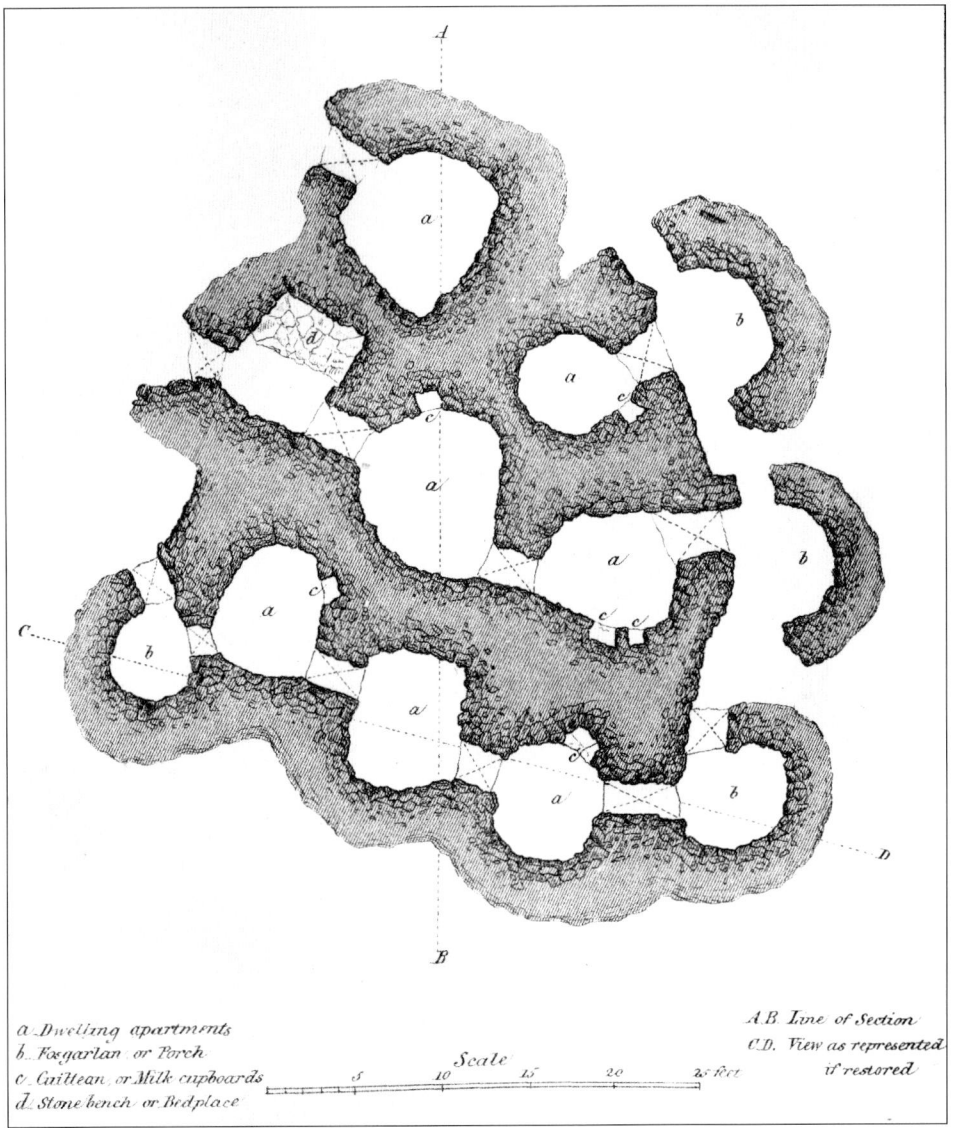

Figure 2.3.2-5: Bothan Gearraidh na h-Airde Moire, H. Sharbau & Capt. Thomas R.N.
Proceedings of the Society of Antiquaries of Scotland, Vol. III (1857-60)
A = dwelling apartments, B = porch, C = milk cupboard,
D = stone bench or bedplace

This historic and unique structure, precariously perched just above the shoreline, has been abused by centuries of storms sending debris crashing into it—fortunately I did not find any rusty bombs. Captain Thomas's work caused some of the domes to collapse, and since then all the rest have fallen. What interior walls remain are, at most, a half-metre high. The following sketch, made in the 1850s, show a cross section along the A-B line of the plan drawing, and a depiction what it looked like, when intact, along the C-D line of the drawing.

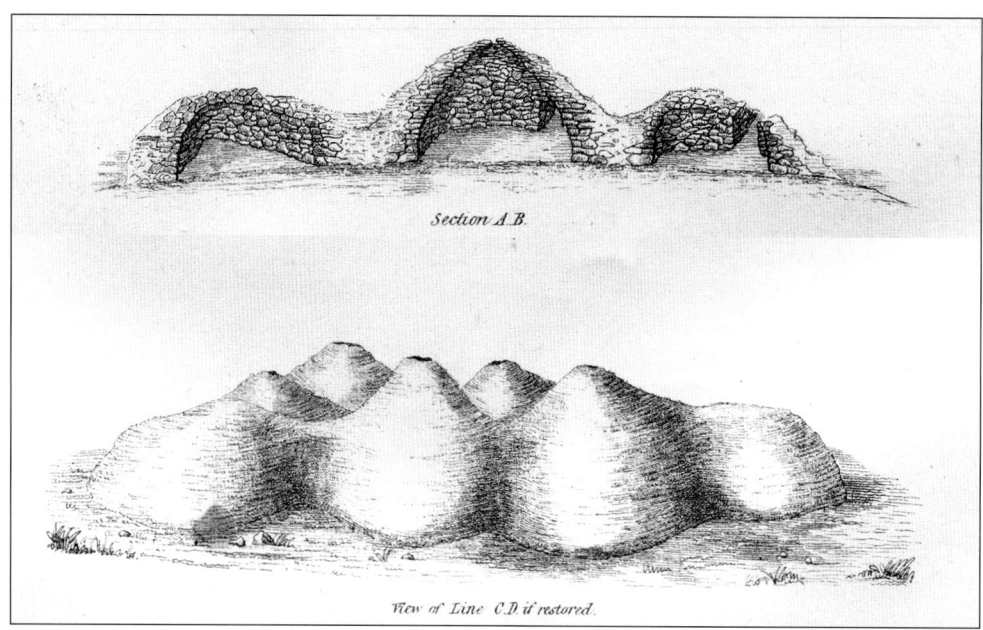

Figure 2.3.2-6: The Both or Shieling of the Garry of Aird Mhor,
H. Sharbau & Capt. Thomas R.N.
Proceedings of the Society of Antiquaries of Scotland, Vol. III (1857-60)

After recording as much as I could about these historic dwellings, sadly decaying in one of the remotest places in the Hebrides, I made my way north to the head of Gleann na h-Airde Mhòire. I could not face retracing my way back to Loch an Ath Ruaidh via all the ups and downs of my route in. I was too tired and overheated—the apple-juice-spiked water in the jug a sweet life saver.

The climb to the head of the glen was rewarded with an expansive view over Loch Tealasbhaigh. A view that brought back delicious memories of an evening fifteen years before. I was on the ship Poplar Diver, anchored for the night in Loch Tealasbhaigh. For supper we had fresh dived scallops that the skipper, Rob Barlow, had gathered from a ledge deep in the icy waters of the loch. My mouth watered at the memory, which allowed me to swallow the energy bar I was munching on. It tasted like sawdust laced with kerosene—according to the label it was scrumdiddlyumptious.

After forcing myself to swallow the last of the bar, I traversed the rocky hillside of Cleit a' Gharaidh, then descended its east side to cross a narrow glen that led to Loch Làmadail. After rounding the hill Sneathabhal Mor I came to the stream that tumbles steeply down from Loch Ruadh. It was a sweltering 27 degrees, with no wind, as I made a slow grind of a climb up the banks of the stream. At the saddle of the pass sat placid Loch Ruadh—its pebbly shoreline a respite from hours of soggy moorland. The tent was a welcome sight when I finally reached Loch an Ath Ruaidh a half-hour later.

Although it was only 5 pm, and there were several hours of daylight left, I decided to call it a day. The tent had been basking in the sun for hours—the inside was like a sauna. I stripped to my shorts, lay on top of the sleeping bag and, after what had been an extraordinary day, fell asleep in ten seconds.

Campsite at Loch an Ath Ruaidh—Loch Bodabhat in the distance

— Day 3 —

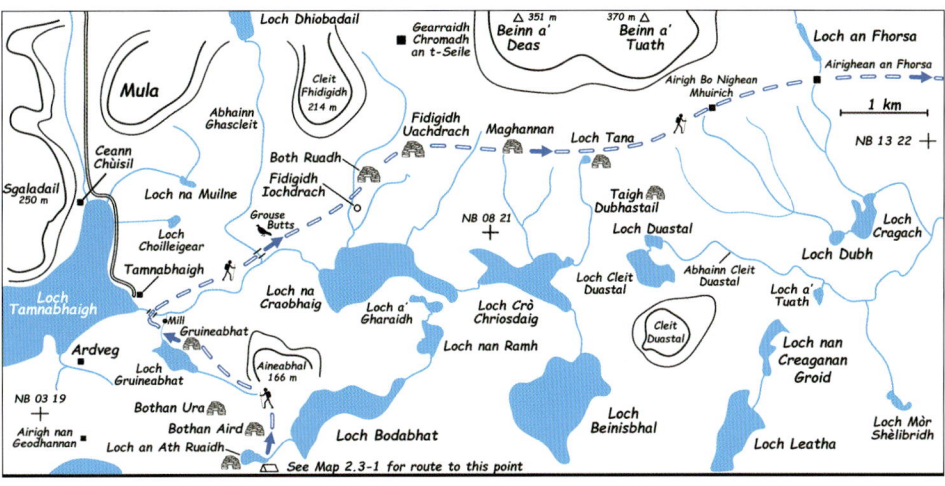

Map 2.3-2: Return from Aird Mhor

The alarm sounded at 5 am. I needed an early start to reach Kinlochrog by 5 pm, the time I'd arranged to meet my wife at the road. After breaking camp I headed north across the shoulder of Cleit na Bothan Aird, resisting the urge to take another look at the high bothies. At Loch Bodabhat I followed the Feadan Gruineabhat to the west, here and there coming across a few of the telegraph poles that date to WWI. No one has harvested them to build a bridge like they've done in Morsgail—not yet, anyway. From Gruineabhat it was an easy walk down the Allt a' Chas Bhraighe stream to its Norse mill, and then on down to the footbridge over the Abhainn Tamnabhaigh.

At Tamnabhaigh I turned right to follow the path that ascends along the north bank of the Abhainn Tamnabhaigh. To help the estate's fishing guests make the long hike to Loch na Craobhaig, planks have been placed over sections of the bog, which sped my progress east. The path eventually reached a footbridge over the Abhainn Ghascleit. I did not follow the path any farther, as I wanted to revisit some of the outstanding beehive cells up in Fidigidh.

I left the path to head northeast. Before I reached the Abhainn Fidigidh I noticed what appeared to be several beehives a hundred metres off to the left. I excitedly headed towards them, thinking I'd discovered cells not marked on any map. On closer examination they were unlike any structure I'd seen before. It was as if someone had taken a beehive, or a shieling of some sort, split it in half, then slid the two halves a few metres apart. I would later learn they were grouse butts, where hunters could lay in wait to ambush unsuspecting wildfowl. I have never had grouse. Curious what it tastes like, I found this description: *The breast is beautifully tender, with the most delicate of gamey tangs, and in the legs a more pronounced kick, but nothing to frighten even the most timid of palates.* My timid palate has never been too appreciative of gamey tangs, no matter how delicate. But it would probably be splendid washed down with a dram of Grouse.

Grouse butts near Loch na Craobhaig

When I reached the Abhainn Fidigidh I found it low, and easy to cross. On its far side lay the half-dozen ruins of Fidigidh Iochdrach (Lower Fidigidh), some of them may have been beehives at one time, but their stones have been plundered. A short distance north I came to Both Ruadh, one of the largest beehives in the Western Isles. It has remained relatively intact due to the fact that, unlike many cells, a good portion of its turf covering remains in place.

I had been to Both Ruadh before (see section 2.2.4), but for old times' sake I stepped inside. Something was different. In one of the stone cupboards lay something colorful—a book wrapped in plastic. I could read its cover: Early *20th Century Poetry*, and a label that said: *Thank you for finding me. I am a special book, travelling around the world and making new friends. Please take me home with you and look inside my cover to find out more.* Written inside was an ID number and website (bookcrossing.com).

Looking at the website a week later, and half a world away, I learned the book had been left in the cell a year before I found it. It seems visitors to Both Ruadh are few and far between. Via the website I also discovered that the book had been left in the cell by Sarah Wilson of Uig. In a quite remarkable beehive-hunter coincidence, Sarah told me she'd been inspired to visit Bothan Ruadh by a blog post I'd written in 2015.

The book had not fared well. The plastic bag enclosing it had been nibbled on by hungry mice, and the book was a soggy mess. I took it anyway, intending to either dry it out or find another copy to release back into the wild. After two years of drying out the book still smelled of mold, so in 2019 I obtained another copy, which was left in St Brendan's Cell, a beehive ruin on the island of Inishglora, two kilometres off the coast of the Mullett Penninsula (County Mayo).

From Both Ruadh I continued north to Fidigidh Uachdrach, one of the best clusters of intact cells anywhere (see section 2.2.4). From there I continued west to another site, Airigh Mhor (the big shieling), a lonely, long abandoned dwelling in an isolated spot on the moorland. From Airigh Mhor it was another kilometer's march east to Màghannan, a level walk, the only obstacle the stream Alt Gil Loch Crò Criosdaig. I had been stopped in this area before by swollen streams, but crossing this one was not a problem. Fifteen minutes later I reached the elusive beehive cell of Màghannan.

2.3.3 Màghannan

Landranger Map: 13 (also see map 2.3-2)
Location: NB 08746 21821
CANMORE ID: 133717
Access: B8011 (near Morsgail Lodge) at NB 1391 2374 – an 8 km walk

The well preserved Màghannan cell lies by its lonesome, 300 metres west of Loch Tana. It is a delightful sight to come across when traversing this lonely stretch of moorland. When I first searched for cells in this area (section 2.2), I only found a rectangular shieling (at NB 08285 21249), 700 metres to the southeast. I had no idea at the time that this beautiful cell was so close.

Its walls stand over a metre high, and the cell-builders made use of a large boulder to anchor the structure. A door faces southeast. What may have been another door on the southwest side has been blocked off. Sitting on the open moorland, at an elevation of 140 metres, the cell has a magnificent view to the west, where the slopes of Tamnasbhal gradually drop down to the sea.

Màghannan—Tamnasbhal in the distance

This is Elspeth Logan's description and plan drawing (fig. 2.3.3-1) of the Màghannan cell: *Beehive structure in fairly good condition with walls standing to height of 1.15m. Roof has collapsed into the interior making a cross section impossible to undertake without moving any of the masonry. One door faces east and it is possible that a large cupboard to the SW may also once have been a door that was subsequently blocked off. Otherwise five cupboards in total and one beside the eastern door which has a strange shape and may have been a fireplace of some sort. This beehive has incorporated a large natural rock outcrop as part of its structure. Situated on open flat ground with Beinn a' Deas and Beinn Mheadhonach behind. Surrounded by fairly boggy ground which may once have been quite fertile.*

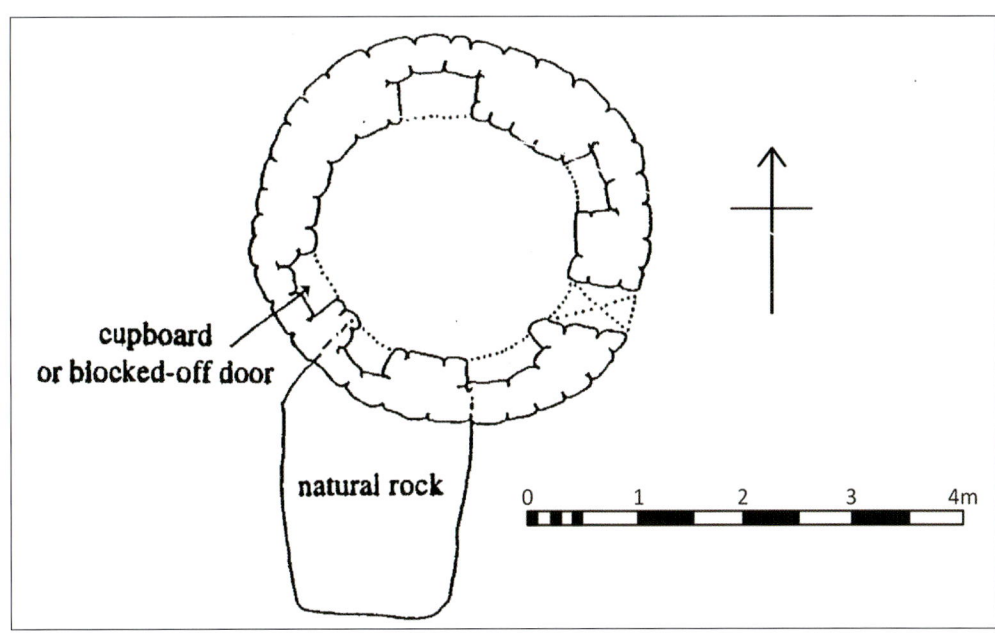

Figure 2.3.3-1: Màghannan plan drawing (Logan site 13)

Màghannan—interior view showing cupboards

Màghannan—showing cupboards and lintel

My next destination was not far, the beehive at Airidh a' Loch Thaine, 400 metres to the east. There were no streams to cross, just gently undulating, heather-clad moorland; wide-open terrain which is a true delight to cross on a sunny day, which it just happened to be.

2.3.4 Airidh a' Loch Thaine

Landranger Map: 13 (also see map 2.3-2)
Location: NB 09095 21705
CANMORE ID: 133718
Access: B8011 (near Morsgail Lodge) at NB 1391 2374 – a 7 km walk

The beehive cell at Airidh a' Loch Thaine lies twenty metres from the southeast corner of Loch Tana (shallow loch). There is not much left, only an arc of foundation buried in heather and grass. If you did not know it was there, you'd walk right by without noticing it (which I did the first time I passed this way). When intact the cell was nearly two metres across. The interior is full of stones, but not enough to account for what would have been the dome.

Loch Tana cell (foreground)

Elspeth Logan described the cell as a *circular feature situated approx. 10m south of the loch. Has arc-shaped wall approx. 60cm high and 90cm wide on its north side. Roughly 1.5m (E-W) by 1.8m (N-S). No entrance or cupboards visible since in very ruinous condition. Interior filled with rubble and vegetation. Marked as ruin on OS map published in 1854. Site is surrounded by good pasture land. Remains of iron triple-footed pot found, similar to remains of pot found at site 6 [Abhainn Fhidigidh Cell 2—see section 2.2.2]. Ruins of a rectangular airidh to the NE on the shoreline of the loch.* Refer to fig. 2.3.4-1 for a plan drawing of the cell.

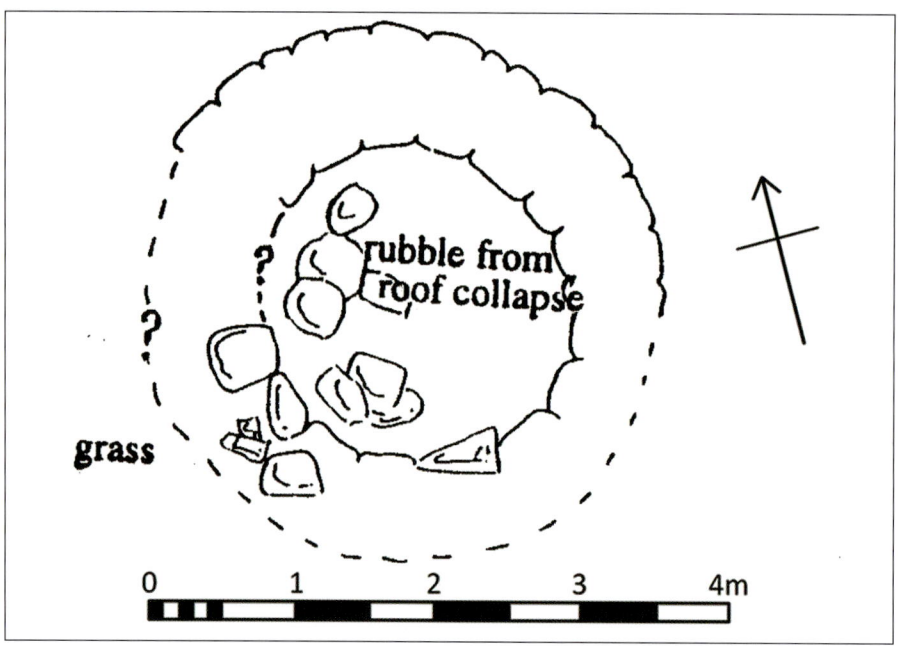

Figure 2.3.4-1: Loch Tana cell plan drawing (Logan site 12)

Loch Tana cell (showing the triple-footed iron pot)

Fifty metres to the north is a rectangular airidh (shieling). It looks quite elegant, standing alone in the middle of nowhere—the large lintel stone over its doorway still in place. The hut is five metres by two, with walls a metre high. One can surmise some of the stones missing from the beehive were used in its construction.

Loch Tana shieling—beehive ruin in the distance (arrow)

From Loch Tana, the evocative beehives of Tighe Dhubhastail lie only a kilometre to the southeast. I say evocative because of Captain Thomas's description of visiting them when occupied by several young women who invited him in for refreshments. Having seen them before (section 2.1.1), I turned to the northeast. Thirty minutes later I came to a very unusual site: Airighean an Fhorsa, the shielings of the waterfall.

Airighean an Fhorsa is a beautiful place; shielings once used by the people of Bhaltos, fourteen kilometers to the north. It is set on an island of sorts below a rocky waterfall. The river, after tumbling down the falls, splits into two streams that flow down opposite sides of the settlement. But it did not look so impressive at the time. The river was dry; the parched stones of the waterfall, and the two streams, waiting patiently for the next rainfall.

I was now on the homestretch. Only two kilometres to Morsgail. Once the lodge came into view I made my way to a gate that gave access to a track, and after fifty hours of exploration I was back on solid ground. I walked the final two kilometres on the track to Kinlochrog, and quickly dropped the pack when I reached the road. I sat on the dry turf, took off soggy boots, and fell asleep. A half-hour later, at the sound of an approaching car, I looked up to see my wife at the wheel. She gave me a kiss before handing me an icy-cold beer. Stored safely in my pack were several memory cards filled with photos, and memories.

2.4 Loch a' Sguair Loop

Nearest Public Road: B8011 at NB 15467 25164
Total distance: 10 km
Sites visited: Tom Ni Bharabhais, Airigh a' Sguair, Gearraidh Coire Geurad, Gleann Marstaig, Airigh Creagan nam Beartan

Whereas our hero Captain Thomas concentrated on the beehives of Southwest Lewis, WM Mackenzie, in PSAS Vol. 38 says with respect to the cells described by Thomas:

Those with which I am about to deal lie farther east where the valley opens out into a scene of pastoral richness, quiet, and beauty, over which the shy deer boldly move among what were once the habitations of men.

A fascinating beehive day-out, to where shy deer boldly move among what were once the habitations of men (and women), starts at Tom Ni Bharabhais, the knoll of the Barvas Cattle. It is just off the B8022, two kilometres east of Kinlochrog. If you drive this road south you can't miss Tom Ni Bharabhais. Atop it, easily seen from the road, stands a slender memorial cairn made of stones robbed from beehive cells that once crowned the hill. These days they would not destroy cells to create a cairn, but attitudes were different in the past. The countryside south of Tom Ni Bharabhais is full of cells, many intact, and from Tom Ni Bharabhais a good day of beehive hunting can be accomplished via a long circular walk around Loch a' Sguair.

WALK START: The B8011 at NB 15467 25164 (500 metres southwest of the turnoff to Scaliscro). From there, follow a rocky peat track 200 metres southeast to where it abruptly ends. Then walk 200 metres to the northeast to reach the memorial cairn on Tom Ni Bharabhais.

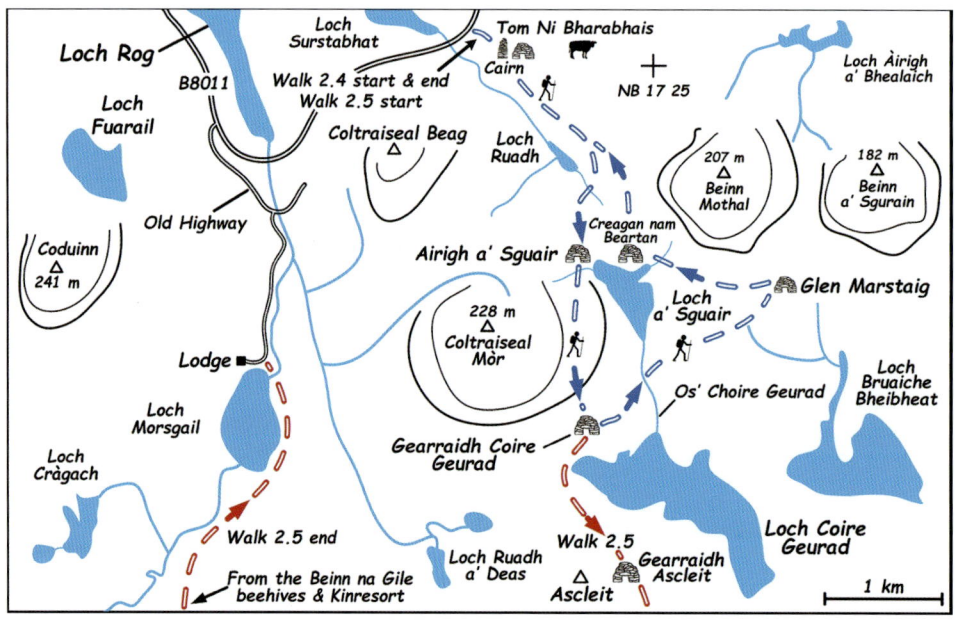

Map 2.4: Loch a' Sguair Loop

2.4.1 Tom Ni Bharabhais

Landranger Map: 13
Location: NB 15744 25154
CANMORE ID: 71057
Access: B8011 at NB 1556 2527 - a 0.3 km walk

This is the story of the cairn on Tom Ni Bharabhais, as recounted by Alasdair Alpin Macgregor in *The Haunted Isles* (1933):

The cairn marks the spot upon which was decided the last encounter in the feud that for centuries distracted the MacAuleys of Uig and the Morrisons of Ness from peaceful pursuits. Two or three hundred years ago the Morrisons, in an attempt to recover a herd of cattle that the men of Uig had driven off from Barvas, set out from Ness for the territory of the MacAuleys, and overtook the cattle-rievers in the vicinity of this hillock. There, according to tradition current in Uig, the Morrisons suffered severe defeat at the hands of the MacAuleys.

There were at least two cells atop the hill, and the cairn was built from some of their stones. In volume 38 of *Proceedings of the Society of Antiquaries of Scotland*, WM Mackenzie describes the beehives on Tom Ni Bharabhais as they were over a hundred years ago as follows:

Of the larger sufficient remains to show clearly the characteristic construction and the circular shape, with a diameter of seven feet between the narrow entrances which look N. and E.S.E. Its companion measures about a foot less.

Cairn atop Tom Ni Bharabhais—beehive ruin to the right—Loch Ruadh in the distance

In the photo you can see the meager remnants of a cell behind, and to the right, of the cairn. Another cairn made from the stones of a beehive can be seen at Tighe Dhubhastail (Walk 2.1). From Tom Ni Bharabhais head 400 metres due south to the barbed-wire fence at NB15741 24759. You need to cross the fence, and this is the only stile. Once over the fence head southeast past Loch Ruadh. At the end of the loch climb south for nearly another kilometer to where, I guarantee, what you'll see will bring a smile to your face: the beautiful beehives of Airigh a' Sguair.

2.4.2 Airigh a' Sguair

Landranger Map: 13
Locations:
Loch a' Sguair **(1)**: NB 16334 23349 (intact)
Loch a' Sguair **(2)**: NB 16380 23333 (intact)
Loch a' Sguair **(3)**: NB 16347 23261
Loch a' Sguair **(4)**: NB 16451 23369 (intact)
Loch a' Sguair **(5)**: NB 16349 23252
CANMORE ID: 72083
Access: B8011 at NB 1556 2527 - a 2 km walk

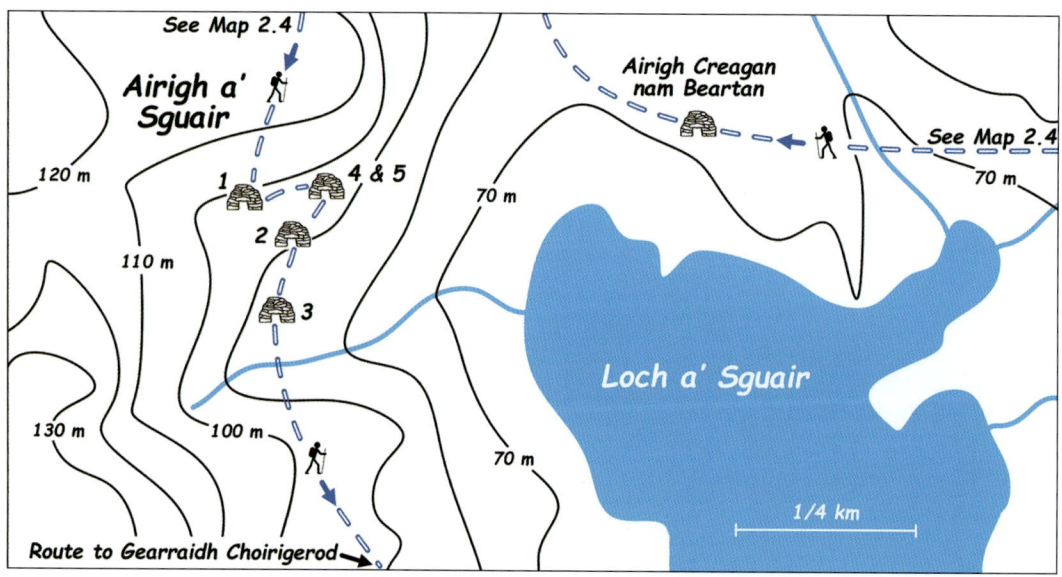

Map 2.4.2: Airigh a' Sguair

The first beehive you encounter when approaching Airigh a' Sguair from the north is spectacular. Airigh a' Sguair **(1)** sits at an elevation of 100 metres, 300 metres west of the loch, with a panoramic view to the southeast. The very top of its dome is missing, which lets in the rain, so the interior can be flooded after any significant rainfall. On the inside there are seven storage niches.

*North-most beehives at Airigh a' Sguair: Cell **(1)** right, Cell **(2)** left*

*Airigh a' Sguair **(1)**—looking to the northwest*

Interior view—Airigh a' Sguair **(1)**

Both at Loch a' Sguair (Cell 1), W.M. Mackenzie
Proceedings of the Society of Antiquaries of Scotland, Vol. 38 (1903-04)

Airigh a' Sguair (1)—same perspective as the PSAS photo

Hiding in a small, rocky cleft 100 metres east of Airigh a' Sguair **(1)**, are two cells, one of them beautifully intact. They are so well concealed, that I completely missed them the first two times I walked this way. The intact cell, Airigh a' Sguair **(4)**, is 3.5 metres in diameter, with much of its turf covering still in place. The top of the dome is nearly 2 meters high, and once inside I was able to stand upright, the top of my head nearly plugging the small smokehole. The cell has a porch protecting its one doorway that faces to the southeast, and inside are five cupboards, one unusually large one at ground level.

*Airigh a' Sguair **(4)** (at right) and **(5)** hiding in their gully—Loch a' Sguair in the distance*

Airigh a' Sguair (4)—front view

I regret my visit to this cell was not during an overnight excursion, as it is the only beehive I've seen to date that I would consider spending the night in. It would be four-star accommodation: wind and waterproof; the floor not littered with fallen stone, or damp, bug-ridden moss. Neither was there a rotting sheep carcass inside. It would rate five stars if it was midge-proof.

Turf-covered Airigh a' Sguair (4) seen from above

Inside Airigh a' Sguair (4)

Both at Loch a' Sguair (Cell 4), W.M. Mackenzie
Proceedings of the Society of Antiquaries of Scotland, Vol. 38 (1903-04)

Airigh a' Sguair (4)—same perspective as the PSAS photo

Airigh a' Sguair **(5)** lies ten metres east of cell **(4)**. Making use of boulders in its foundation, it is oval in shape, some three by two metres. Not much is left, but six cupboards are visible. In the near vicinity there are said to be footings of three other cells, but I was unable to locate them.

Airigh a' Sguair (5)—seen from the east

Eighty-five metres southwest of the cells hidden in the gully is Airigh a' Sguair **(2)**. From a distance it looks completely intact, but as you approach you'll see that the top of the dome has fallen. Inside are six storage niches.

Airigh a' Sguair (2)—looking west with cell (1) on the horizon

Airigh a' Sguair (2)—looking east to Loch a' Sguair

*Airigh a' Sguair **(2)**—front view*

*Interior of Airigh a' Sguair **(2)***

Eighty metres south of Airigh a' Sguair **(2)** is cell **(3)**. It has collapsed, but two cupboards are still visible.

*The tumbled Airigh a' Sguair **(3)**—seen from the west*

Leaving Loch a' Sguair behind (if you can), carry on a kilometre south to the east end of Loch Coire Geurad. Hiding here, to the south of a rocky knoll, are the ruins of Gearraidh Coire Geurad. Although none of the cells are intact, this beautiful site overlooking the loch is stunning

2.4.3 Gearraidh Coire Geurad

Landranger Map: 13
Location: Centered at NB 16609 21985
CANMORE ID: 133750
Access: B8011 at NB 1556 2527 - a 3.5 km walk

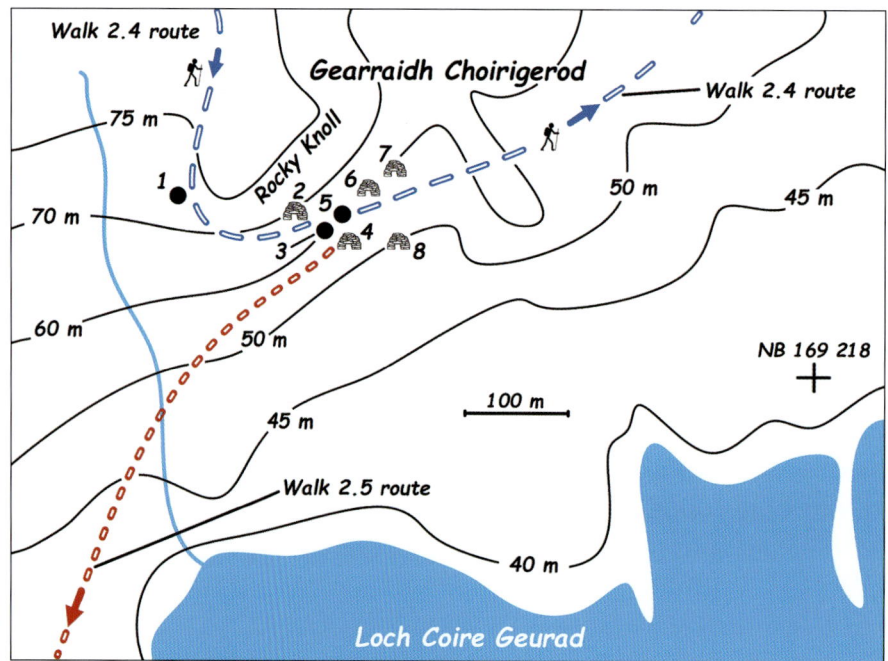

Map 2.4.3: Gearraidh Coire Geurad

This is WM Mackenzie's description of Gearraidh Coire Geurad from PSAS Vol. 38 (1904):

About a half mile further south (from Loch a' Sguair) we reach the ample margin of Loch Choirigerod. Where the gently sloping meadow terminates abruptly, at the foot of a rocky ridge to the west, stands a compact group well suiting in their appearance the comparison to a Kaffir kraal, and strangely impressive in their suggestion of former residence and present abandonment. There are seven in all, of which two are in a state of fairly good preservation.

Coire Geurad does resemble a Kaffir kraal, an African village with enclosures for livestock. Of all the beehive sites I've seen over the years, this is one of the most interesting—a communal setting nearly as charming as Loch an Ath Ruaidh. Although none of the cells are intact, the location is spectacular.

The settlement lies nestled below a rocky knoll. If you are following my route (approaching from the north) the knoll blocks the site from view. It is only once you stand atop the summit of the knoll that you'll know anything is there. And what you'll see is astonishing. On the sloping terrain leading down to Loch Coire Geurad lies a close-knit group of cells and pens.

Cells 2, 3, 4, and 5 seen from the knoll

Off by its own, fifty metres west of the settlement, is a small structure, Coire Geurad **(1)**, that may have been a pen, although there are slight signs of corbelling (see map 2.4.3). From your vantage point atop the knoll, descend its west side to start your tour of the site at Cell **(1)**.

Gearraidh Coire Geurad (1)—possibly a pen

From Cell **(1)**, none of the other structures are in sight. It's only when you circle east around the knoll that the rest of the cells come back into view. The western cell of the main settlement, Cell **(2)**, is very large, over two metres in diameter, with walls still a metre high that still show signs of corbelling. There is a photo of the cell when it was intact in PSAS Vol 38 (1904).

Both at Loch Choirigerod, W.M. Mackenzie Coire Geurad (2)
Proceedings of the Society of Antiquaries of Scotland, Vol. 38 (1903-04)

Coire Geurad (2)—same perspective as the PSAS photo

Coire Geurad (2) from the south

Just below Cell **(2)** is Coire Geurad **(3)**, its low stone walls making use of natural rock. There are no signs of corbelling, and the structure may have been a pen, as it is similar to Coire Geurad **(1)** described earlier.

Coire Geurad (3) from the east

The largest diameter ruin here is Cell **(4)**, nearly three meters across. A section of wall stands a metre high, but most of the stones are gone—possibly taken to maintain the other cells. The base diameter of this structure is so large that it may have been a pen.

Coire Geurad (4)—looking east

Coire Geurad (4)—looking west

A few metres east of Cell **(4)** lie the scant remains of a small, odd structure **(5)**, built against several boulders. It is too small to have been a cell, and was possibly for storage, or a time-out pen for unruly children.

Coire Geurad (6) seen from the west

Cell **(6)** lies thirty-five metres northeast of **(5)**. Like the others, its stones are mostly missing. A lintel spans what may have been a low doorway. But that may have been put there by a wandering hiker (not me).

Coire Geurad (6) seen from the north

Coire Geurad **(7)** lies fifty metres from **(6)**, and marks the east end of the settlement. Its western walls, which have signs of corbelling, stand 1.5 metres, but the rest has collapsed.

Coire Geurad (7)—east end of the settlement

Lying fifty metres due south of cell **(7)**, down the slope towards the loch, lies the last cell on the site, Coire Geurad **(8)**. It is a jumble of stones in a beautiful location.

Coire Geurad (8) overlooking Loch Coire Geurad

Although the cells of Coire Geurad are ruinous, taken as a whole, this compact settlement on the slopes above the loch is beautiful. The photos used are from visits in 2016, 2018, and 2019. Someday I hope to once again wander to the delightfully remote shores of Loch Coire Geurad.

If you are just out for the day, and not making an overnight excursion farther south (Walk 2.5), it now is time to change course: time to turn northeast and aim for Gleann Marstaig.

After crossing the waters of Òs *Choire Geurad*, a lumpy kilometer of walking over the Druim Mòr ridge leads to Gleann Marstaig. Note that along this route you'll pass near two shieling sites, both named Airigh Druim Mhòr (NB 1727 2300 and NB 1751 2283). I have not visited these shielings on the big ridge, and they may be worth a look at if you have the time (and energy).

2.4.4 Gleann Marstaig

Landranger Map: 13
Location: NB 18197 23017
CANMORE ID: 133745
Access: B8011 at NB 1556 2527 - a 3 km direct walk

Like Gearraidh Coire Geurad, none of the cells in Gleann Marstaig are completely intact. There are six cells, but only one is recognizable as a beehive. Its walls stand over a metre high, and some corbelling is evident. This is WM Mackenzie's description from PSAS Vol. 38: *On the hillside above Glen Marstaig... one (cell) in a rather better state of preservation, shows traces of adaptation to the more modern type in that its top had been adjusted to permit of rafters and a roof of heather or turf.*

Donald MacDonald, in *Tales and Traditions of The Lews* (chapter 85) says: *The Glen Marstaig 'boths' were used as summer shielings in 1832, and were so used until 1872, when the outer moor was taken from the Bernera people and the grazings made into a deer forest as far as Loch Langavat* (Glen Marstaig) *and Scaliscro.*

So what were they used for prior to 1832? An intriguing question. Donald MacDonald, in the same chapter, says: *boths' were used by the early hunting inhabitants, and then by a semi-pastoral people, who lived for months in them, making butter and cheese, salted' for winter use, from the milk of the black Highland cows.* A use that could date to the Bronze Age.

Gleann Marstaig cell—interior view

Both at Glen Marstaig, W.M. Mackenzie
Proceedings of the Society of Antiquaries of Scotland, Vol. 38 (1903-04)

Gleann Marstaig cell—same perspective as the PSAS photo

From Gleann Marstaig head northwest across the boggy slopes of Beinn Mothal. Your destination, the last on the Loch a' Sguair Loop, is Airigh Creagan nam Beartan.

2.4.5 Airigh Creagan nam Beartan

Landranger Map: 13
Location: NB 16780 23436
CANMORE ID: 74698
Access: B8011 at NB 1556 2527 - a 2 km direct walk

Airigh Creagan nam Beartan lies above the northernmost point of Loch a' Sguair, a half-kilometre east of the beehives of Loch a' Sguair. Here you'll find the substantial remains of a large cell. Partially embedded in an earthen mound, it looks like a stone-lined volcanic crater. There is said to be a rectangular shieling hut nearby, made from some of the cell's stones, but on my two visits to the site I was unable to find it.

Airigh Creagan nam Beartan—looking southwest to Loch a' Sguair

Airigh Creagan nam Beartan

With the knowledge of the other sites you've seen on this walk, and from the vantage point atop the mound, you can truly appreciate the complex set of settlements surrounding Loch a' Sguair. Another nearby village of cells, not visited on this walk, lies high on the east shoulder of the hill Ascleit, 2.5 km to the south. You could make it part of this walk, but that would increase the total distance to 15 km. (Ascleit is visited in section 2.5.)

From Airigh Creagan nam Beartan, return to the road by backtracking the way you came: north along the shore of Loch Ruadh, and then up the banks of Abhainn Sùrstabhat to the B8011. Having reached the road safely, congratulate yourself on having done one of the most rewarding short beehive walks on Lewis.

2.5 Bo'h Hunting in Morsgail

Sites visited: Loch a' Sguair, Gearraidh Coire Geurad, Gearraidh Ascleit, Both a' Gharaidh, Airigh a' Chlàir Mhòir, Both a' Chlàir Bhig, and Gearraidh Bheinn na Gile
Total distance: 26 km

NOTE: This journey begins at the same point as Walk 2.4, and revisits the cells at Loch a' Sguair and Gearraidh Coire Geurad. Refer to section 2.4 for descriptions of those sites.

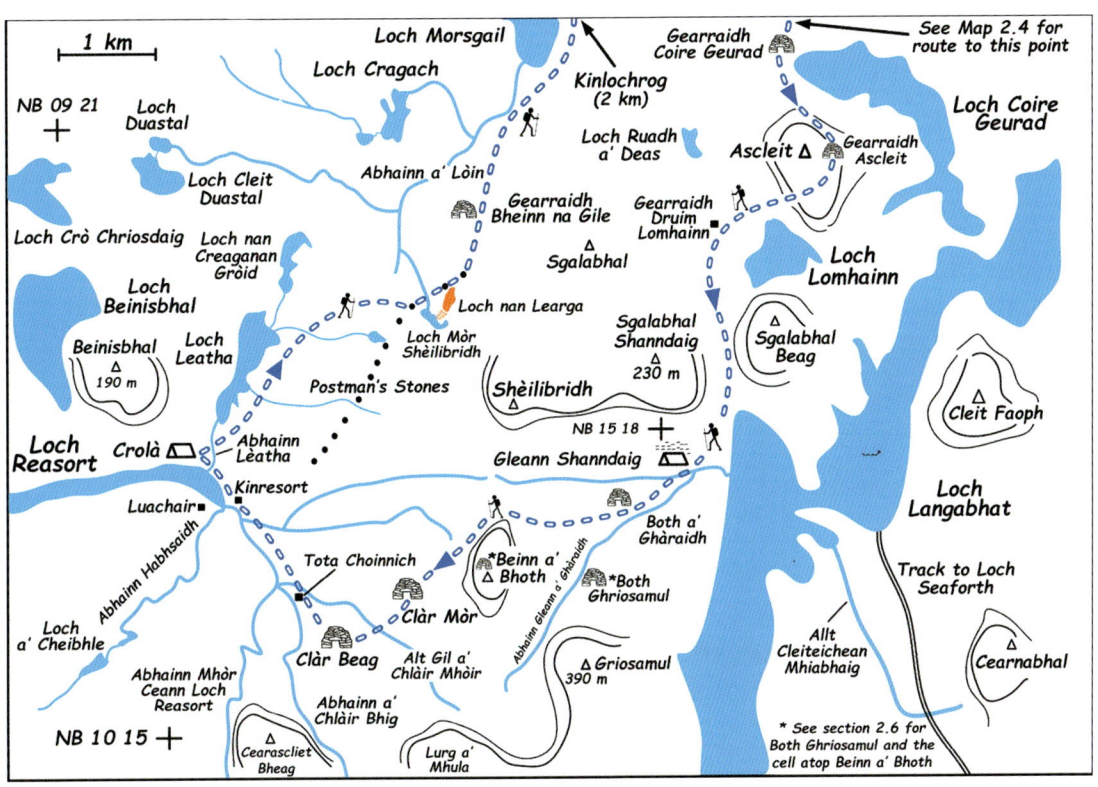

Map 2.5: Bo'h Hunting in Morsgail

Since 1998 I've made some thirty day-hikes, and over a dozen multi-day hikes, to the remoter parts of Lewis. Every year the backpack seems to get heavier, the terrain harder, the hills higher, the distances farther. The explanation could be I am getting older and less fit. But I blame the natural expansion of the universe: the hills *are* getting higher, and the distances farther. As I set off from the Uig road in the summer of 2018, the pack felt heavier than ever, as it was stuffed with sleeping bag, tent, extra clothes, two cans of beer, and food for three days.

— DAY 1 —

From the Uig road (the B8011 at NB 15467 25164) I hiked south along the banks of Abhainn Sùrstabhat where, on a knoll to the left, stood the memorial cairn atop Tom Ni Bharabhais. A half hour later I passed the south end of Loch Ruadh, where I changed course to head for the corner of Loch a' Sguair. Many beehive sites deserve a second visit, and Loch a' Sguair is one of them. I had visited the intact cells before, but I paused to look once again at these beautiful structures on the hillside above the loch. The same goes for the village of cells at Gearraidh Coire Geurad, a kilometer and a half to the south, which I passed an hour later.

From Coire Geurad a half-hour hike over soggy terrain to the southeast, and a climb of sixty metres, led to something wonderful: the airy beehive village of Gearraidh Ascleit.

2.5.1 Gearraidh Ascleit

Landranger Map: 13
Location: Centered on NB 1678 2082
CANMORE ID: 133726
Access: B8011 at NB 15467 25164 - a 5 km direct walk

Gearraidh Ascleit is one of the most awe-inspiring set of beehives in the Hebrides. A large settlement on the eastern shoulder of Ascleit, it overlooks Loch Coire Geurad from an elevation of 110 metres, nearly as high as the cells of Bothan Aird. The cells here are marked **(1)** through **(8)** on Map 2.5.1. The best-preserved cells are **1**, **3**, **4** and **8**. Cell **(1)** is the first you come to when approaching from the north. It is, to put it mildly, spectacular.

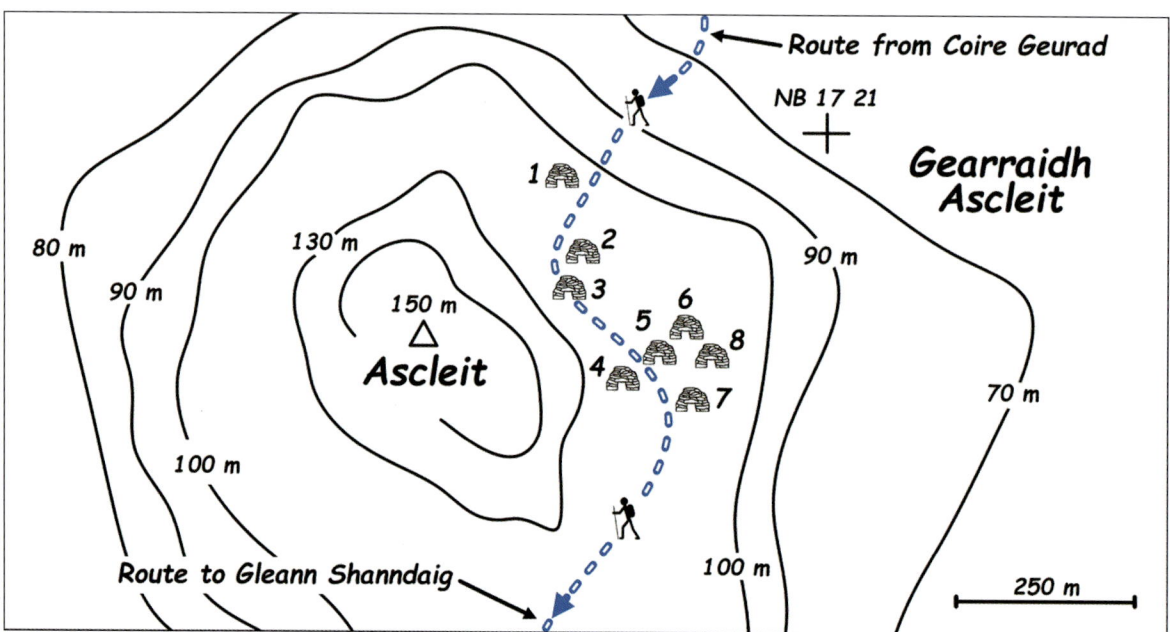

Map 2.5.1: Gearraidh Ascleit

Ascleit 1: NB 16707 20918 (intact)

Ascleit **(1)** with its intact dome, and a base nearly three metres in diameter, is one of the most impressive cells anywhere. Its turf coat is gone, but the half-metre high kerb that encircles the base, which once supported the turf, is still in place. Its single doorway faces north. After crawling through it, you will find the top of the dome to be two metres high, more than enough to stand upright. Embedded in the walls are seven stone cupboards.

Ascleit (1)—front view

Ascleit (1) looking east—Loch Langabhat and Roineabhal in the distance

Ascleit (1)—side view

Ascleit 2: NB 16698 20834

An eighty metre walk south from Ascleit **(1)** leads to ruinous cell **(2)**. One side stands about a metre high, but the rest has long since fallen. Most of its stones appear to have been robbed to maintain the other cells.

Ascleit (2)

Ascleit 3: NB 16698 20805 (intact)

Thirty-five metres south of Ascleit **(2)** stands intact cell **(3)**. It is oval in shape, two metres by three, with a dome just under two metres high. Its capstones have fallen, leaving a metre-wide gap at the top of the dome. Like cell **(1)**, its door faces north, and there are seven cupboards inside. Be careful if you crawl into the cell, as the stonework above the door is quite fragile.

Ascleit (3)—side view

Ascleit (3)—front view

Inside Ascleit (3)—it would not take much of a disturbance to bring it all tumbling down

Ascleit 4: NB 16772 20723

One hundred and twenty metres southeast of Ascleit **(3)** is another nearly intact cell, Ascleit **(4)**. In layout and size it is nearly identical to cell **(3)**. The top courses of the dome have fallen, but it still stands a metre and half high. The doorway faces north, and built into the walls are five cupboards.

Ascleit (4)—side view

Ascleit (4)—looking east to Roineabhal

Northeast of Ascleit **(4)** lie two very ruinous cells **(5)** and **(6)**, and seventy metres to the southeast lies another ruinous cell, Ascleit **(7)**. They are just sad piles of stone. [Ascleit **(5)** NB 16796 20716; Ascleit **(6)** NB 16808 20728; Ascleit **(7)** NB 16862 20689]

Ascleit 8: NB 16861 20747

The last cell in the village, Ascleit **(8)**, lies eighty-five metres east of **(4)**. Its circular wall is a meter thick and three in diameter. Although the dome has collapsed, you can still make out the single doorway that faces south. Like Ascleit **(1)** its turf covering is gone, but the kerb encircling the base that supported it is partially in place.

*Ascleit **(8)***

Gearraidh Ascleit, with its intact cells and panoramic views over the vast interior of Lewis, would be a fascinating place to camp. But there was still a lot of daylight left, and I wanted to carry on to Glean Shanndaig, four kilometres to the southwest. Getting there from Ascleit involves following a zig-zaggy route. First you have to cut across the south shoulder of Ascleit to ford the stream that flows into Loch Lomhainn. From there, fifteen minutes of hiking leads to the interesting ridge-top settlement of Gearraidh Druim Lomhainn.

Gearraidh Druim Lomhainn

Location: Four cells centered at NB 15675 20170
CANMORE ID: 133747
Access: Kinlochrog, just off the B8011 at NB 1391 2374 – a 6 km direct walk

The ruins at Gearraidh Druim Lomhainn are so tumbled it is hard to tell if they were corbelled structures. But the circular foundations hint at it. The settlement is a linear layout of four cells straddling a ridge above the northwest side of Loch Lomhainn. Set twenty-metres higher than the loch, they command a view over the surrounding terrain.

Looking south from the north-most cell—Gearraidh Druim Lomhainn

Second cell (or pen) from the north—Gearraidh Druim Lomhainn

Third cell (from the north)—Gearraidh Druim Lomhainn

Southmost ruin—Gearraidh Druim Lomhainn

From Druim Lomhainn it is not a straightforward route to Gleann Shanndaig where I wanted to camp for the night, as 230 metre-high Sgalabhal Shanndaig blocks the way. Its flanks, guarded by the cliffs of Creag Maralltan and Speireag, force you to head south over the saddle between Sgalabhal Shanndaig and Sgalabhal Beag (though if you are a glutton for punishment, you could climb across the hills). From the saddle it's an easy hike down to Gleann Shanndaig.

The low terrain in the glen is confusing: a maze of streams winding to and fro between grass-grown mounds of sand and gravel—glacial debris. The first ruin I came to was a large tumbled double beehive at NB 15023 17514. It stood alone above a small peninsula, nearly an island, surrounded by an oxbow loop of the Abhainn Gleann Shanndaig. The grassy peninsula looked like a good campsite, or so my weary legs were telling me. When I dropped the heavy pack on the ground, the earth quaked—I think it was a 7.0—which stirred up the blood-lust of a million slumbering midges.

Word spread fast that supper had arrived. The air soon thickened with ecstatic midges as I set up the tent. The bug-net had to be donned in a panic, then I filtered some peaty water from the stream. With chores taken care of it was time to wander around the glen to look for beehives. I did find a half-dozen rectangular shielings, but no beehives. I also ventured south to a larger stream, Abhainn Gleann a' Ghàraidh. There were ruins there too, but none of them beehives.

I returned to camp to have my supper, and it was not long before the midges came looking for theirs. It was time to seek sanctuary. After zipping open the tent I walked away, stood for a minute to let the bugs find me, then dashed back to the tent, slid in, and hurriedly zipped it shut. Once comfortably ensconced in my little home on the moor I wadded sheets of newspaper and stuffed them into the boots. Although I had not made a false step into a bog, one boot was starting to separate from the sole, letting water in. The newspaper and fresh socks would let me start the next day with dry feet.

It was a quiet evening—just the trickling waters of Abhainn Gleann Shanndaig breaking the dark silence. The Perseid meteor shower peaked that evening. But if there were any shooting-stars high in the heavens, their sparkling tails were hidden behind heavy gray clouds.

– DAY 2 –

I was up at 7 am. So were the midges. After smearing on some repellent, and donning the bug-net, I stepped out into midge hell. Under overcast skies I rolled up the tent and strapped it to the pack; my hands soon blackened from midges, dying by the hundreds on insecticide drenched hands. Once on the move I'd left the bugs behind, but the world seemed a little blurry. So I stopped long enough to take off the bug net, but not long enough for the thirsty horde to catch up.

Without the net distorting my vision, the world was back in focus. I carried along up the banks of the Abhainn Gleann a' Ghàraidh to the first destination of the day: Both a' Ghàraidh. Based on its name, I'd hoped to find an intact cell. But all I found was the purple heather-clad foundation of a massive cell that had been robbed of its stone long ago (NB 14455 17021, CANMORE ID 133867). From there I made a soggy traverse around the northern flank of Beinn a' Bhoth. My next destination: the beehives of Airigh a' Chlàir Mhòir.

Note: I would later learn I'd missed an outstanding beehive cell at Both a' Ghriosamul, a kilometre southwest of Both a' Ghàraidh. I would also discover that, as I traversed the northern flanks of Beinn a' Bhoth on the way to Airigh a' Chlàir Mhòir, I'd passed directly below one of the most spectacularly placed cells in the islands. I would return a year later to see both of these cells (see section 2.6).

2.5.2 Airigh a' Chlàir Mhòir

Landranger Map: 13
Location: NB 12088 16043
CANMORE ID: 352042 & 133871
Access: The A 859 at Bogha Glas (NB 1861 1154) – a 12 km walk
The B8011 at Kinlochrog (NB 139 237) – a 10 km walk

Airigh a' Chlàir Mhòir is the Epsilon Lyrae of beehive sites; a double-double star, two double cells standing next to the Allt Gil a' Chlàir Mhòir. The eastern double **(1)** is astounding. It consists of an intact giant cell, one of the largest anywhere, connected to a smaller collapsed cell. And the western double cell **(2)** is as beautiful as they get.

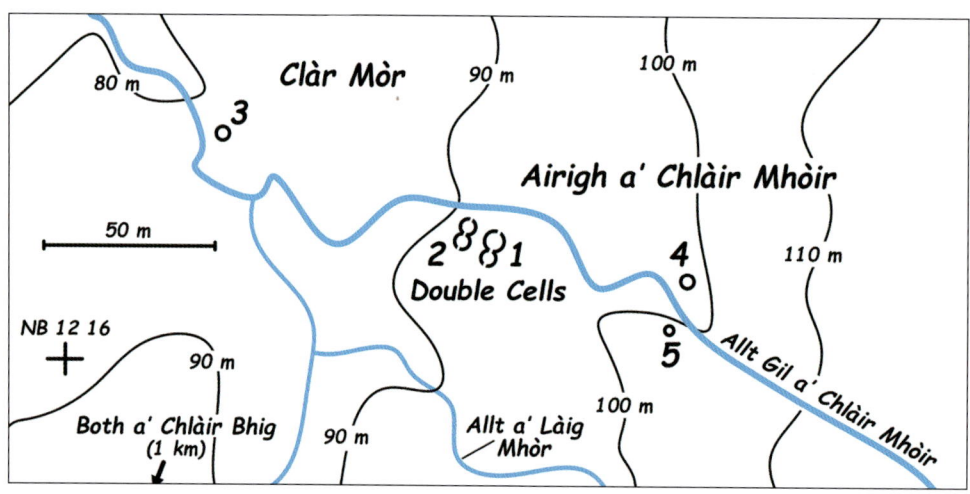

Map 2.5.2: Airigh a' Chlàir Mhòir

The two double cells seen from the north—Airigh a' Chlàir Mhòir

The eastern cell **(1)** is built atop a mound that may hide the remains of previous dwellings. After crawling through the door on its northwest side, you will discover that the inside is spacious, some three metres in diameter and two high. Opposite the entrance is a passageway to the collapsed second chamber, which when intact had been two metres in diameter.

The east cell (1)—collapsed chamber in the foreground

Inside the east cell (1)—Airigh a' Chlàir Mhòir

The western double cell **(2)** is beautifully constructed of tightly packed stones. Once inside its northern door you find yourself in a large chamber. The very top course of the dome has fallen, so you can stand up, your head rising above the top like a curious puffin peeking from its burrow. Stooping back down you can puffin-waddle across the large, slippery moss-grown stones that have fallen from the dome, to reach the connecting cell. The top of its dome has also fallen, but the inner walls are strong, walls that should stand for centuries. From the second chamber the puffin waddled outside via its southern entrance.

*West cell **(2)** at left, cell **(1)** at right—Airigh a' Chlàir Mhòir*

*Inside the western double cell **(2)**—Airigh a' Chlàir Mhòir*

Dome of the northern chamber of the western cell (2)—Airigh a' Chlàir Mhòir

There are three other ruinous structures here. The first lies eighty metres downstream from **(1)**, and is the remnant of a double cell (marked **(3)** on the map, at NB12016 16076). Sixty metres upstream from **(1)** you'll find two small structures: a pen **(4)** on the north side of the stream at NB12149 16025, and across from it, hidden high above the stream, the low walls of a tiny cell **(5)** at NB12144 16018.

The Allt Gil a' Chlàir Mhòir flowing past the cells

I now had a decision to make. Crolà, my destination for the night, lay two kilometers to the northwest—I could be there in an hour. But the double beehive of Both a' Chlàir Bhig was a kilometre out of my way to the south. I was bagging beehives, so why would I skip Both a' Chlàir Bhig? The answer is that I'd been there before. Back in 1998 they were the first cells I'd made a long-distance hike to see, as described in Chapter 17 of *Skye & Tiree to the Outer Isles*. Exactly twenty years had passed, an anniversary of sorts, so I decided to celebrate that anniversary. I would go take a look to see how the beehives had held up over two decades. After hiking south for another hour I rounded a hillside corner, and there, along with another smile, I found the double cell of Both a' Chlàir Bhig.

2.5.3 Both a' Chlàir Bhig

Location: NB 11668 14742 (on the Lewis/Harris border)
CANMORE ID: 75023
Access points: A859 at Bogha Glas (NB 1861 1154) – 11 km walk
B8011 at Morsgail (NB 139 237) – 13 km walk

The double beehive at Clàr Beag was one of the best-preserved cells in the Hebrides. So well preserved that the OS map still labels the site as 'Beehive Huts'. The only definitive identification of beehives on any map I know of. Along with the cells there are also the ruins of several shielings and pens. As to the question of how the cells have held up after two decades, the answer was: not well. The dome of the smaller cell had collapsed since my last visit.

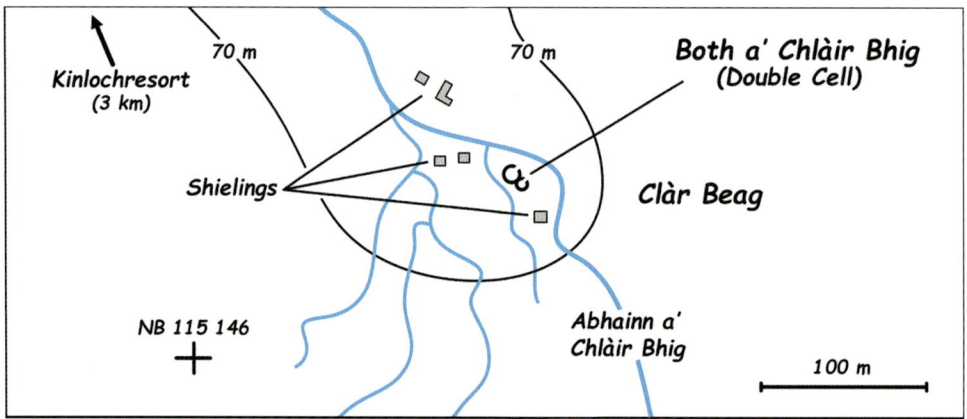

Map 2.5.3: Both a' Chlàir Bhig

A young hermit emerges from Both a' Chlàir Bhig in 1998

The two adjacent sub-rectangular beehives lie along the meandering Abhainn a' Chlàir Bhig stream, which marks the Lewis/Harris border here. When I visited in 1998 the two cells were nearly 100% intact, and you could crawl into both chambers. But in the intervening years the dome of the smaller cell has collapsed. As I'd done twenty years before I crawled into the larger cell through the entrance on the northeast side. It was very spacious inside, as the cell measures three metres by two, with walls a metre thick and nearly two metres high.

Both a' Chlàir Bhig in 1998 when the dome of the smaller cell was intact

Both a' Chlàir Bhig in 2018

The collapsed cell—Both a' Chlàir Bhig

The fallen dome of the small cell—Both a' Chlàir Bhig

Dome of the large cell—Both a' Chlàir Bhig

Front view of the large cell—Both a' Chlàir Bhig

Cupboards inside the large cell—Both a' Chlàir Bhig

I was done *bo'h* hunting for the day. Time had come to make a beeline to Crolà to camp for the night, three kilometres to the northwest. From the cells I descended along the north bank of Abhainn a' Chlàir Bhig to the ruin of Tota Choinnich. (See chapter 17 of *Skye & Tiree to the Outer Isles* for the story of Tota Choinnich.) Here the Abhainn a' Chlàir Bhig joins the Abhainn Mhòr Ceann Reasoirt, a substantial river that is not easy to cross after any significant rainfall, which there had been all week. Fortunately I didn't have to cross and continued along its banks to the old house at Kinlochresort.

The house at Kinlochresort is not a place you can count on for shelter in the great back of beyond, as they've gone to a great deal of trouble to prevent anyone from getting in. Built around 1850, a place more heavily defended from bog-weary intruders would be hard to find. Most of the doors and windows are securely covered with padlocked metal shutters. Those not so covered are tightly blocked up with stone.

From the house I made my way along the north shore of Loch Reasort. Only one more obstacle lay in the way: the Abhainn Lèatha. The stream, in heavy spate, forced me to climb the hillside to find a fording place. A hundred metres north it split to flow around a small island. On each side of the island flowed a narrow stretch of cascading water I could ford. I was almost across when I made a misstep; one boot slipped off a slick rock to plunge into the icy water.

After cursing myself for the mistake, I descended to the shore of Loch Reasort and the ruin of the postman's house at Crolà (Croleatha —the broad enclosure); a picturesque place where I'd camped in 2010. (For that story, and more on the postman Murdo Crolà, see chapter 22 of *Skye & Tiree to the Outer Isles*, and the Islands Book Trust publication *Murdo Crola—A learned man and a very talented postman*.)

Pitching the tent at Crolà was easy and relaxing. In other words there were no bloodthirsty midges on the attack—a brisk sea breeze kept them away. Before sliding into the snug, warm, welcoming sleeping bag, I stuffed the boots with the last of the newspaper. That earlier misstep had left one a bit soggy. I slept like a midge with its blood-lust sated, waking once to the sound of a deer barking as it took a nighttime drink at the stream. I am used to nights not being very dark that time of year in the Hebrides (early August), but due to the cloud cover, the sky was pitch black when I stepped out at 2 am. Us old guys step out of the tent a lot at night—to see if the stars are out, of course. I was asleep again in an instant: the lap of the surf, the pitter-patter of rain on the tent, both narcotic-like sleep aides.

Crolà on the shore of Lochreasort

It was still raining in the morning as I packed everything up before stepping out of the tent. A biting sea wind chilled my hands as I shook water off the tent, strapped it to the pack, then set out to the north. Having made the walk from Kinlochresort to Morsgail several times over the years I was on familiar territory as I headed up to the eastern shore of Loch Leatha. Along the way I had to cross the Abhainn Leatha again, but I did it this time without getting my feet wet.

At the north end of Loch Leatha I turned east to search for the Postman's Stones that mark the route through the bogs. Near Loch Mòr Shèlibridh I finally came across one, and then several others were soon spotted, which I followed to the northeast. The final stone is placed near a vague quad-bike track that leads to Loch Morsgail, which I followed to the bridge of telegraph poles over the Abhainn Bheinn na Gile. On the other side of the bridge lay the triple beehive of Beinn na Gile. These cells are a delight to see—walking past them always marks the beginning of an adventure, or the end of one.

From there the going is straightforward—north up the side of Loch Morsgail to the footbridge over the Kinlochrog River, then a final stretch along the winding tarmac track to Kinlochrog. The track ends near the old bridge at Kinlochrog, which overlooks one of the most beautiful spots in Lewis; the salmon pool of Morsgail, where the river flows under the bridge before cascading past a grove of tall pine trees to the sea. A more beautiful place to end a walk would be hard to find.

Where the Kinlochrog River flows to the sea

2.6 Return to Beinn a' Bhoth

One of the frustrations of finding beehive cells is when you come across a mention of one that gives absolutely no information to help find it. An example of this is in Donald MacDonald's *Tales and Traditions of the Lews*; a book posthumously published by his wife in 1967, six years after his death. The book includes an all-too-short chapter, basically a compilation of notes, entitled *The Beehive Huts on the Uig and Harris Hills*, which ends with the following cryptic sentence: *On the side of Ascleit are a group of boths still with the roofs on and one on Beinn a' Bhoth.*

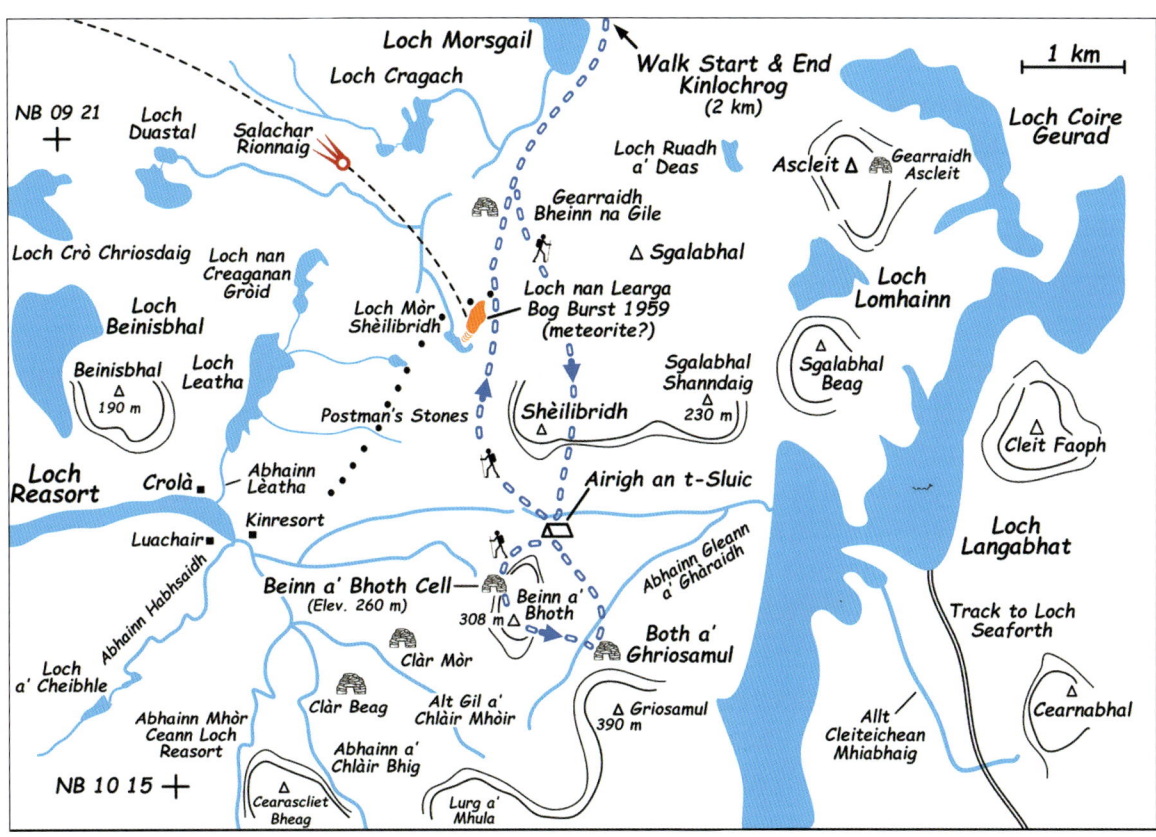

Map 2.6: Return to Beinn a' Bhoth

I had easily found the Ascleit cells on a walk in 2018 (section 2.5.1). But the cell MacDonald mentioned on Beinn a' Bhoth was a complete mystery. Beinn a' Bhoth (the mountain of the beehive) is 308 metres high and spans over three-square kilometers. The CANMORE database does not show any sites on the hill. Neither does the 1854 OS map, which is usually a good source to find ruins. I knew I would not have the energy to walk over every square metre of the hill, especially after the long trek in, so I spent some time looking at the aerial photography overlays available on CANMORE.

In scanning the images I noticed what looked like a small pimple on the north shoulder of Beinn a' Bhoth—possibly a beehive without its top. At 260 metres it was very high up, only 48 metres below the summit, and during the walk described in section 2.5 I had passed right below it. While looking at the aerial images I also noticed what appeared to be an intact cell at Griosamul. It was only a kilometer southeast of the summit of Beinn a' Bhoth, and I had also missed it on my previous walk through the area.

And so a return to Beinn a' Bhoth became a must-do. It would require a round-trip walk of 18 kilometres from Kinlochrog. A bit far for a day-trip over boggy terrain with lots of ups and downs. So I decided to make it an overnighter. What I found was truly astounding.

2.6.1 Beinn a' Bhoth

Landranger Map: 13
Location: NB 13317 16944
CANMORE ID: None
Access: Kinlochrog, just off the B8011 at NB 1391 2374 – a 9 km walk

I was on familiar territory as I headed south along the track to Morsgail Lodge and on down the eastern shore of Loch Morsgail. At the Beinn na Gile beehives I turned southeast to follow a very old track up to the saddle between the summits of Shèlibridh and Cleit Shèlibridh. From there an easy descent south took me to the shielings of Airigh an-t-Sluic (CANMORE ID 133866). This was where I would camp for the night in a few hours. To lighten my load for the rest of the day's hiking I dropped my tent and sleeping bag next to one of the ruined shielings. Looming above me was Beinn a' Bhoth, the mountain of the beehive.

The north and west sides of Beinn a' Bhoth are a mix of steep, grassy slopes and craggy cliffs. I entered the grid coordinates into my GPS of the object on the aerial photo, and then let the GPS guide me to it as I ascended to the southwest. As I climbed a grand view west to the sea gradually opened up. When the GPS indicated I had 20 metres to go, I saw something, and gasped. At an elevation of 260 metres, lying half enveloped in heather, moss and grass, stood a very old beehive.

The cell stood on a sloping, grassy ledge, 50 metres below the summit. It is so isolated and hidden that it had to be a lookout post or a hermitage, with a spectacular view west to Loch Reasort and the Atlantic. A more perfect place to spy on unwanted arrivals by sea would be hard to find. The upper courses of the dome have collapsed, and the interior is filled with a mound of grass and moss that has grown over the fallen stones. The mound is like an island; surrounded by a moat of stagnant water a half-metre deep between it and the cell walls.

The cell below the summit of Beinn a' Bhoth

The cell is at the highest elevation of any beehive I've encountered; twice as high as the high bothies of Bothan Aird, which lie eight kilometers to the west. I regretted leaving my tent at Airigh an t-Sluic, as this would be a memorable place to camp. But it was for the better, as the severe winds I experienced that night would have been much stronger at this elevation.

The Beinn a' Bhoth cell—filled with an island of turf

Beinn a' Bhoth—looking to the northwest

The sun blazed down relentlessly as I left the cell to spiral up to the summit. A joyful surprise startled me when I crested a small rise. On its far side was a large pond; in it a dozen deer lazily enjoying a cool soak. When they noticed me they jumped up in unison, causing sprays of water to erupt into the air. Then they elegantly sprinted away at breakneck speed. Within five seconds the only sign of their presence were ripples slowly spreading across the surface of the pond.

The view west over the cell to Loch Reasort

I took some time to enjoy the 360-degree view from the summit of Beinn a' Bhoth, then headed down its grassy eastern slopes. It was a 100-metre drop to the boggy floor of Gleann a' Ghàraidh (they are all boggy) where I forded the Abhainn Gleann a' Ghàraidh. As I ascended the hillside east of the stream another shout of joy burst forth—which scared a snoozing grouse out of the heather. Crowning a large mound stood a compact triple beehive cluster, one of the cells 100% intact. I had reached Both a' Ghriosamul.

2.6.2 Both a' Ghriosamul

Landranger Map: 13
Location: NB 13931 16086
CANMORE ID: 133872
Access: Kinlochrog, just off the B8011 at NB 1391 2374 – a 10 km walk

There were once three beehives clustered close together atop the mound at the center of the site, two of them interconnected. Only one of the three stands complete, and it is one of the best intact cells anywhere. After crawling inside I could see that the only large gaps in its dome were the smokehole at the top, and a small window to let the occupants keep an eye on what's going on down in the glen. Having a window opening is unusual, the only other cells I know of with windows are St Ronan's Cell and one of the beehives at Gearraidh Aineabhal.

Both a' Ghriosamul

Both a' Ghriosamul—collapsed cells in foreground and at right

The smokehole—Both a' Ghriosamul

Inside Both a' Ghriosamul—window opening right of centre

I am glad the users of this shieling site left one of the cells intact, for there was no mystery as to where the stones of the other cells had gone. At the base of the mound stood the ruin of a newer, oval shieling hut, obviously made from the pillaged stones of the other cells. And fifty metres to the north lay the foundation of another beehive almost completely plundered for its stone.

Both a' Ghriosamul—one of the two collapsed cells in foreground

The triple at Both a' Ghriosamul—collapsed cells in foreground and at right

After leaving a note for the next visitor I crawled out of the cell, and then made a level crossing of the wide glen back to the shielings at Airigh an t-Sluic, where I'd stashed the tent and sleeping bag three hours earlier. As the sun started dipping west I pitched the tent by the meager remnants of a shieling hut. I fell asleep atop the sleeping bag in the hot, sun-baked tent, only to wake shivering at midnight as a storm blew through.

Camp at Airigh an t-Sluic—Loch Langabhat in the distance

Lashing rain and howling winds came and went all night. In the morning I put off getting up as long as possible, hoping the rain would stop. But it didn't. It was only after rolling up the wet tent, and strapping it to my pack, that the rain decided to stop. It was time to return to Morsgail, but only after making one more stop.

I headed northwest over a mist-shrouded ridge to find one of the old paths that lead north to Morsgail. These old, mostly abandoned paths are more interesting to follow than the muddy, quad-bike tracks that scar the moorland. Here and there these old routes cross substantial, and in some cases elegant, stone-slab bridges built in the early years of the estate. After crossing one of those bridges I came to a large, sunken, brown swath of moorland, 600 feet long and 200 wide, that marks the site of a vanished loch.

Here I stopped to gaze skyward, hoping that a flaming interplanetary traveller would not plunge down on me, as it's said a meteorite destroyed the loch that once lay here. In 1959 the missing loch, Loch nan Learga, collapsed in what is known as a peat slide, or bog burst— its water draining into nearby Loch Mòr Shèlibridh. But what triggered it? It was possibly heavy rainfall, but at the Aird Uig radar base, twenty kilometres northwest of the loch, a giant "burning ball of hell" reportedly flew overhead. An expedition to the area discovered that the loch had drained. But there was no sign of any meteoritic debris.

Fortunately, no meteorites plunged down on me as I carried on across the bog—talk about going out in a blaze of glory—oh, to think how the books would sell after that! Near the vanished loch a pillar-stone stands atop a large mound, visible for quite a distance. It is a significant stone, a guide-stone, the last of the Postman's Stones that lead you across the bogs from Kinresort to Morsgail. From there it was an easy trek back to the Beinn na Gile beehives, and then on to the quiet road at Kinlochrog.

Vanished Loch nan Learga and the final Postman's Stone

Section 3 - Harris and North Uist

This section describes journeys to the beehives of Sròn Smearasmal on Harris, and the solitary cell inside Dun Charaigearaidh on North Uist. There are other cells on these islands, but to date these are the only ones I've been able to visit.

The Sròn Smearasmal cells were the first beehives Captain Thomas visited in the 1850s. In his report he mentions others to the west. I have searched that area, but could not find any cells other than some ruinous (but beautiful) cells at Glen Hallidail (NB 03067 09313). The far north of Harris must have beehives, but it is so remote that, other than the section between Direascal and Luachair, I have not had a chance to explore the area. Aerial photos hint at what may be a half-dozen cells at Abhainn Lon na Graidhe (CANMORE ID 122272), an extremely remote place I hope to visit someday.

North Uist, too, has other cells. In addition to Dun Charaigearaidh, Erskine Beveridge wrote of four on an island in Loch Hornaraigh reached by a submerged causeway; a cell on an Island in Loch Fada; two on an island in Loch Dun an t-Siamain; and two on an island in Loch a' Gheadais. (See Appendix A for more on these cells.) Although I've only visited a subset of the sites on Harris and North Uist, the two locations described here are stellar and well worth a visit.

3.1 Bothan Sròn Smearasmal – Harris

Landranger Map: 13
Location: NB 09006 07456
CANMORE ID: 313882
Access: B887 at the head of Loch Mhiabhaig (NB 10035 06252) - a 2 km walk

Note: The North Harris Eagle Observatory (NB 1004 0879) is 1.3 km north of where you leave the track to visit Bothan Sròn Smearasmal. If you are visiting the observatory (a 5.3 km round-trip walk), a detour to the cells adds 2 km distance and 140 m of elevation gain.

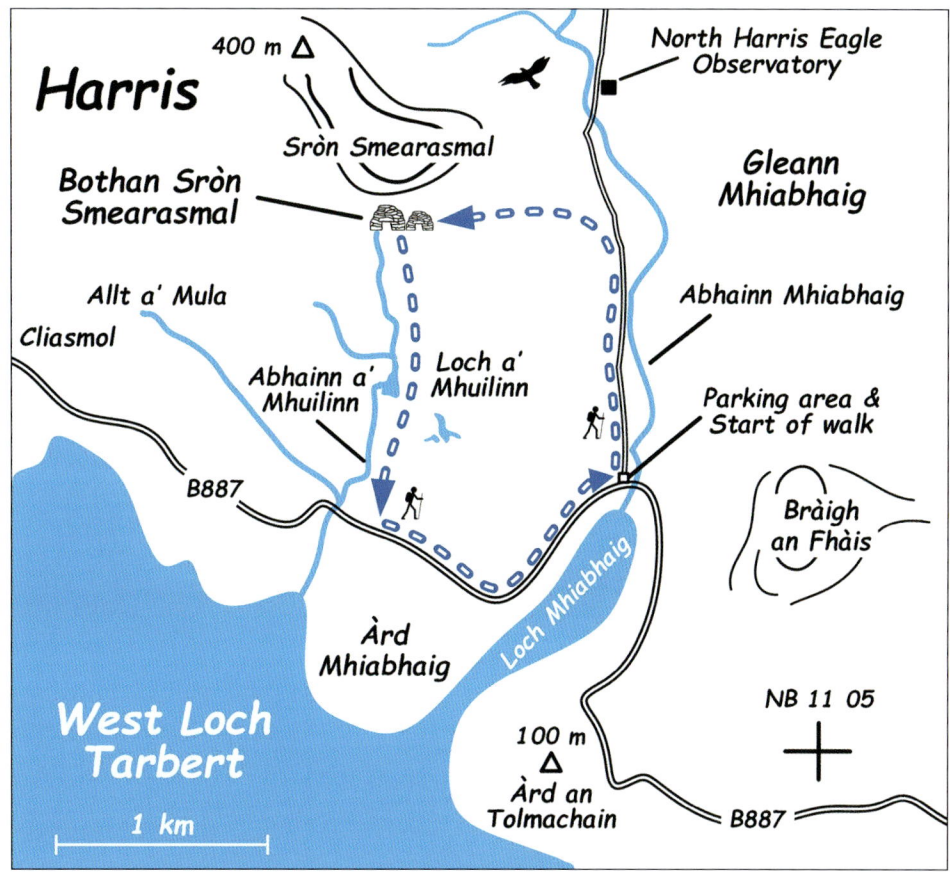

Map 3.1: Sròn Smearasmal

The Bothan Sròn Smearasmal cells, also known as the Cliasmol cells, are a two-kilometre hike up Gleann Mhiabhaig, eight kilometres west of Tarbert. They are important to the modern beehive hunter in that they were the first cells seen by Captain Thomas, that prolific explorer of beehives in the nineteenth century. Here is how the captain begins his report on the cells:

I was informed that on the moor, about a half mile from the head of this loch (Loch Mhiabhaig), there was a circular house, roofed entirely with stone and without a bit of wood in its construction… these 'bothan,' as they are called in Lewis, are from a short distance hardly to be distinguished from the granite blocks around, and in fact I was unsuccessful in finding them on my first search.

I visited Sròn Smearasmal during a week's stay at a B&B on Scalpay. It was a quiet Sunday—the only kind they have on Scalpay—as I drove over the bridge to Harris, turned left, and drove through Tarbert to make my way to the B887 road to Huisinis. I followed that narrow, windy road past the ruins of the whaling station at Bunabhainneadar, and then on past what is the most remote tennis court in the UK. Even if I had been in the mood for some tennis, I was out of luck—the court is closed on Sundays. After another five minutes of driving I crossed the bridge over the Abhainn Mhiabhaig, then found a place to park next to the gated track that leads to Loch Bhoisimid.

After hiking a kilometer north I left the track, at around NB 1000 0745, to head west up the grassy shoulder of Sròn Smearasmal. The beehive settlement was easily spotted, a kilometer to the west, at an elevation of 180 metres. One cell is completely intact, but only the foundation remains of the second. The intact cell is four metres in diameter at its base, two metres high to the top of the dome, and has four cupboards built into its lower walls.

The intact cell—Bothan Sròn Smearasmal

Bothan Sròn Smearasmal—collapsed second cell at right

*Beehive Houses (Bothan) Meahbag, Forest of Harris, Capt. Thomas R.N.
Proceedings of the Society of Antiquaries of Scotland, Vol. III (1857-60)*

Although the second cell has collapsed it still has a unique feature. It is built against a large boulder that had somehow been moved here, and a rectangular compartment (Captain Thomas speculated it may have been a sleeping place), had been built between the boulder and the main compartment. Here is how Thomas described it:

. . . the roof has fallen in, but the walls are still 5 feet in height. It differs from No. 1, first, that the walls of the chamber begin to close in from the base-line; and secondly, in having a prolongation, probably a sleeping-place, on one side. The chamber of No. 2 is circular in plan, and 6 feet in diameter. On the west side is a cell 4 feet long, from 1 to 2 feet broad, and 2 feet 4 inches in height. The sides of the cell are formed by placed stones, and the roof by single stones laid across. The end or head of the cell is the rough face of a large (naturally placed) transported block of gneiss.

The collapsed second cell—Bothan Sròn Smearasmal

A storm blew in just as I reached the cells, the stinging, half-frozen rain, blowing horizontally. Needing shelter I crawled into the intact cell. Although there were gaps in the roof, it kept the storm at bay. Once inside I enjoyed the stunning view the cell-dwellers had over the rolling terrain that gradually drops south to the sea.

Comfortably sheltered, I lived like a hermit-monk for an hour, listening as the storm roared past. After things calmed down the hermit-monk got thirsty. He crawled from his cell, stretched his cramped legs, then went in search of a warm pub and a cold beer. But he'd forgotten it was Sunday and failed in his quest. He eventually settled for a banana sandwich and cup of tea, provided by his B&B hostess on Scalpay. But only after sitting in the car for an hour waiting for her return from church, as the B&B was locked. They don't usually lock their homes on Scalpay. The hermit-monk had been suitably punished for venturing out on the Sabbath.

Walk note: Don't return from Bothan Sròn Smearasmal as you came. For a truly spectacular walk, follow the gradually descending terrain south past Loch a' Mhuilinn and on down to the highway. Then return to the head of Loch Mhiabhaig by following the road east

3.2 Dun Charaigearaidh – North Uist

Landranger Map: 18
Location: NF 92195 64070
CANMORE ID: 10429
Access: A867 at NF 897 680 - a 15 km round trip

Alternatively, if you can arrange to be dropped by boat on the south shore of Lochmaddy, it is an easier 4 km walk from NF 926 672. An even shorter route, though it's up difficult terrain, is if you can be dropped on the north shore of Loch Euphort.

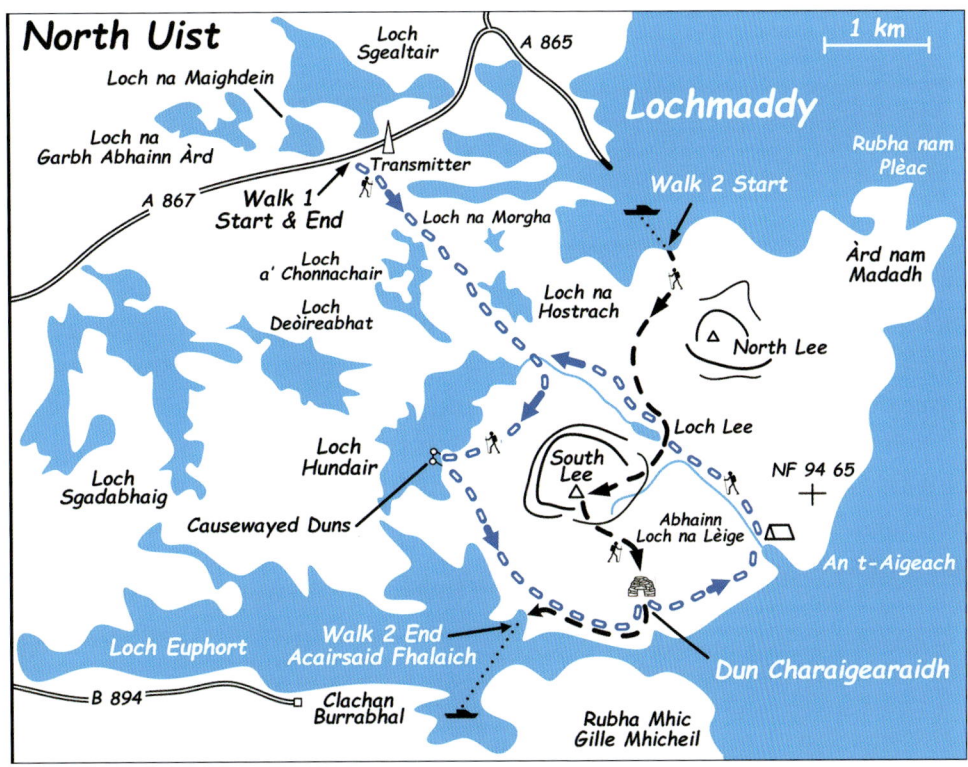

Map 3.2: Two journeys to Dun Charaigearaidh

Have you ever planned a long overnight hike in very remote country to see a historic site? Did you plan it months in advance to be the centerpiece of a fortnight's holiday? And to reach your final destination, did you set out on foot across the bogs, with fifteen kilos of gear strapped to your back. Did you look forward with every step to seeing something you've only read about, the only photos of it a century old? And when you finally reached this much anticipated place, did it disappoint? Was it nothing like you pictured it?

That's what happened in the May of 2015 when I went in search of an unusual beehive cell that sits atop the ruin of a prehistoric fort on the slopes of South Lee (North Uist). The fort is called Dun Charaigearaidh, and the only photos of its beehive were taken by Erskine Beveridge over a hundred years ago (see p.163 of his book *North Uist*).

— North Uist - Walk 1 —

On that failed hike I started from the A876 road at NF 897 680, two kilometres southwest of Lochmaddy. From there it was a boggy march southeast past Loch a' Chonnachair, Loch na Hostrach, and Loch Hundair. At the south end of Loch Hundair I took a slight detour to walk out onto its causewayed duns (forts).

Causewayed duns—Loch Hundair

From Loch Hundair I made a beeline southeast to traverse the slopes of South Lee to reach the narrows of Loch Euphort, where the waters of the Minch enter the loch. From there I started up the heather-clad hillside. After climbing 100 metres I came to what I thought was Dun Charaigearaidh. It was a stone structure much smaller than I'd envisioned, topped with a small, semi-circular, ruined drystone cell that could barely be described as a beehive. I was so exhausted after marching across miles of bog, that I convinced myself I'd found what I'd come to see. After taking a few photos I disappointedly went in search of a campsite.

What I initially thought was a beehive ruin near Dun Charaigearaidh

From the ruin I descended east to the sea, then followed the coast north. A cold wind was howling from the east. A few great campsites looking out over the sea, with short grass growing on solid, dry turf, had to be bypassed as being too exposed. Then I came to an inlet south of the headland An t-Aigeach. It was sheltered, with a little beach where the Abhainn Loch na Lèige tentatively trickled to the sea: the perfect Hebridean campsite.

Campsite—Abhainn Loch na Lèige

Just as I set up the tent the rain started to fall and would not stop for fourteen hours. In the wet morning, with waves lightly breaking on the shore below, I set out to climb the pass between North and South Lee. It appeared deceptively easy from sea-level, as it looked like an old peat track climbed to the summit, which would make for an easy hike. But on closer examination it was not a track, but a giant bank of heather covered peat with swampy ground on each side. I had no choice but to slowly follow it to the top of the pass. From there a similar peat bank dropped down the west side to the vast moorland I'd crossed the day before. Although there was still four kilometres to go, I was fortunate: the sun came out, there was no rain, and I had an easy walk back to the road.

When I returned home a week later I compared my photos to the one Erskine Beveridge took of the cell. It was readily apparent that what I'd found was not the beehive. More research revealed that fifteen metres below Dun Charaigearaidh there is a small outbuilding, perhaps a guard cell. That was what I'd found. I'd been so close—only a little farther up the hill and I'd have found the beehive. After realizing my mistake I thought it would be a very long time before I'd have another chance to visit that remote part of North Uist.

As things turned out, three months after that missed opportunity another chance arose: one that would allow me to see the real Dun Charaigearaidh without fifteen kilos of gear strapped to my back.

— North Uist - Walk 2 - A Second Chance —

That second chance occurred when I was on the ship Hjalmar Bjørge in August 2015. After visiting St Kilda we motored around to Lochmaddy, where the skipper, Tim Wear, and First Mate Craig Robinson, ran me the short distance across the harbour to the base of North Lee. They then took Hjalmar Bjørge for a 15 km motor around to Loch Euphort, where I'd meet up with them after walking over the hills.

The distance to Loch Euphort was five trackless kilometres. But that's as the sea eagle flies. The route I had in mind would be eight kilometres. I wanted to reach the top of South Lee, find the beehive in Dun Charaigearaidh, and then drop down to the shore to be picked up at Acairsaid Falach, a small hidden harbour (as its name means) in Loch Euphort.

Having climbed North Lee before (see chapter 15 of *Skye & Tiree to the Outer Isles*), I decided to bypass it and head directly for Loch Lee, which lies in the pass between North and South Lee. From the loch it was a straightforward, but rocky climb, to the top of South Lee. The view from the summit, of the hundreds of lochs that dot the interior of North Uist, is surreal. A view that took me back in time to the spring of 1968, when I watched with eyes wide the movie *2001—A Space Odyssey*. Some of the psychedelic scenes, where Astronaut Dave Bowman passes through the stargate were filmed by flying over this other-worldly terrain.

From the rocky top of South Lee I descended to the southeast. It was slow going—the hillside cloaked in tall bracken and dense heather. At an elevation of ninety metres I came to a narrow gully with a wall of defensive stonework on its opposite side. It was obviously man-made, it was Dun Charaigearaidh.

Inside the fort stood a beautiful beehive chamber. The very top of its dome had collapsed, and looking down into the cell I could see it had been built atop a two-metre deep hidey-hole in the ground. I would have slid down into it, but the stonework looked fragile. The cell is nearly two metres in diameter, and its walls stand a metre above the surrounding heather. This is Erskine Beveridge's description of the cell from his book *North Uist*:

Within the centre of Dun Caragarry, amidst a vigorous growth of heather, was found a domed cell in nearly perfect condition, so closely preserving its original character that a couple of slabs laid across its top would suffice to complete the fabric.

The dun-dwellers here had a panoramic view to the east over the mouth of Loch Euphort. It was easy to envision the fort as a strategic outpost monitoring the entrance to the vast inland sea of Loch Euphort. I had to laugh at myself when I noticed a small stone structure just down the hill. It was what I'd mistakenly thought was the beehive three months before.

From the cell it was a hard battle down the hillside, a non-stop bash through thick bracken, brambles, and heather to the shore of Acairsaid Falach. Fifteen minutes later I heard the sound of an outboard. It was Tim and Craig, and in short order I was back aboard Hjalmar Bjørge. I had been incredibly fortunate. Events had conspired to let me rectify a mistake and visit one of the hardest to reach and most beautifully situated beehive cells in the Hebrides.

Dun Charaigearaidh—Eaval in the distance

Beehive cell in Dun Charaigearaidh—mouth of Loch Euphort in the distance

Beehive seen from the north—Dun Charaigearaidh

Section 4 – Inner Hebrides

Surviving beehives in the Inner Hebrides are scarce. That said, the largest of the Hebridean cells are the monastic ones on Eileach an Naoimh of the Garvellach Isles. In this section we visit five sites in the Inner Hebrides.

4.1 Eileach an Naoimh

The massive cells on Eileach an Naoimh are the only Scottish cells comparable to the large Irish Cloghauns. Built for monastic use, they may date to the seventh century.

4.2 Islay

The hidden cells at Allt nam Bà on the remote northwest tip of Islay may also be early Christian, associated with the monasteries of nearby Kilnave and Nave Island.

4.3 Scarba

On the west coast of Scarba lie the slight remains of a half-dozen cells. Seeing them firsthand there were no signs of corbelling, and they appeared to have been plundered for stone long ago. I include them here because Patrick Gillies in his 1909 book *Netherlorn, Argyllshire and its Neighbourhood* described them as beehives, and the site as a possible location of St Columba's mysterious Hinba.

4.4 Eigg

Concealed in a remote ravine at the southwest end of Eigg lies an intriguing set of ruins, possibly monastic. When I visited them in 2006 no signs of corbelling were visible from the outside, and the structures were so unstable that I could not crawl in for a closer look. They are included here because they were described as beehives in 1964, and signs of corbelling were still visible in 2001.

4.5 Canna

Hidden below the southwest cliffs of Canna is Sgòrr nam Bàn-naomha, a Celtic Christian cashel, one of the oldest such sites in the Hebrides. At its centre stands the foundation of a large, two-chambered structure, possibly once a beehive-cell oratory, and next to it is a partially corbelled cell that was either a mill or a bathhouse.

4.1 Eileach an Naoimh – Garvellachs

Landranger Map: 55
Location:
Double cell: NM 64117 09715
Underground cell: NM 64032 09733
CANMORE ID: 22361
Access: Best visited as part of a multi-day cruise of the Southern Hebrides. A private charter, or a friend with a boat, may be your only options for a day-trip.

It was a quiet Sunday morning in 1997 when I arrived in sleepy Cullipool on the island of Luing. I had made arrangements with Lachie MacLachlan to take me to Eileach a Naoimh, but was not sure where to meet him. That question was soon answered—the early-morning calm shattered by the rumbling of a boat motor starting up. Lachie invited me to join him, and in short order we sped away from Cullipool Pier at full throttle. Lachie took the scenic route to Eileach an Naoimh, showing me the islands of Fladda, Belnahua, Dun Connel, and Garbh Eileach. All islands it would take many years to eventually set foot on.

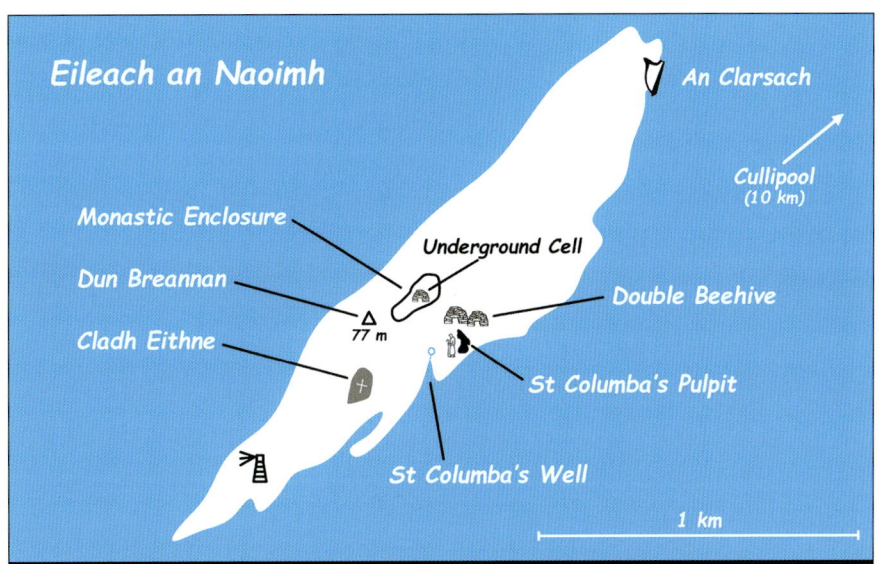

Map 4.1: Eileach a Naoimh

Lachie nosed the boat up to a smooth section of rock on the east side of Eileach an Naoimh, where I could easily jump ashore. After bashing through dense heather and passing St Columba's Pulpit (a natural pillar-stone with an overhang), I came upon the seventh century double beehive cell. Constructed from large slabs of sandstone, the cells span a distance of thirteen metres. With interior diameters of over four metres and walls a metre thick, these are the only cells in the Hebrides comparable to the large monastic beehives (*Clocháin*) of Ireland. Their corbelled stone roofs have collapsed, and at some point the cells were altered for use as a sheep pen. After that misuse some restoration work was done in 1937. There are still plenty of missing stones, probably taken to build the later-period buildings a hundred metres to the west.

The Garvellach cells from the north

The cells are built in a figure 8 shape, and partially embedded in the sloping hillside. Each has its own doorway, and a square passageway connects the two. It is possible they date to when the monastery was founded by St Brendan, and that the island was the mysterious monastic site of Hinba. If so, it may have been in these cells that the 'Mass of the Saints' was held by Columba, Cormac, Brendan, Kenneth, and Comgall, where St Brendan reported a column of fire rising from Columba's head. (See section 4.3 for a visit to another possible Hinba site on Scarba.)

The cells from the south

The passage between the cells

The cells and Columba's Pulpit

The cells seen from above

The beehives are in an isolated area, 100 metres east of the monastery. I hiked inland, and on reaching the top of a small rise the entire monastic site became visible. It covers an area 120 metres long by 30 wide. As I approached I heard voices. There was no one in sight, so where were the voices coming from?

Buried in the ground within the monastery enclosure is a hidden beehive. (Illustrated in TS Muir's *Characteristics of Old Church Architecture*—see Appendix C). The cell is a focal point for pilgrims visiting this holy island, and there were two people praying inside. The buried

Entrance to the underground cell

beehive is oval in shape, 1.6 metres by 1.4 metres, and 1.2 metres high. Once inside you'll discover a small shelf set halfway up the wall; a perfect place to light a candle and spend a few moments of solitude.

There is a strange story that the buried cell was a prison, the unlucky convict having their hands pinned under a rock wedge—though why a monastery would have a prison is a mystery. Or is it? *Bad, bad, monk, what were you up to in Oban over the weekend? Go to the punishment cell now young man, no guga for you tonight.* As opposed to a prison, the tiny structure may have been cold storage, or a sanctuary hidey-hole to escape raiding Ragnars.

In the underground cell

After exploring the rest of the monastic site, including a visit to Cladh Eithne, the grave of St Columba's mother, I heard the sound of a boat. My time was up, and Lachie was motoring in. We sped at full throttle back to Luing, as Lachie was in a hurry. Evening service was in an hour, and he coaxed every knot possible out of the boat to get to Cullipool in time.

Being late spring there was still plenty of daylight left for a walk. After he put on his Sunday best Lachie drove me to the ruin of Kilchattan Chapel at the south of the island, and then headed off to church. The day ended on that late Sabbath afternoon with a walk up the spine of Luing. Although there wasn't another soul in sight, I had some company—the lilt of psalms drifting on the wind.

4.2 Allt nam Bà – Islay

Landranger Map: 60
Location:
West settlement: Wall chambers **(A)** NR 21867 71164, Cell **(B)** NR 21862 71131
East settlement: Cell **(C)** NR 21961 71247
CANMORE IDs: 37513
Access: B8018 at Sanaigmore (NR 236 707) - 4 km round-trip walk

On the northwest coast of Islay, six kilometres from Kilnave, lies a complex site, part of which may have been a hermitage associated with the monasteries at Kilnave and Nave Island. The OS Name book from 1878 records the site as *Alt nam Bà,* (with one 'l'), and says the name means Valley of the Cows. Being a steep, narrow chasm below the cliffs, it's hard to imagine cows being able to get there. Current maps call the site *Allt nam Bà*.

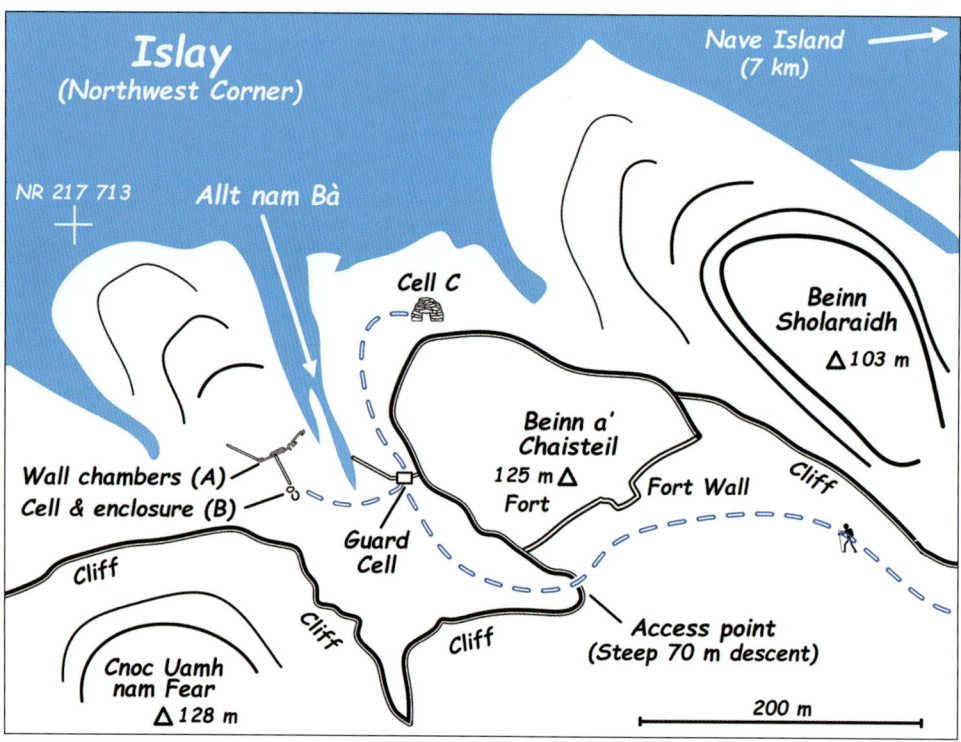

Map 4.2: Allt nam Bà—Northwest Islay

To get there I started walking west from the small parking area at Sanaigmore. After following the coastline for 0.75 kilometres, I traversed to the southwest up a series of lumpy knolls following a quad-bike track that made the going easier. After following the track for 0.75 kilometers I came to an old stone wall at NR 2239 7100. It was time to leave the track and follow the wall up through rough terrain to where it made a 90-degree left turn (NR 2225 7116). After following the wall a further 0.2 km to the southwest I came to a break in the wall at NR 22088 71045. After stepping through the break, a short walk led to a viewpoint over the Alt nam Bà peninsula.

Peninsula seem from the cliffs—Allt na Bà inlet to the right

The remains of a promontory fort lie atop nearby Beinn a' Chaisteil. But what I wanted to see required dropping seventy metres down a steep ravine to reach the peninsula. On the neck of the peninsula, and visible from the cliff, is an enclosure with a cluster of odd kidney shaped structures and a complex beehive cell.

Enclosure wall with cellular structures—beehive at lower centre

Halfway down the ravine I reached a wall with a linteled chamber. The wall blocks the route if you want to head north, but I was headed west. A gatekeeper here once warded off unwelcome visitors, but these days you'll only encounter a few wild goats manning the guard cell.

The guardhouse

From the guard cell I continued on down the slope to the left. Halfway down the peninsula I came to several kidney shaped dwellings **(A)**, and a triple beehive cell **(B)**—refer to Map 4.2 for locations. The remoteness has kept their stones from being robbed, but time has taken its toll and the domes of the beehive have fallen in.

The triple cell—view 1

The triple cell—view 2

The most unusual ruins are several kidney-shaped structures built onto each other that form a wall two metres thick. I poked my head into the largest, about 1.5 metres long by a half-metre wide. It did not look stable, so I had to settle for the view from outside. After seeing the ruins in the enclosure I climbed back to the guard cell. The return to the car would be mostly downhill, except for the first bit, the steep climb to the top of the cliff. I'd had a good day afoot. But nearly a decade later I learned I'd missed seeing another beehive, and a completely intact one at that, by just 100 metres.

Kidney-shaped corbelled structure built into the wall

I learned of the other cell several years after my visit to Allt nam Bà when the RCAHMS Inventory of Islay became available online. Along with some informative text on Allt nam Bà, there was a truly informative photo. It showed an intact cell on the headland east of where I'd been. There was only one thing to do. And so, nine years after my visit to Allt nam Bà, I found myself once again descending that steep ravine. But this time, when I reached the guard cell, I climbed over its walls and carried on down a steep, grassy slope.

At the bottom of the slope, twenty-five metres above the sea, lay a broad ledge littered with scree fallen from the cliffs over the centuries. At first sight no cell was evident. I did see a mound of stone, but it appeared to just be a collection of scree, as there was no visible doorway.

I had brought with me the photo from the RCAHMS Inventory, and was able to line up the mound with an odd, block-shaped outcrop of rock shown in the the old photo. The photo showed a doorway, and on closer examination of the mound I found that a large triangular slab had been inserted to keep sheep and goats out of the cell. The slab was easily lifted to reveal the doorway. Unfortunately, another large stone still blocked much of the entrance, a stone that was supporting the lintel. To enter the cell would have meant trying to squeeze past that pillar. Not wanting to disturb the structure, and possibly have it come falling down, I decided not to go inside. But it was easy enough to see the interior from the outside. The cell was quite spacious; oval in shape, 2.5 metres long and just over a metre wide, with an interior height of 1.3 metres.

*Cell (**C**) - seen from the south*

Not many people make the effort to visit this historic place, which is probably for the better. After replacing the slab that sealed the cell's doorway I started back. The climb to the top of the cliff was much harder than it had been nine years before—somehow it had managed to get steeper. Even so, it had been well worth returning to rectify a mistake and see the most intact beehive in the Southern Hebrides.

Note: Near where the walk to Allt nam Bà starts is a monument to a sea tragedy in 1847 when the brig Exmouth wrecked on the shore a kilometre from Allt nam Bà. The plaque on the monument, Gaelic on one side, English on the other, reads: *This memorial is dedicated to the memory of 241 Irish emigrants who lost their lives on the 28th April 1847, when the brig 'The Exmouth of Newcastle' out of Derry and bound for Quebec Canada at the time of the great famine, was wrecked on the N/W coast of Islay. 108 bodies, mostly women and children (63 under the age of 14, and 9 infants) were recovered and are buried under the soft green turf of Traigh Bhan. May their souls rest forever in the Peace of Christ.*

Tràigh Bhàn is a kilometre and a half south of Allt nam Bà. If you want to extend your walk, go the extra mile to seek out the soft green turf above the beach at NR 214 700, where you will find another memorial that marks the final resting place for 241 souls seeking a new life in Canada.

*Cell (**C**)–Interior view*

*Cell (**C**)–front view*

4.3 Port nan Urrachann – Scarba

Landranger Map: 55
Location:
Cell ruins found: NM 67941 04478
1880 OS map site: NM 68054 04542
CANMORE ID: 22368

Access: Aside from a boatman willing to drop you at Lurach Bay, your only option is a difficult twelve kilometre round-trip hike from Kilmory on the northeast corner of Scarba. A stalker's path takes you the first five kilometres, but from its end (near NM 6867 0380), there is still a kilometre of difficult, trackless terrain, to descend to the bay.

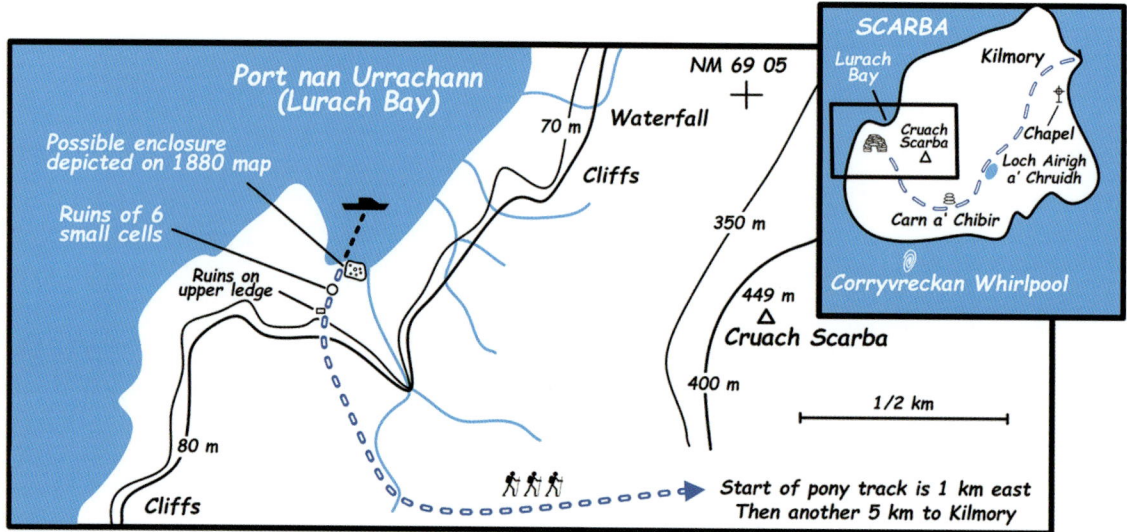

Map 4.3: Port nan Urrachann—Scarba

Prior to my first visit to Scarba, in 2002, I'd read of sightings of beehive cells on the northeast side of the island. But I could not find any when I was there. A few years after that I came across Patrick Gillies' *Netherlorn, Argyllshire and its Neighbourhood* (1909). In the chapter on Scarba he describes a set of six cells on the west side of the island, and conjectures the site may have been St Columba's *Muirbulcmar*, the monastery of Hinba. This is what Gillies had to say:

Six beehive cells, of a nature similar to those found in Eilach a' Naoimh, but in a more ruinous condition, are clustered together on a sheltered depression leading down from the terrace to the bay called Lurach, the only landing place on this side (west side) of the island. It may be that these cells formed the hermitage of Muirbulcmar; no such name has been preserved to us in the place-names of the district; but the probable derivation of the words (Muir, the sea; bolg, surging or soft; mor, great: the great surging sea) would indicate proximity to such a wild ocean as may be seen so frequently from this spot, caused by the rush of the tidal waters of Coirebhreacain.

One of the mysteries of the Hebrides is the location of Hinba. The usual contenders are Colonsay, Oronsay, Jura, Canna, Seil, and Eileach a' Naoimh. Patrick Gillies' book suggests Scarba belongs on that long list. And so a visit to Lurach Bay to search for its beehives became a must do. But I'd not the slightest idea when I'd ever have the chance to land on the remote western shore of Scarba.

A few years passed, then I discovered some discouraging information. It was a report on a visit to the site in 1970 (which you can find on the CANMORE website). It said: *A perambulation of the area around Port nan Urrachan failed to find any evidence of beehive cells, but a few crude bothy-type shelters lie scattered round the bay.*

Discouraging indeed, and I so crossed Scarba off as a place to look for cells. Another year passed and OS maps from the 1880s became available on-line. Lurach Bay was covered on sheet 87, and a look there showed something astonishing: what appeared to be a rectangular enclosure just above the shore. It was roughly 18 metres by 12, with what appeared to be a large circular structure at its center, surrounded by five smaller ones. Although the enclosure was not oval, it had the look of a Celtic Christian cashel. But there was something not quite right. The depicted enclosure was at sea level, not on a terrace twenty-five metres above the sea as described by Patrick Gillies. A mystery, indeed. All this meant that getting to Lurach Bay once again became a must do.

Good things come to those who wait. In 2016 I was aboard the ship *Elizabeth G* with members of the St Kilda Club. We were visiting the islands of the Southern Hebrides when I mentioned the possibility of cells at Lurach Bay. That appealed to fellow passengers Christina and Chris. After a visit to the raised beaches of Jura's West Loch Tarbert we headed up the west side of Scarba, where the three of us were set ashore at Lurach Bay. The skipper, Rob Barlow, then motored off to find an anchorage off Kilmory on the other side of the island. After searching for the beehives, Christina, Chris, and I, would hike over to Kilmory.

Under bright but unsettled skies, we started searching the foreshore of Lurach Bay. It was here that the 1880 map showed an object that looked like a cashel, but there were no structures to be found. I can only surmise the 19th century surveyors were either depicting some unusual rock formations on the shore, or cells that have been swept away by the sea in the intervening 140 years.

But we were not inclined to give up the search. Patrick Gilles described the cells as lying on a terrace just above the sea, so we made our way to a level bit of ground west of the beach. And sure enough, snuggled between a natural rock wall, two-metres high, and a cliff with a large cave, we discovered a cluster of a half-dozen small cells.

Site of the small cells—Lurach Bay

Remnant of a cell—Lurach Bay

All the cells were tumbled, but still recognizable under brittle fronds of dead bracken. The moss-grown ruins were small, and possibly the 'crude bothies' found in 1970. Were these the cells described by Patrick Gillies over a hundred years ago? I was hoping they would be, but after seeing them firsthand I'm not sure. Even so, finding these cells on Scarba, hiding in this beautiful secluded spot, was one of the highlights of twenty years of beehive hunting.

The weather made a turn for the worse as we climbed up from the terrace of the cells—fog and misty rain were moving in. We then came to another and larger terrace. This one covered with ruins of several large rectangular structures buried under heavy turf and bracken—perhaps another part of the monastery. We continued climbing and, after taking a last foggy look down to the bay, headed up into the mist to make our way to Kilmory.

4.4 Gleann Chàradail – Eigg

Landranger Map: 39
Location: NM 4510 8570
CANMORE ID: 22160
Access:
1. End of Grulin Iochdrach track near NM 4465 8510 – a hard 1 km walk
2. The Eigg M1 at NM 4763 8730, where the path to Laig starts – 5 km walk
3. The path to An Sgurr (from NM 4738 8407) – 3 km walk

Hidden high in the hills of Eigg, in a curved ravine at the head of Gleann Chàradail, lie a series of mysterious structures. I include them here because, due to slight signs of corbelling reported twenty years ago, they may have been beehive cells. There are six cells in the narrow glen, 200 metres upstream from a shieling site with a half-dozen ruins. The cells are quite advanced structures. Obviously built for concealment, they lie atop a channeled stream that flows out of Lochan Nighean Dugaill.

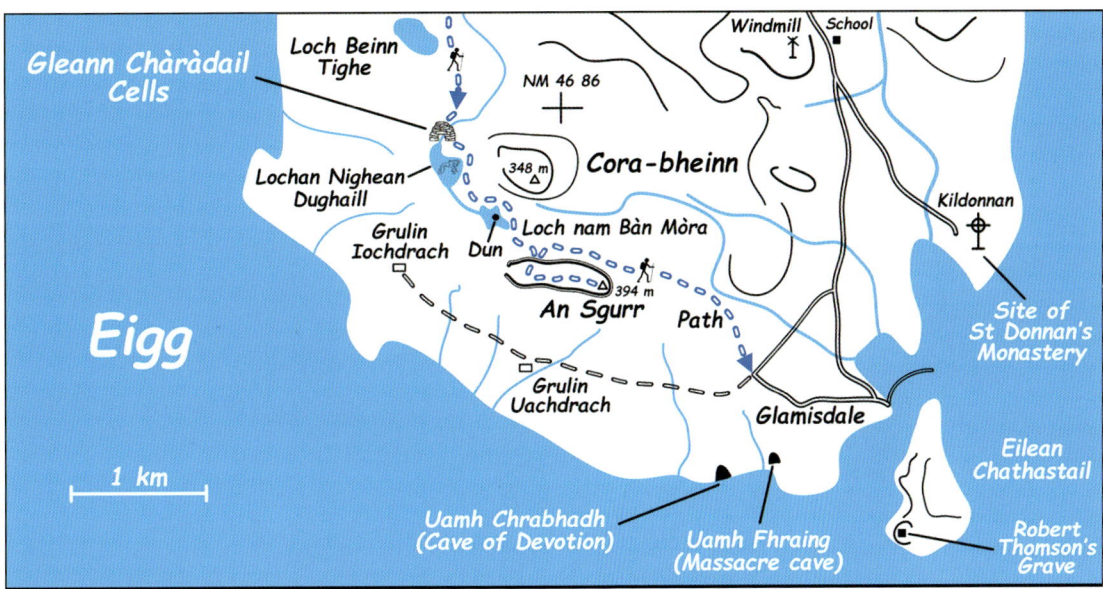

Map 4.4-1: Gleann Chàradail—South Eigg

*Looking towards Gleann Chàràdail and Rum from An Sgurr
Loch nam Bàn Mòra in the foreground*

I visited Gleann Chàràdail (possibly the glen of the twisting valley) as part of a long walk from Cleadale, but a shorter route is to take the Sgurr path starting at NM 4738 8407. The walk from Cleadale involves following the road south to Cuagach (NM 476 873). From there the path to Laig farm quickly drops down a ravine to cross the stream of the washer woman, then rounds the cliffs above a small loch shaped like a foot; the footprint of a giant according to an old island tale. After a couple hours of walking I reached the headwaters of Abhainn Gleann Chàràdail and the most intriguing ruins on Eigg.

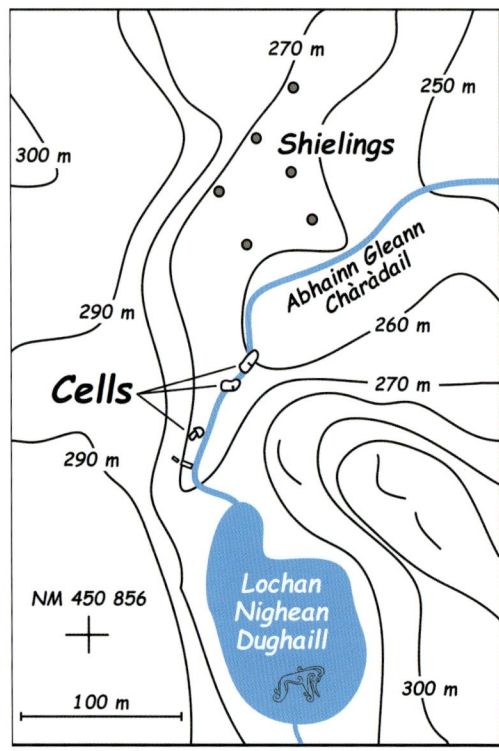

Map 4.4-2: Gleann Chàràdail settlement

In Chapter 4 of *Wanderings in the Western Highlands and Islands* (1921), MEM Donaldson describes a walk through Gleann Chàràdail. She makes no mention of any structures, but they could have been hidden by vegetation at the time. (The CANMORE website says the ruins were uncovered in 1964.) Although it does not say so, the photo facing page 246 of *Wanderings in the Western Highlands and Islands*, captioned *A Miniature Pass on the Heights of Eigg*, appears to be near the site.

There has been some speculation that the cells, built atop the flowing waters of a stream, were a form of cold storage. But they seem too elaborate to be simply refrigerators of a sort. Could they have been monastic? Denis Rixson, in his book *The Small Isles*, says: *There is absolutely nothing to prove that these structures have early Christian context, but there are several features that are striking.* To summarize these features:

Concealed and remote
Signs of corbelled construction
Well built—implies permanency, and not temporary (shieling) usage
Engineered manipulation of water flow beneath the structures implies institutional (monastic) knowledge

Rixson goes on to draw a comparison between these structures, and those of Canna's Sgòrr nam Bàn-naomha (see section 4.5). The similarities include the characteristics noted above (especially the waterworks), along with nearness to a site associated with women; in this case Eigg's Loch nam Bàn Mòra (Loch of the Great Woman), which lies a half-kilometre from Gleann Chàràdail.

Looking north from the hidden settlement—Gleann Chàràdail

The cells seen from above—Gleann Chàràdail

The cells seen from the north—Gleann Chàràdail

Access portal to the waterworks in Gleann Chàràdail

From the glen of the cells I hiked to the source of its stream, Lochan Nighean Dughaill, the little loch of Dougal's daughter. Said daughter met an unhappy end, devoured by the *Each Uisge*, the water horse that lived in the loch. There was no sign of the beast as I hoofed my way along the western shore of its lair. Continuing to the southeast, I followed another stream to Loch nam Bàn Mora with its island fort. From there it was an easy two kilometre walk along the Sgurr path to the road at NM 4738 8407.

Sadly, the historic structures of Gleann Chàràdail are falling apart. If you visit, please treat them with care.

4.5 Sgòrr nam Bàn-naomha – Canna

Landranger Map: 39
Location: NG 22991 04395
CANMORE ID: 10766
Access: 12 km round trip walk from Canna Pier

I almost did not make it to Sgòrr nam Bàn-naomha (the cliff-girt terrace of the Holy Women). A *Sgòrr* is an isolated terrace above the sea, and Canna's coastline has several. On this one lies the ruins of a seventh-century Celtic Christian cashel. The site is surrounded by an oval wall two metres thick, enclosing an area 32 by 39 metres across. My first walk there was in 2002, during a cruise on the ship Poplar Diver. We had spent the night in Tobermory Bay, and after the four-hour cruise to Canna I jumped ship to see if I could get to the cashel.

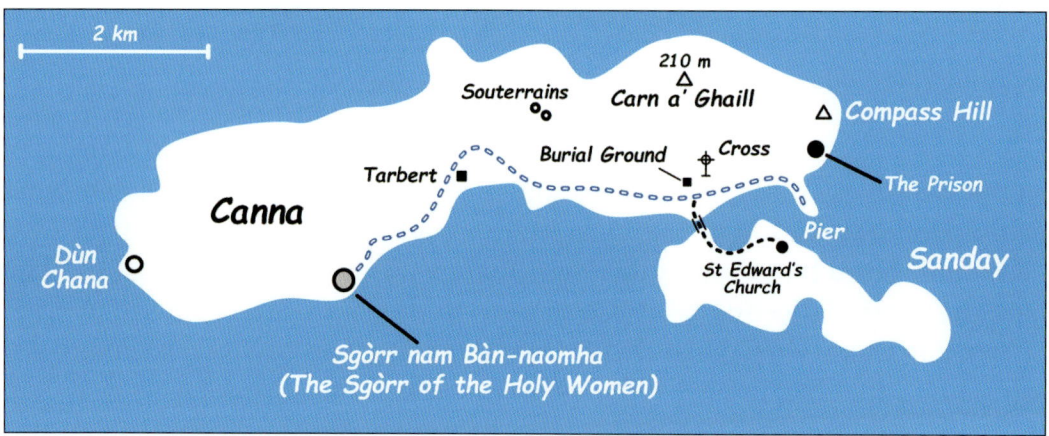

Map 4.5: Canna

But a depression set in when reached the cliffs overlooking the site. Not a weather depression, a mental one. There appeared to be no way down the 100-metre cliffs. I had come so close, but the cliffs seemed a final, impassable barrier. A narrow gully had looked promising. But after tentatively starting down, the small stones underfoot started to avalanche. One slip and I would find myself landing in eternity, so I scrambled back to the top. Thinking I'd have to settle for the view from above, I sat at the cliff-edge overlooking the cashel to eat my packed lunch. Seen from above, the cashel seemed to be a mis-mash of ruins, some that looked like sheep-pens.

I had just started back to the ship when I noticed several small white dots far below. Sheep were grazing on the terraces at the foot of the cliffs. Now how did they get there? Could there be a sheep track down the cliffs? I went farther east, and as I did the faint trace of a path appeared that came up around a promontory (NG 2328 0461). I followed the path downward, and that depression lifted when I realized it continued down the face of the cliff. The path eventually leveled out on the boulder-strewn ground at the foot of the cliffs. And there, in front of me, lay the centuries-old monastic ruins of Sgòrr nam Bàn-naomha.

Cashel seen from the cliffs

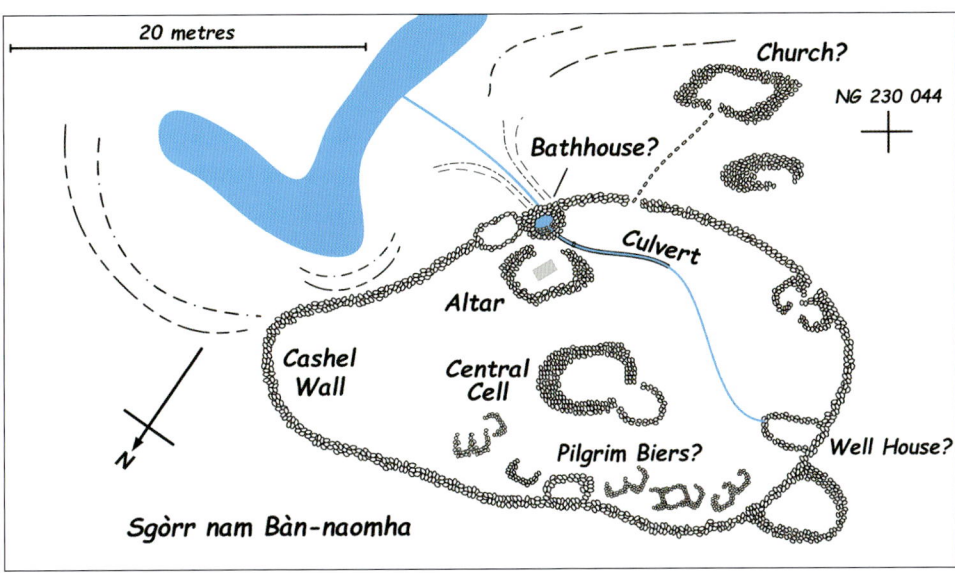

The cashel as viewed from the cliff

The central cell of the cashel, possibly once a beehive-oratory, is five-metres in diameter with walls over a metre thick and a meter high. Adjacent to it is the outline of a small chamber three-metres in diameter, possibly a lobby or porch.

The two-chambered central ruin—Rum in the distance

Ten metres southeast of the central cell lie the two most intriguing structures on the site. One is referred to as 'The Altar.' The other has been called either a bathhouse or a mill. The Altar lies at the centre of what appears to be the remnants of either a wall or some sort of large structure, about five metres in diameter. The Altar itself, composed of thin slabs of stone, is D-shaped, some two by three metres in size.

The ruin of the Altar with the 'bathhouse' cell behind and to the right

An article about The Altar, written by the Rev JE Somerville, appeared in PSAS Vol. 33 (1899). A photo in the article shows what appears to be a small beehive, which the author describes as *a 'cella' in which are placed a quantity of votive offerings, consisting of smooth round stones selected from the shore. As they lay, they looked much like the eggs of some large bird in a nest.*

It could be that The Altar was a *leacht*, a stand-alone altar of stone. Although they are gone today, the rounded stones described by Somerville are similar to those found on the *leachts* in Inishmurray cashel off the coast of Sligo. But the old photo makes me wonder if it was not originally an altar, but a beehive cell occupied by some venerated monk long ago. A cell that, over time, became a pilgrimage station.

The Altar, Canna, Rev J.E. Somerville
Proceedings of the Society of Antiquaries of Scotland, Vol. 33 (1898-99)

Next to the altar, built against the cashel wall, is a partially corbelled cell. It has been referred to as either a bathhouse or a mill, although to my knowledge no millstones were ever found in it. The structure is two metres in diameter, with walls a metre high. A channeled stream, from what may have been a well house on the opposite side of the cashel, flows through a culvert into the structure. The stream then pours through a linteled drain before cascading down to the sea.

It is interesting to speculate on the use of this structure. There is a local tradition on Canna that pilgrims crawled through the culvert that leads to the bathhouse. A plunge into cold water is in the tradition of the Celtic sweat lodge. Could one of the building here have been a *Taigh an Fhalluis*, a sweat house, and at its centre a *Leac an Teine* (the hearth stone)? After sweating out their sins the pilgrim could go to the adjacent bathhouse and plunge into a pool of cold water.

I base this speculation on the description of the *Taigh an Fhalluis* on Inishmurray. Its sweat-house is a corbelled cell at the north tip of the cashel set next to the water gate. In *A Description of the Western Isles* (1703), Martin Martin writes:

The ancient way the islanders used to procure sweat was thus: A part of an earthen floor was covered with fire, and when it was sufficiently heated the fire was taken away, and the ground covered with a heap of straw; upon this straw a quantity of water was poured, and the patient lying on the straw, the heat of it put his whole body into a sweat. To cause any particular part of the body to sweat, they dig a hole in an earthen floor, and fill it with hazel sticks and dry rushes; above these they put a hectic-stone, red hot, and pouring some water into the hole, the patient holds the part affected over it, and this procures a speedy sweat. Their common way of procuring sweat is by drinking a large draught of water gruel with some butter as they go to bed.

And there is this from William Frederick Wakeman's *A Survey of the Antiquarian Remains on the Island of Inishmurray* (1893):

When about to be used, a great fire of turf or brushwood was made inside; when this had burned out the ashes were swept out, and the patients took their place crouched on sods of turf. In several cases the bathhouse had adjoining it a deep artificial pool, in which after the hot-air bath the patient took a plunge.

Or, less picturesque, perhaps the 'bathhouse' was a latrine. The vestigial remains of a dozen other cells lie scattered along the north and west sides of the cashel. These may have been *Leaba Cràbhach* (pilgrim biers), where the penitents rested after their treatment. Fifteen metres south of the cashel lies the foundation of a large rectangular building—possibly a church—that has a doorway in its north wall, directly across from the entrance to the cashel.

The cashel seen from the east

When I was last on Canna (2016) the precarious path down to the cashel had been severely undermined by rabbits, so I do not advise using it. But do be sure to make the walk to see the site from above. Sgòrr nam Bàn-naomha was selected as one of Scotland's Treasured Places, and even from a distance it is an impressive sight. A more impressive sight would be how it looked 1400 years ago, when monks, or nuns, lived an eremitic life in their stone cells beneath the high cliffs of Canna.

Section 5 – Remote Outliers

The hardest to reach cells, remote and intriguing, are on the islands of Rona, Sùlaisgeir, St Kilda, the Flannans, and Eilean Fir Chrothair. Access requires a boat, knowledgeable crew, and lots of luck (meaning calm wind and seas). I have yet to set foot on the remotest of these, Sùlaisgeir, though not without trying. What follows are stories of journeys to the other outliers, and a close look at Sùlaisgeir from the sea.

5.1 Rona – Teampull Naoimh Rònain & Fianais

Landranger Map: 8
Locations/CANMORE IDs:
Ronan's Cell HW 80916 32329; CANMORE ID 1472
Fianais Cell (westmost): HW 8138 3301; CANMORE ID 320016
Fianais Cell (eastmost): HW 8148 3308; CANMORE ID 320017
Access: Boat only

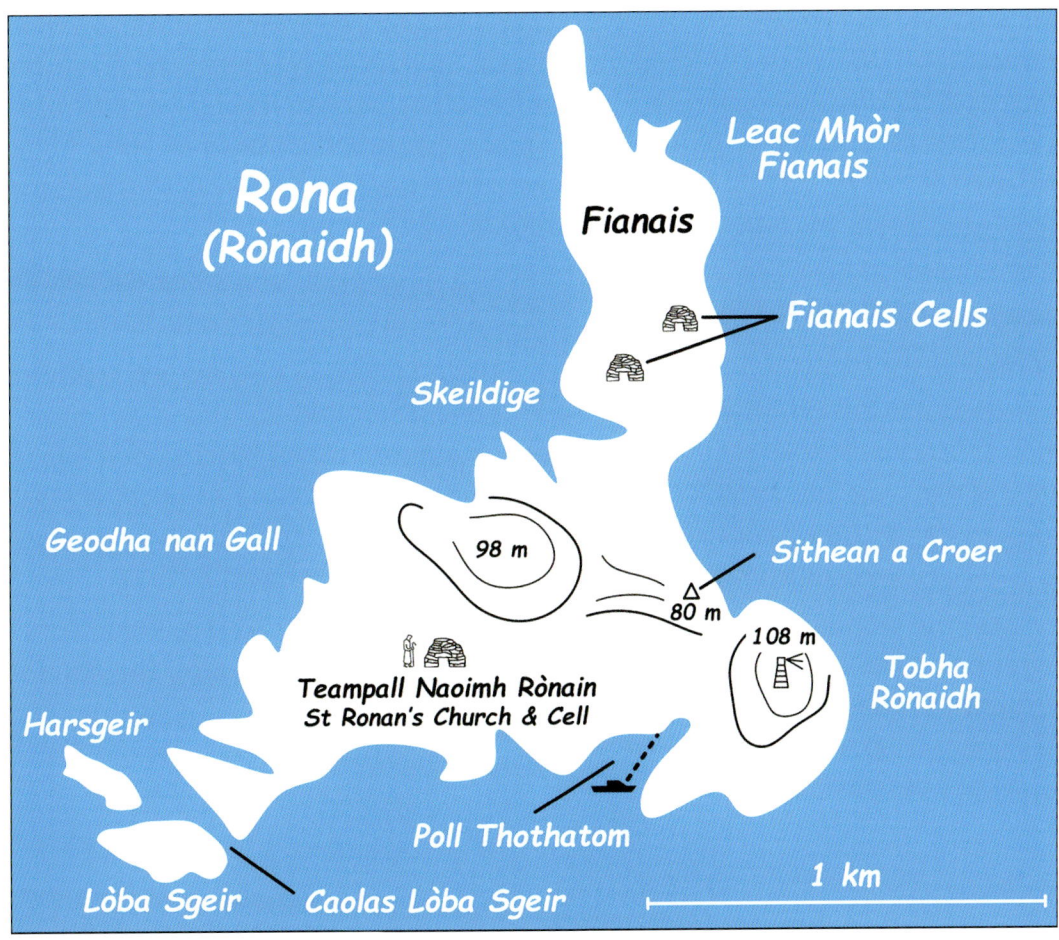

Map 5.1: Rona

Teampull Naoimh Rònain, along with the cells of Eileach an Naoimh and Canna, may be the oldest in Scotland. Fraser Darling, in his book *Island Years*, describes Teampull Naoimh Rònain (also referred to as St Ronan's Cell) as he found it in 1938, before doing extensive repairs to the cell and adjacent church:

The east and west walls are almost perpendicular, but the longer north and south walls slope inwards rapidly, and at a height of over eleven feet are bridged by rectangular slabs of gneiss to finish the roof.... the inside edges of the flattish stones are set a little higher than those reaching to the outside, so that all water draining on to the top of such a wall must drain outwards and the inside surface remains dry and free from condensation.

During his restoration work Darling found a green, egg-shaped stone, with veins of light green running through it: a talisman of some sort. It was buried under the altar and he believed it to be Iona marble. Here is his description of the stone from *A Naturalist on Rona*:

As I was digging at floor level beside the altar my spade was deflected from a rounded stone which, even in the dim light of the cell, showed green. My first thought was—Iona Marble—a stone of which I am familiar, for I always carry some small pieces in my pocket. I picked up the stone, washed it, and found a piece of smooth, dark-green marble about the size and shape of a sheep's heart. There was an intricate veining of lighter green. No rock of this kind occurs naturally on Rona, and, found in this place of all others, I wondered if St Ronan had been to the collage of Iona and had brought this piece of stone to his church on Rona to be a symbol of the mother foundation. This stone has left Rona with me, so that it may be seen by antiquaries and men of science, and that it may not be lost. But it must go back to its place as part of Ronan's altar and not be kept by me or placed in a museum. I have left a token of good faith of my present custodianship by burying three of my own pebbles of Iona marble in the masonry of the altar. Fanciful, perhaps, but it has pleased me so to do.

In DDC Pochin Mould's *Irish Pilgrimages* there is a description of a stone strikingly similar to the one found in Ronan's cell:

Martin Martin (1695) tells of St Moluag's Ball ... this is Moluag of Lismore, who was originally a monk of Bangor in Ireland before crossing to Scotland. The stone was round and green, about the bigness of a goose egg; it was used for swearing oaths, for curing stitches, and for throwing at enemy's armies, the opposing force being flung into confusion and at once running away. Macdonald of the Isles was said to have carried the stone and always to have been victorious when he had it with him. The stone had a hereditary keeper of the Clan Chattan.

This makes me wonder if St Moluag's Stone somehow found its way to Rona. Fortunately for us, after being buried for centuries, and then hidden away for decades, the Rona stone is now on display at the Museum nan Eilean in Stornoway.

— Journey to Rona —

On the first day of Summer 2011 the ship Hjalmar Bjørge left Oban: destination Rona. There were nine passengers, and one dog aboard. *Seven*, the ship's dog, has been on more islands than many an island-bagger. And as we set out, beside what was for dinner, *Seven* and I had one thing on our minds. Would we be able to land on Rona? The odds were against us, for the wind and sea must be calm to get ashore on that island, sixty-five kilometres north of the Butt of Lewis. The ten-day cruise improved those odds, allowing time to wait for a break in the weather.

Our first night was a calm anchorage in Canna's Tarbert Bay. The following morning, as we cleared the north of Skye, a strong westerly started to blow, and it continued as we approached the Shiants. The wind made the usual anchorage between the islands untenable, so we dropped the hook off the west side of Garbh Eilean. A few hours were spent ashore exploring the Bronze Age roundhouse ruin at Annait, and climbing Glaic na Crotha (cattle hollow) to the summit of the island, where we were rewarded with a view over the Minch. Verdant Eilean Mhuire, with its large puffin colony, lay a kilometre east; to the south was Rubha Hunis (the northern tip of Skye), and beyond Skye lay South Rona. But there was no sign of that other Rona, the one we were headed for, 150 kilometres north.

The next morning, as we motored past the Butt of Lewis, the sea-state worsened as the ship ploughed her way through large swells that occasionally broke over the bow. On nearing Rona we saw that the only possible landing site would be Poll Thothatom, an inlet on the southeast side of the island.

Then, surprisingly, the sea calmed, the sun came out, and we were blessed with a true summer day. The inflatable was lowered, and our skipper, Mark Henrys, guided it to a spot on the rocky shoreline. One by one, we jumped off the bouncing RIB onto Rona. Once ashore we climbed a steep hill to reach the lush blanket of grass that covers the south half of the island. My first destination was the village. As I walked towards it, I was attacked. A sudden whoosh overhead, and then a sharp *kark-kark*, as two great skuas started a series of strafing runs, trying their best to scare me away. The attacks ceased as I neared the village.

The cashel enclosure surrounded by cultivation ridges

The village consists of clusters of cells and rectangular structures built along the south side of the monastic cashel. At times upwards of thirty people lived here, surviving off the birds, seals, and the island's seventeen arable acres. It was a hard life, and the entire population starved to death at least once. In the early 1800s only six acres were under cultivation, and the last permanent residents left in 1839.

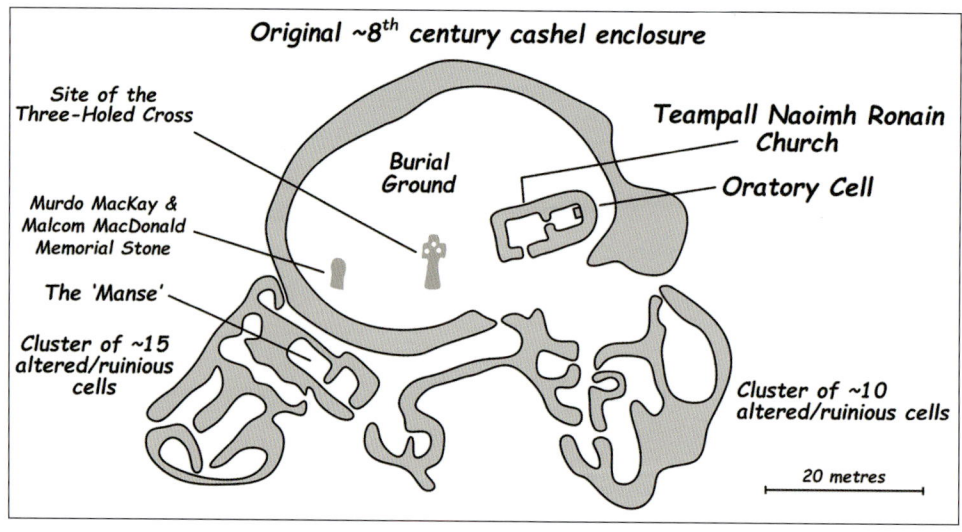

Monastic cashel and later enclosures

The stellar attraction of the village is St Ronan's Cell and Church. The cell dates to the seventh or eighth century; the church added to its west end in the thirteenth century. The only entrance to the cell is low in the east wall of the church. Several inches of muck usually cover the ground, and as the portal is only a metre high you have to squat down to enter. Once inside it is clear this is not an ordinary beehive. The high rectangular interior, similar to some of the large beehives on Skellig Michael, and one of the cells on the Flannans, signifies it as an oratory.

Ronan's Cell (left) and later church

The cell is 3.5 metres long by 2.5 wide, 2.5 metres high, with a window opening over its low entrance. Getting down on all fours I crawled into the cell, which Fraser Darling rightly called the Heart of the Island. A fulmar was nesting inside and I stood as far from it as possible. The interior was spacious, most of it below ground level. The small window above the entrance lit the stone roof, and the slab-remnants of the altar lay at ground-level along the eastern wall.

Entrance to St Ronan's Cell

Inside the oratory—St Ronan's Cell

The window opening above the entrance

Propped against the wall stood three beautiful stone crosses. One of the crosses did not look like a tombstone, and may have once been mounted near the altar. Missing from the collection is the mysterious three-holed cross taken away in the 1930s, and is now in the museum of the Ness Historical Society.

Cross stones in Ronan's Cell
Inset: The three-holed cross no longer on Rona (not to scale)

Fulmar nesting next to the altar

The fulmar was nestled snugly next to the altar. If it hadn't been there I'd have stayed longer; but the fulmar was getting nervous, turning in circles and occasionally jabbing its beak at me. Not wanting to get spit on, or further disturb the fulmar, I crawled out of the cell to continue my look around the old village. There are other beehives here, but aside from Ronan's Cell they are in a sorry state. There is also a rectangular structure here called the Manse, adjacent to the cashel wall, built from the stones of a dozen beehives that once stood there. And just north of Ronan's cell are two mounds that mark the sites of beehives cannibalized to build the church.

Beehive ruin—Sùlaisgeir in the distance

Once a beehive cluster—The 'Manse' (with roof-pole) at centre
Ronan's Church & Cell at right

After paying my respects to the generations that lived, and sometimes starved on Rona, I left the village and climbed the central ridge of the island. How I wish I could have seen what Fraser Darling saw up there in the winter—seals lounging on the ridge sixty metres above the sea. I then descended to Fianuis, the narrow peninsula at the north of the island, and walked to a sheep fank near the cave that penetrates halfway through the peninsula. Fraser Darling and his family lived near here to study seals in the late 1930s. Darling estimated there were 5000 seals, but now, in summer, not a single one was hauled out on the low, rocky ground.

Near the fank there is an odd, sloping hole in the ground. As I neared it a strange sound grew louder. I stopped and listened. It was exactly like what you hear when you put your ear to a conch shell: the sound of the sea. Marked as a 'gloup' on the OS map, the hole leads down to the sea cave. Darling described descending the hole, some fifteen metres to the cave. But it would be dangerous to do that without a rope, so I passed on by.

A hundred metres north of the gloup I came to a large altered beehive. Darling described this unusual cell, and its neighbor, in *A Naturalist on Rona*:

There are other relics of a stone-age culture on Rona, not contemporary with the megalithic period but a relic of its culture all the same. These are the beehive shielings which remain on the stark northern penninsula of Fianais and the one on Sceapull. I believe they of relatively recent construction, built as shelters for the sealers from Ness... one of these shielings (the westmost) is in a fairly good state of preservation, and we ourselves have repaired it and cleaned out the floor, so that it could be used as an emergency lodge if the huts blew down.

The cell measures about 4m by 2m on the inside, and would still be a good place to pitch a tent if you were going to spend a stormy night on the island. The second cell on Fianais Darling mentions lies twelve metres to the northeast. It is more dilapidated, but slight signs of corbelling and a cupboard are still evident. I have searched for the cell referred to at Sceapull, on the southwest corner of the island, but was not able to find it.

Large altered cell—Fianais (westmost cell)

Interior view of the large cell—Fianais

Smaller (eastmost) cell—Fianais

With just an hour left of our time on the island I started back up the ridge. No bonxies attacked, and neither did I have the distraction that tempted St Ronan. While climbing this ridge with his sister Saint Brianuil, Ronan blurted out "What beautiful legs you have." Brianuil decided isolation was taking its toll, so she packed up and moved to Sùlaisgeir. On reaching the top of the ridge the bonxies noticed me, and so I held a fist high in the air to ward them off before starting down to the landing. An enticing small lump of stone rose from the sea 20 kilometres to the west; the place where Saint Brianuil sought solitude, and where she would die alone. It was our next destination: Sùlaisgeir of the gannets.

St Ronan's Cell—Sùlaisgeir in the distance

5.2 Sùlaisgeir – A Desert Place in the Sea

Landranger Map: 8
Location: HW 6212 3058
CANMORE ID: 1470
Access: Boat only

After leaving Rona we floated for an hour off Sùlaisgeir, looking in awe at the thousands of gannets nesting along the southern half of the island. Also visible from the sea were the cairns built by the men of Ness, who come every August to hunt the young gannets.

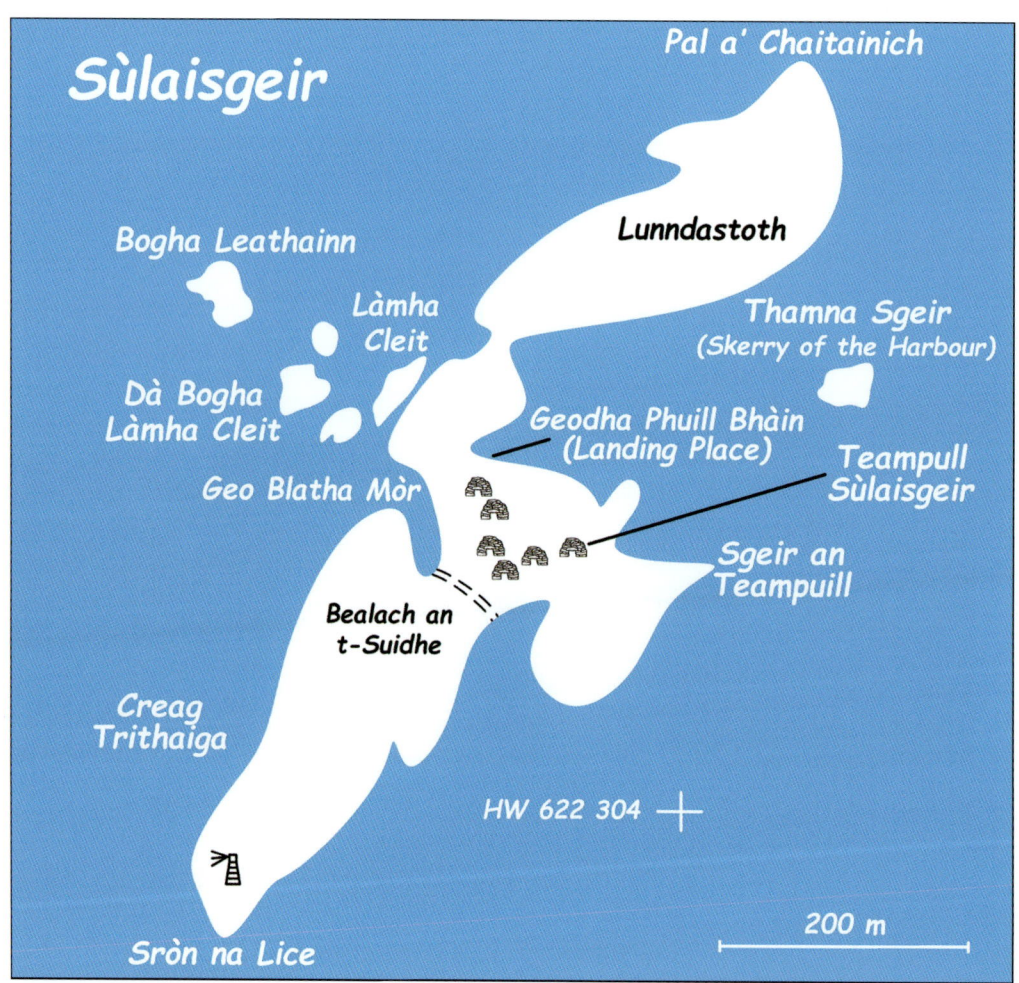

Map 5.2: Sùlaisgeir

One cairn in particular, known as *Suidhe Brianuil*, stood out from the rest. It is said to mark where St Brianuil died. As the story goes, she lived here in self-exile after leaving her brother on Rona. *Suidhe* means seat, and the placenames *Bealach an t-Suidhe* and *Suidhe Brianuil* refer to where she sat, and where her skeleton was found with a shag nesting inside. It is interesting that the story involves a shag (a species of cormorant) and not a gannet, as gannets were known in Ness as Brianuil's Bird.

Sùlaisgeir from the east

There are six cells on Sùlaisgeir. Five of them may have been built by the fowlers who come for the gannets—but the east-most cell is older. TS Muir, when he visited in 1860, named it *Teampull Sùlaisgeir*, and another name for it is *Tigh Beannaichte* (blessing house). There is no proof this was a church, but Muir reported seeing an altar under its eastern window. Unfortunately, that side of the cell has since collapsed, and the dome fell in 1984.

Teampull Sùlaisgeir in 2008—Photo © john m macfarlane (cc-by-sa/2.0)— licensed for reuse https://www.geograph.org.uk/photo/1032175

Some of the cells on Sùla are used as shelter during the annual hunt, when the men of Ness come to harvest their allotted 2000 guga. (Guga is Gaelic for a fat, clumsy fellow—the young gannet.) The cells lie at an elevation of thirty metres, and as we floated off the island we were able to see the north-most cell, which lies just above the landing place of Geodha Phuill Bhàin. More visible were the cairns of the Nessmen, and a larger cairn topped by a stone pillar. Every guga hunter has his own cairn, but the larger one is older: Saint Brianuil's Cairn.

North-most cell—Sùlaisgeir

Cairns of the Nessmen—St Brianuil's cairn at right

True or not, the tale of St Brianuil brings up the question of who first set foot here to build these cells: a mystery that will never be solved. Perhaps it was guga hunters centuries ago. But as Sula was readily visible from the monastery on Rona, it may have been their hermitage retreat. St Adomnan, in his *Life of Columba*, writes:

It was one characteristic of the asceticism of the early Irish Church, that its Clergy were in the habit of retiring to some desert place, to lead the lives of hermits, completely isolated from all intercourse with their fellow creatures for a certain number of years; and we find that almost all their leading Saints, at least once in their lives, retired to some solitary spot, where they led the lives of hermits for some years.

In the same work we find passages such as the *Prophecy of the holy man Baitan who had sailed out looking for a desert place in the sea,* and *Cormac, a soldier of Christ, attempted for the second time to reach a desert place in the ocean.* There could be no better Desert Place in the Sea than Sùlaisgeir.

We were unable to land, but it was a magnificent summer day, and we circled the island as thousands of gannets circled us. Over 10,000 birds nest here, and the highlight of our sail-by visit was when a massive sea of white gannets, disturbed by our presence, avalanched off the rocky side of the island to take flight.

South end light beacon—Sùlaisgeir

5.3 Calum Mor's House – Hirta, St Kilda

Landranger Map: 18
Locations: Calum Mor's House NF 10065 99484, Cleit 123 NF 09929 99503
CANMORE IDs: 9700 Calum Mor's House, 9677 Cleits 122 & 123
Access: Boat only

In 2015 I signed up for an August cruise to St Kilda on the ship Hjalmar Bjørge operated by Northern Lights Cruising Company. As the date approached I started paying attention to the weather news from Scotland. It was, to say the least, dismal. Due to the bad weather a record number of cruises to St Kilda had been canceled. A week before the trip the weather still looked horrible, and none of the boat operators had been able to get to St Kilda.

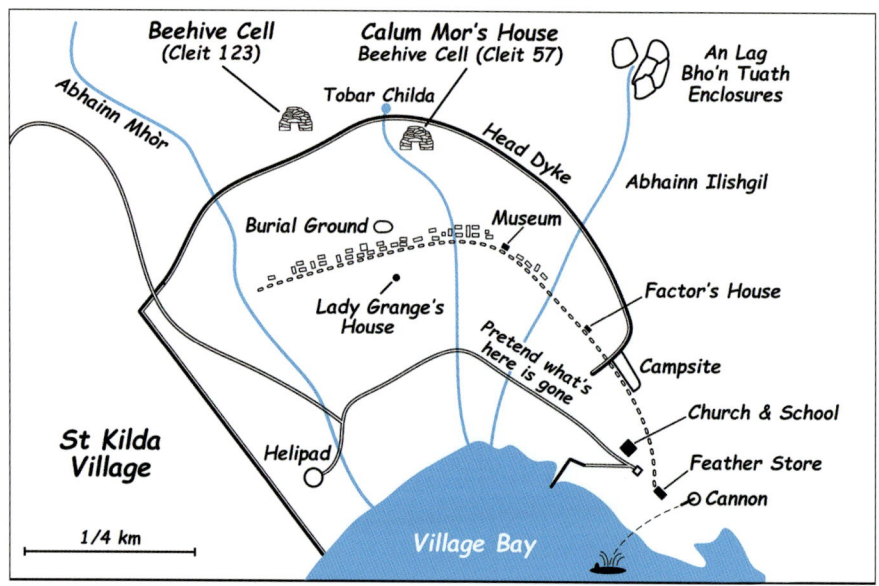

Map 5.3: St Kilda Village

But we were lucky. The weather took a turn for the better as we set out from Oban. After a short interlude on Canna we were able to reach St Kilda. That was the good news. The bad news was that every other cruise operator had taken advantage of the good weather. In addition to Hjalmar Bjørge, there were five day-boats anchored in Village Bay. The population of St Kilda on that beautiful August day was over 100.

To escape the crowd I made a long hike around the island, but only after paying a visit to the beehive cells in the village. One of the most studied and written about cells in the islands lies here on far-off St Kilda. It is a large beehive known as Calum Mor's House, that lies 100 metres north of the burial ground. Half-embedded below ground, its dark oval interior is 4.5m by 2m, and 2.5 metres high.

The cell is constructed with some very large stones, a few weighing in excess of 400 kg—hence the legend that it was built by the strongman Calum Mor (Big Malcolm), a story that dates to the 1800s. There are slight remnants of adjoining cells on its south and west side, and corresponding lintel stones inside the cell hint that the three chambers had once been interconnected.

The cell's survival over the centuries has been somewhat due to its protective turf covering. But that covering is at risk. Last time I saw the cell several sheep were lazily munching away on the tasty grass growing on the dome. Another danger is water damage. The interior is often flooded, which can be a deterrent to anyone wanting to enter the cell. That is partly a good thing. So many people visit St Kilda that if they all went into the cell it would certainly be damaged.

Calum Mor's House

In the catalogue of St Kilda structures Calum Mor's House is listed as Cleit 57. But it is not a cleit—storage cells built to allow the wind to blow through them. (There are over 1200 cleits on St Kilda.) For comparison a photo of Cleit 122 is provided, which has its own interconnected beehive cell annex, only accessible via the larger cleit. This stunning double structure lies 140 metres northwest of Calum Mor's House. (The little beehive annex, two-metres inside diameter, is listed as Cleit 123.)

Cleit 122 at right—connected beehive (Cliet 123) at left

There are many other cellular structures on St Kilda, but Calum Mor's house is unique: possibly one of the oldest surviving dwellings in the Village Bay area. Remarkably similar to the beehives of Lewis and Harris, it is one of the most authentic ruins in the village, as it has remained unchanged over the years, looking today as it did 400 years ago.

After seeing the cells I headed up into the hills of Kilda. An extraordinary thing to do. A dream hike on a dream island. Fortunately, it was not a dream. If you want to visit St Kilda and make a hike like that there are day-trips from Skye and Harris, and six to nine-day cruises from Oban, Ullapool, and Lewis. Do it. Just do it. It is an experience to remember forever.

5.4 Eilean Mòr – Flannan Isles

Landranger Map: 13
Locations: Teampull Beannachadh: NA 7263 4683, Bothan Chlann 'ic Phail: three-chambered cell NA 7232 4689, single cell NA 7231 4688
CANMORE IDs: 3971: Teampull Beannachadh   3973: Bothan Chlann 'ic Phail
Access: Boat only—good luck, for even if you get near the chances of landing are slim. If you do land, congratulations! But keep an eye out for rogue waves.

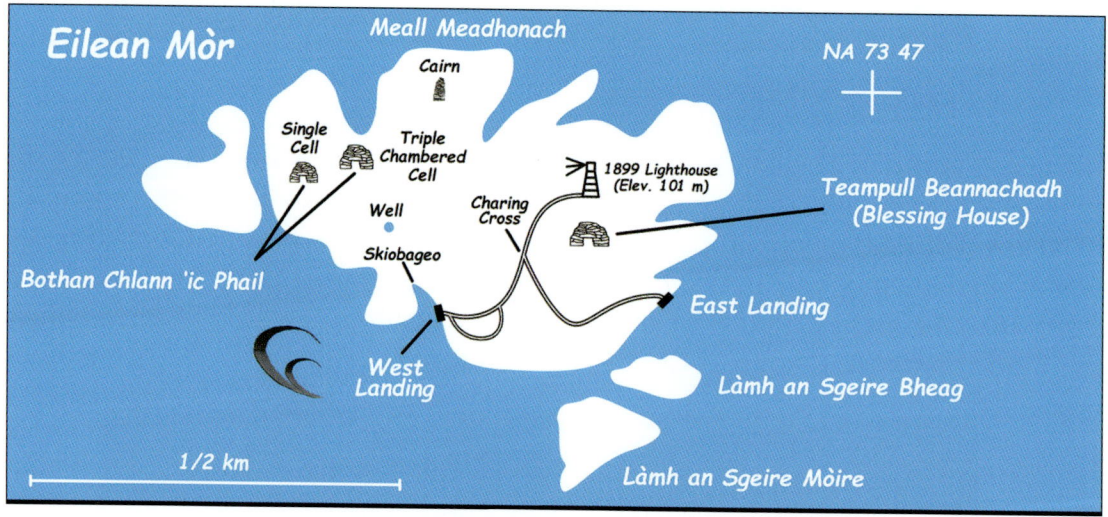

Map 5.4: Eilean Mòr of the Flannan Isles

On Eilean Mòr, the largest of the Flannan Isles, you will find the golden lichen-stained remains of three beehives. They are complex structures, and possibly built to house a monastic settlement as far back as the eighth century. Two are called *Bothan Clann 'ic Phail*, the bothies of Clan MacPhail. The third is *Teampull Beannachadh*, the Church of Blessing, sometimes referred to as St Flannan's Chapel. St Flannan, whom these islands may have been named for, was a seventh century prince of Thomond in the west of Ireland. He became an abbot and went on a pilgrimage to Rome, possibly visiting the Hebrides during his travels.

My first visit to the Flannans was in 2003, as recounted in *Skye & Tiree to the Outer Isles*. After two subsequent failed attempts, in 2004 and 2015, I made a second successful landing in

2017. I was aboard the ship Hjalmar Bjørge, skippered by Mark Henrys, and as we approached the island landing looked problematic. Although the swell was less than a metre, the cement steps up to the east landing, built 120 years ago, have been scoured away by the sea.

It also looked like the rusted ladder-rungs embedded in the face of the landing platform, that I'd used to get ashore in 2003, were unsafe. I had resigned myself to not getting ashore when skipper Mark said he had a cunning plan. He lowered the inflatable, and with rope in hand Mark and Anna (Mark's wife, and First Mate of Hjalmar Bjørge) went to take a closer look.

Through binoculars we saw Anna leap ashore with the rope, and Mark soon followed. We watched as they attached the rope to iron stanchions embedded in the rock, remnants of handrails long since rusted away. Even with the rope it was going to be a steep, slippery scramble to land. Five of us gladly volunteered for shore leave. One by one we used the rope to steady ourselves as we inched up to where the steps were still intact, ten metres above the rolling sea. From there seventy steep steps led to the base of a tram track.

Setting the rope at the East Landing

For sixty years a tram hauled supplies to the lighthouse from the two landings, winched up via a cable. A speaking-tube allowed someone at the landing to tell the keeper when to start the winch. I've often wondered if that speaking-tube was used to alert the men in the lighthouse to a problem on that day in 1900, when the three keepers disappeared.

Once atop of the island we made our way to *Teampull Beannachadh*, the Blessing House. Once you crawl inside and look up at the corbelled dome, you can see this structure is at its heart a beehive cell. Built from granite blocks it is four metres long, a little over two wide, and its 'gable' ends stand two metres high. The roof collapsed at some point and has been rebuilt. Viewing the chapel from the outside it reminded me of the Gallarus Oratory in Dingle, as it's built in the shape of an upturned boat. Another similarity is that the Flannan cell was built to the same proportions; its length, width, and height, each half that of Gallarus.

Dating the oratory is difficult. Based on the following discussion of oratory evolution (from Peter Harbison's *Pilgrimage in Ireland: The Monuments and People*), it may well be 1200 years old:

For many years, such oratories were seen as a halfway house, architecturally, between the beehive hut and the church with upright walls... In such a scheme, oratories of Gallarus type had to be placed at the beginning of church development, and therefore sometime before the eighth century... But the oratories can equally well be seen as an adaptation of the idea of the rectangular stone church of non-Irish origin to the local methods of corbelled construction practiced in the beehive huts... which would allow us to place the oratories anywhere between the ninth and twelfth century.

Teampull Beannachadh

The top of the dome—Teampull Beannachadh

The monk's view—Teampull Beannachadh

Readers of Peter May's *Coffin Road* will recall the story of how the body of a murder victim was found here. Thankfully all I found in the chapel on my visit in 2003 were obtrusive sacks of building material, which I was glad to see were gone in 2017.

Three hundred metres west of the chapel stand the two cells known as *Bothan Clann ic' Phail*, the cells of the Clan MacPhail. One is a complex three-chambered beehive, the other a single cell. The larger cell is similar to a structure on Luchruban, a rock stack near the Butt of Lewis (CANMORE ID 4420). The Luchruban structure, very likely monastic, is eight meters long with a square chamber, an oval chamber, and a small lobby. The Flannan cell is nine metres long, and contains three similar chambers.

Three-chambered cell in 2019—seen from above

Three-chambered cell in 2019—seen from below

Three-chambered cell seen from the west (2003)

Describing the three-chambered structure from east to west, we first have an entrance passage a metre long. The passage leads to a chamber that has been referred to as a 'lobby'. From the lobby, another metre-long passage leads to a square cell, 2.5 metres on each side. This cell has a small hearth and its upper dome is partially intact. From that chamber a 1.5 metre passage leads west to an oval room, 2 by 1.5 metres, with a mostly collapsed corbelled dome. From there a metre-long passage exits the structure at its west end. The central chamber may have been a rectangular oratory, and the western chamber a circular living cell. The dome of the oratory was intact when TS Muir visited in 1859.

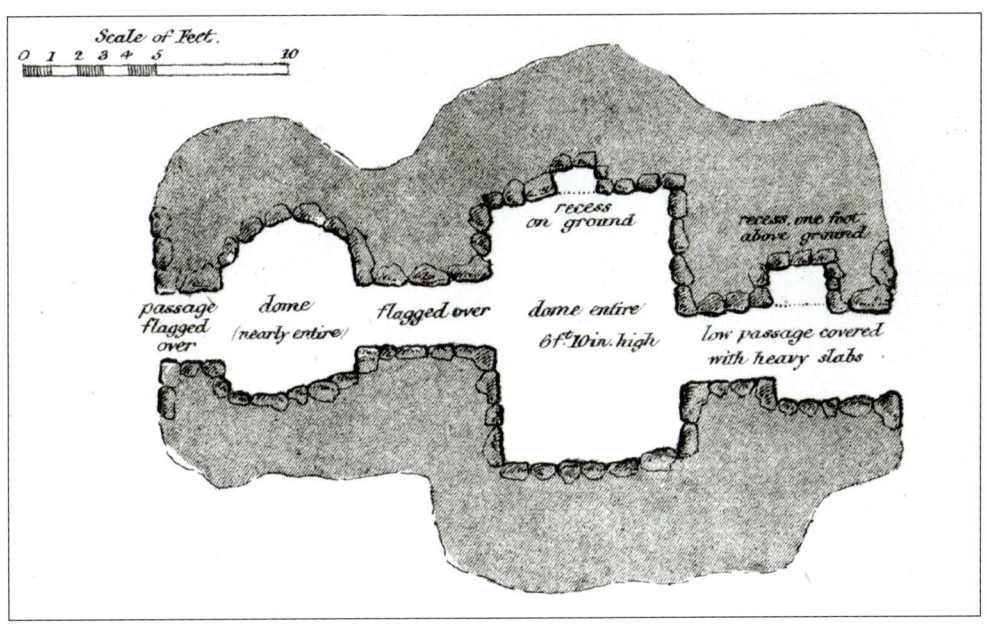

Bothan Chlann 'ic Phail, Eilean Mor, Flannan Isles, T.S. Muir
Proceedings of the Society of Antiquaries of Scotland, Vol. VII (1866-68)

Three-chambered cell seen from the east—2019

Interior view of the eastern chamber (lobby) of the triple cell—2019

The other beehive, a single cell ten metres to the southwest, is two metres by one, portions of its walls a metre high. If you are fortunate to land on the Flannans in late spring or early summer you will encounter hundreds of busy puffins standing atop this cell, bickering and sharing the news of the day. The puffins are the highlight of a visit to the Flannans. This was especially so in July 2019. In my 30 years of travelling to the Hebrides, I have never seen as many puffins at one time. The island was completely covered in burrows, the sky filled with more of these delightfully busy birds than even the Shiants or Lunga.

The single cell seen from the west chamber of the triple cell—2019

The single cell (puffin-less) in 2003—island of Soray in the distance

Puffins on the single cell—2019

The single cell seen from above

The single cell—three chambered cell in the distance (left)

For fresh water the cell dwellers had a small well 100 metres to the southeast. Surrounded by sea pinks it is a delightful spot. But when I last saw it, in 2019, it was sparsely filled with scummy water and puffin pooh.

Looking north from the well to Bothan Chlann 'ic Phail

Our allotted hour ashore flew by, and time came to return to the landing. Going down the steep steps, with no handrail, and the sea directly below, was more exciting than the climb. Especially the final stretch where, with a rope in case, we slid down into the waiting RIB.

Descent to the East Landing

5.5 Eilean Fir Chrothair

Landranger Map: 13
Location: NB 13992 41896
CANMORE ID: 270625
Access: Boat only—the beehive can be seen from the north end of Little Bernera

Eilean Fir Chrothair is not easy to reach. It lies 150 metres off the shore of Little Bernera, so is too far to swim (for me, anyway). A kayak or canoe could get you there, but it would be difficult to land on the rocks that surround the island. Perhaps that's why some monk built a cell there centuries ago. Your best bet is to arrange a charter from Seatrek, which operates out of Miabhaig. But if that's not possible you can get a distant view of the cell from the north end of Little Bernera.

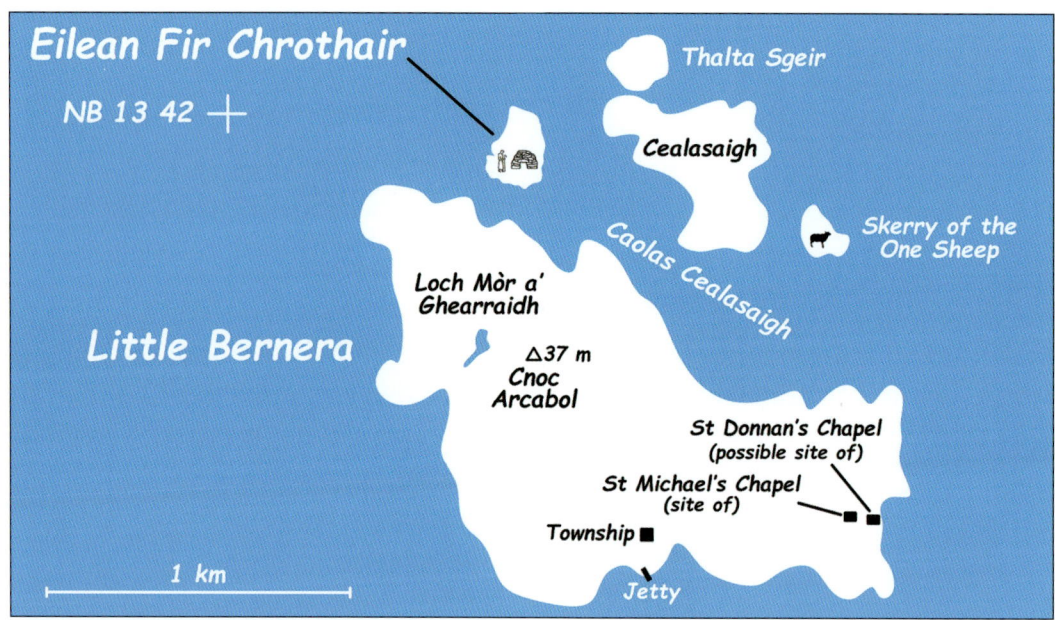

Map 5.5: Eilean Fir Chrothair & Little Bernera

Getting to Little Bernera itself requires a boat trip, but it is worth the effort just to see Little Bernera. There you can linger on white sandy beaches, stroll through hidden meadows of wildflowers, explore the old burial ground of St Donnan's, and climb dozens of rocky knolls, each offering a different view over the isles of Loch Rog. (In summer there are regular day-trips to Little Bernera).

In 2015, wanting to see the cell on Eilean Fir Chrothair, John Randall (former chairman of the Islands Book Trust) and I arranged a charter with Seatrek. From Miabhaig we motored up the west side of Great Bernera. Then a sharp turn to starboard took us past the Bosta Tide Bell and through the enchanting narrows between Little and Great Bernera.

We then rounded the east side of Little Bernera, where we could see the old burial ground above Traigh an Teampull. Once around the north of Little Bernera we slowly approached the rocky shoreline of Eilean Fir Chrothair. Skipper Kenny nosed the RIB into some rocks where John and I could scramble onto the island. Once ashore we both smiled. Adorned by clusters of sea-pinks growing beside its low entrance, the beehive was absolutely beautiful.

The cell on Eilean Fir Chrothair

Looking across to Little Bernera

We took turns crawling into the perfectly intact cell—locally referred to as *An Beannachadh*, the blessing place. It is small, about 1.5 metres in diameter at its base, and would have uncomfortably sheltered one person at most. The cell partially collapsed over a hundred years ago. Since then someone has done a great job of restoration.

Both on Eilean Fir Chrothair, W.M. Mackenzie
Proceedings of the Society of Antiquaries of Scotland, Vol. 38 (1903-04)

Eilean Fir Chrothair—from the same perspective as the PSAS photo

After crawling out of the cell, we spent some time admiring the view over the galaxy of islands in Loch Rog. It's possible that with a lower sea-level some of these islands were once connected. In addition to Little Bernera, with its association to St Donnan, there may have been a monastic settlement on nearby Cealasaigh (Church Island). The CANMORE record for Eilean Fir Chrothair refers to it having a chapel, but during our time on the island we saw no sign of any structure other than the beehive. The cell is too small to have been a chapel, so perhaps it was a place of retreat, a Desert Place in the Sea where a monk could get away from the hustle and bustle of Little Bernera.

The cell—Uig hills in the distance

Looking east to Cealasaigh and Laimisiadair

Parting Words

This has been the story of twenty years of beehive hunting. The hunt continues, as there are over a dozen Hebridean sites I still hope to visit (see Appendix A). The search has been profoundly rewarding—the days and nights spent in remote corners of the Hebrides as memorable as the search itself. Another reward has been the intimate, firsthand knowledge of island terrain gained from hiking in those remote areas.

For example, twenty years ago I thought of the vast interior of Lewis, between Morsgail and the Ardveg, as forbidding, treacherous and, practically speaking, unreachable for the average hiker. It can indeed be forbidding and treacherous. But with good planning, stout equipment, lots of practice at heather-hopping over soggy stretches of bog, and, most important, knowing when to turn back, the remote sites are reachable. But to truly enjoy hiking through this difficult terrain you have to have a purpose. Without that purpose the physical demands, the persistent depredations of thirsty midges, and the overwhelmingly wet terrain tend to discourage most people from venturing out more than once.

There are, of course, purposes other than beehive-bagging that draw us to these remote areas. Be it photography, hoping to capture sunset shadows from the Dibidale cliffs; or wildlife encounters, hoping to spot a golden eagle wheeling high over Loch Reasort. That said, the beehive hunter can also enjoy all the fascinating things this terrain has on offer. Sunsets from the heights of Ardveg. The drumming of elusive snipe. Or the heart-stopping shock of a startled grouse taking sudden flight from thick heather.

Not many venture into these remote areas, which is fine with me. In twenty years of beehive hunting I've only encountered three people: two were estate gillies out doing their jobs, the third a shepherd at the gathering. I don't think any of them would ever think of spending their holidays hiking across bogs and feeding midges, and I'm sure they thought I was crazy to spend mine doing just that.

I hope the journeys presented here will encourage you to explore the land of beehives. If you do, and happen to encounter a solitary figure on the hills of the Hebrides, huffing and puffing his way up a rocky knoll in the middle of nowhere, be sure to say hello. Don't be put-off if he's wet, midge-bitten, and exhausted: telltale signs of a beehive hunter. He may also seem a bit crazy; he's not—well, maybe a little. He just happens to find joy in visiting centuries old relics of a past way of life, relics out there waiting to be appreciated in those Blue Isles, from the Skerries to the Lews, with heather honey taste upon each name.

Appendix A: Cells Unseen

The search goes on. Here are sites unseen (I am sure there are more).

1. Sùlaisgeir, HW 6212 3058, CANMORE ID 1470: Discussed in section 5.2.

2. Luchruban, Lewis, NB 50781 66013, CANMORE ID 4420: On the rock stack of Luchruban, near the Butt of Lewis, is a ruinous structure similar to the Flannan triple cell beehive/oratory. It is an easy walk to see the stack, just head south along the cliffs from the Butt of Lewis lighthouse for a kilometre. I have read of people descending the steep gully to the shore and then climbing the stack, but it looks quite dangerous. Over the years I have been to the cliff-top opposite Luchruban three times, each visit ten years apart. Each time the scary climb deterred me from even trying. A very long ladder, and some rope, would come in handy—a helicopter even handier. Luchruban is also known as the Pygmies Island. The word Luchruban is related to the word leprechaun, and at one time someone reported finding small bones there, hence the legend of pygmies. See the following references for more on Luchruban:

A Desert Place in the Sea: The Early Churches of Northern Lewis (1997), M Robson, Chapter 1 *The RCAHMS Ninth report with inventory of monuments and constructions in the Outer Hebrides,* 9, No. 22, Fig. 37
Notes on the Pigmies Isle, at the Butt of Lewis, with results of the recent exploration of the "Pigmies' Chapel" there, PSAS vol. 39 (1904-5), 248-58

3. Allt na Smuide, Skye, NG 3200 5484, CANMORE ID 71214: Three shieling huts, each with a corbelled cell attached. Sounds very interesting, but I have not had the chance to see it. A four kilometre round-trip walk from Greshornish.

4. Annait, Skye, NG 2721 5272, CANMORE ID 10918: Four cells in a monastic site built atop a fort. It lies along the west bank of the Bay River, a kilometre north of the Fairy Bridge.

5. Cashel Eilean Chalium Chille, Skye, NG 3770 6879, CANMORE ID 11187: On the island of Skye Martin Martin mentions *Several little stone houses, built above ground, capable of only one person, and round in form. One of them is to be seen in Portree, another at Lincro (Eilean Chalium Chille), and at Culuknock (Kilmartin on the northeast side of Trotternish). They are called Tey-nin-druinich, i.e. Druid's House. Druinich signifies a retired person, much devoted to contemplation.* The Portree cell is long-gone, and I know of no cells near Kilmartin, but the cashel ruin in drained Loch Chaluim Chille may reward a visit.

6. Dun Ban, Grimsay, NF 8698 5693, CANMORE ID 10182: Four beehives built onto the walls of an island fort in Loch Hornary reached by a submerged causeway. They were seen by Captain Thomas (see Archeology Scotland, Vol 5 (1890), 401), and are described in Erskine Beveridge's *North Uist* (p.172) as *an agglomeration of beehive cells embedded in a circular tower.* You would need a boat to visit the site, or be willing to swim thirty cold metres.

7. Loch Fada, North Uist, somewhere near NF 863 713, CANMORE ID none: A cell on an island at the west end of Loch Fada. It is described as follows in Beveridge's *North Uist* (pp.154-155): *Hidden amidst the heather is a small oval erection...probably a dwelling or hiding place. The interior of this cell or chamber, at a level apparently half-way up its original height, measures about 54 by 36 inches, disjointly contracting upwards with the rise of the wall into a domed, or beehive form, although its upper half is now lost.* There are several small islands at the west end of Loch Fada. Beveridge does not say which one has the cell.

8. Dun an t-Siamain, North Uist, NF 8859 5949, CANMORE ID 10179: Two cells on an island fort in Loch Dun an t-Siamain. They are described as follows in Beveridge's *North Uist* (p.170): *close to the east edge (of the dun) there seems to be traces of a circular cell measuring 51 inches across. At the north, partly in the thickness of the outer wall, are the remains of another cell which has been dome-shaped, with a base diameter of 4 feet, contracted to 3.5 feet at its present top.* You can get onto the island as the causeway is above water. Loch Dun an t-Siamain is a hard eight kilometre round-trip walk from the road end at Cladach Chairinis at NF 8555 5892.

9. Loch a' Gheadais, North Uist, NF 9135 5938, CANMORE ID 10403: A cell, and the slight signs of a second, in a fort on an island in Loch a' Gheadais. They are described on p.58 of *The RCAHMS Ninth report with inventory of monuments and constructions in the Outer Hebrides* as: *a ruined circular cell, about 5 feet in diameter internally, with a drystone wall about 2 feet thick, which seems to have been of beehive shape; impinging on it to the south is a mass of stone, possibly the remains of a second structure of the same character.* The site is also described on p.170 of Beveridge's *North Uist*. Loch a' Gheadais is an eight kilometre walk from Cladach Chairinis (NF 8555 5892). You would probably have to settle for the view from the shore, as the causeway is mostly submerged.

10. Boreray, St Kilda, NA 15248 05078, CANMORE ID 3968: John Sands, in *Out of this World; or, Life in St Kilda* (1875), reported there were three beehive houses on Boreray occupied by the women who snared birds. Kenneth Williamson and J. Morton Boyd in *A Mosaic of Islands* (1963), mention the circular foundations of beehive bed-chambers, and a beautifully corbelled vault, entirely underground, which appeared to be intact. Getting ashore on Boreray and climbing to the top to see the site would be quite an accomplishment, and beyond the realm of possibility for most of us.

11. Abhainn Lon na Graidhe, North Harris, NB 04335 14557, CANMORE ID 122272: Aerial photos hint at a half-dozen cells. It is about as remote as you can get in the Western Isles. The journey involves a fifteen-kilometer round-trip hike from Amhuinnsuidhe (NB 05266 07825), a hike that also has 500 metres of elevation gain. It might be possible to get there from Huisinis, but I am not sure if you can safely cross the river that flows to the sea from Loch a' Ghlinne.

12. Loch Monica, Rum, NM 3329 9656, CANMORE ID 21927: A linear arrangement of six corbelled structures, one with an intact dome (in a report from 1983). Loch Monica is a kilometre northwest of the Bullough's mausoleum at Harris, on the remote west side of Rum. Unless you can entice a friendly skipper to drop you at Harris, the site would be a long walk across Rum. That in itself would be an amazing day afoot.

13. Uishal, Lewis (north end), NB 26600 41800: I have long neglected looking for cells in the north of Lewis. But one site calls for a visit: Uishal, five kilometres east of Carloway. A photo of a beehive at Uishal appears in a remarkable work entitled *A Swedish Field Trip to the Hebrides in 1934*. The frustrating thing about that photo is that Uishal is a large area, and no specific location for the cell was listed. On my one walk through the area I was unable to find it.

14. Cearascleit Bheag, Lewis, centered at NB 1075 1555, CANMORE ID 133833: Three cells nestled within an oxbow bend of the Kinlochresort River. I walked past this site in 1998. I did not know about it at the time, and was so focused on crossing the mountainous peat hags that I missed the cells by 100 metres. They are mentioned in Leonie Charlton's *Marram* (p.218).

15. Eilean Tighe, Flannans, NA 7288 4635, CANMORE ID 3974: A ruined cell at the apex of a gully that cuts into Eilean Tighe from a small inlet on its west side. Two-hundred feet to the northeast is a stone lined well.

And then there are the lost beehives of Teampull na Trionaid in North Uist (NF 818 604). No one will ever see them, as they were destroyed by subsequent construction on the site. See note 2, p.287, of Beveridge's *North Uist*.

Appendix B: Essentials for overnight beehive excursions

Air mattress/sleeping pad
Bug net and midge repellent
Camera with spare memory card & spare battery (consider taking a spare camera)
Candle
Compass
Fire starter
First aid kit with tick extractor
Flashlight
GPS with spare battery
Maps
Newspaper (for a fire or to dry soggy boots)
Notebook & several pens
Pack rain cover
Gloves
Hat
Knife
Medication (ibuprofen and any prescription medication)
A can of beer (maybe two)
Mobile phone & spare battery
Pillow case (to stuff sweater in for a pillow)
Rain coat
Rain pants
Toiletries
Toothbrush & paste
Hiking poles (don't leave home without them)
Twine/string
Sleeping bag in waterproof container
Soap
Socks (one pair/day)
Strapping (duct) tape for repairs
Sunglasses
Sun hat
Sunscreen
Sweater
Tent and ground cover sheet
Thermal underwear/spare underwear
Washcloth
Water bottle
Water filter
Waterproof matches/lighter
Water shoes (for fording and wearing in camp)
Whistle
It would also be good to take some food.

Most important of all, be sure to file a flight plan with a friend.

Appendix C: References

1 Cnoc Dubh
The Hebrides: A Cultural Backwater, EC Curwen, Antiquity (Sept 1938), 274–275, Fig. 3 & Plate 3
On the Primitive Dwellings and Hypogea of the Outer Hebrides, FWL Thomas, PSAS Vol. 7 (1866), 161 and Fig. 8 of Plate XXXI
Notes on certain Structures of Archaic Type in the Island of Lewis—Beehive Houses, Duns, and Stone Circles, WM Mackenzie, PSAS Vol. 38, 179–182, Figs. 6–8
West Over Sea (1953), DDC Pochin Mould, Chapter XIX, 262-263
Poacher's Pilgrimage (2016), Alastair McIntosh, Chapter 15
RCAHMS Ninth Report with Inventory of Monuments and Constructions in the Outer Hebrides (1928), Fig. 7

2 Southwest Lewis
2.1 Journey to Aird Bheag
2.1.1 Airighean Tighe Dhubhastail
Hebrides: A Cultural Backwater (1938), EC Curwen, 276
A Swedish Field Trip to the Hebrides (1934), Part 1 & Fig. 10
The Past in the Present (1878), Arthur Mitchell, Lecture III, 58–62
On the Primitive Dwellings and Hypogea of the Outer Hebrides, FWL Thomas, PSAS Vol. 7 (1866), 161–162, Fig. 9 of Plate 31
Someone Else's Story (2018), Michael Robson, 24
A Study of Beehive Structures in the Uig Area of the Isle of Lewis (1996), E Logan, Sites 18 & 19

2.1.2 Loch an Ath Ruaidh
Notice of Beehive Houses in Lewis and Harris, FWL Thomas, PSAS Vol. 3 (1859), Plate XI, Figs. 1 & 2 of Ath Ruaidh (5), Fig. 4 of Ath Ruaidh (1)
The Past in the Present, Arthur Mitchell, Lecture 3, 65–66
A Study of Beehive Structures in the Uig Area of the Isle of Lewis (1996), E Logan, Sites 20–25
Ordnance Survey Name Book (1852), Vol. 97, 106-108
Regarding the 'Bothan Ruadha' naming, the OS Name Book from the 1850s (Vol 97, p.106) says "3 shielings in ruins which gives names to several objects adjacent."

2.1.3 Bothan Aird
West Over Sea (1953), DDC Pochin Mould, Chapter 19, Plates 11 & 12
Notice of Beehive Houses in Lewis and Harris, FWL Thomas, PSAS Vol. 3 (1859), 138–139, 143–144, Plate XIII Figs. 1–3 Bothan Aird (1), Figs. 4–6 Bothan Aird (2)
A Study of the Beehive Structures in the Uig Area of the Isle of Lewis (1996), E Logan, Sites 26 & 27

2.1.4 Bothan Ura
West Over Sea (1953), DDC Pochin Mould: Chapter XIX, 264–5
Notice of Beehive Houses in Lewis and Harris, PSAS Vol. 3 (1859), Plate XIII Fig. 7 of Both Ura (1)
A Study of the Beehive Structures in the Uig Area of the Isle of Lewis (1996), E Logan, Sites 28 & 29

2.1.5 Gearraidh Cleit Gruineabhat
West Over Sea, DDC Pochin Mould describes the mill in Chapter XIX

2.1.6 Ceann Chùisil
Lewis -The West Coast in History and Legend (2008), Bill Lawson, 238

2.2 Journey to Fidigidh
2.2.1 Gearraidh Bheinn na Gile
Hebrides: A Cultural backwater, EC Curwen, Antiquity Magazine (Sept 1938), 276 & Fig. 4
Dolly Doctor (2009), The Islands Book Trust, 8 (photo)

2.2.2 Fidigidh Iochdrach
The Past in the Present, Arthur Mitchell: Lecture III, 64
A Swedish Field Trip to the Hebrides—1934, Fig. 6
Notice of Beehive Houses in Lewis and Harris, FWL Thomas, PSAS Vol. 3 (1859), 137–138
& Plate 12
A Study of the Beehive Structures in the Uig Area of the Isle of Lewis (1996), E Logan:
Sites 6 & 14

2.2.3 Both Ruadh
West Over Sea, DDC Pochin Mould, Chapter XIX, 264
A Study of the Beehive Structures in the Uig Area of the Isle of Lewis (1996), E Logan, Site 2

2.2.4 Fidigidh Uachdrach
A Study of the Beehive Structures in the Uig Area of the Isle of Lewis (1996), E Logan, Sites 3–8

2.2.5 Bothan Mileabhat
Walking on Harris and Lewis (2010), Richard Barrett, Walk 20

2.2.6 Both Cleit na Crich
No references found

2.3 Journey to Aird Mhòr
2.3.1 Bothan Loch na Airigh
No references found

2.3.2 Gearraidh na h-Àirde Mhòire
West Over Sea, DDC Pochin Mould, Chapter XIX & Plate XIV
Notice of Beehive Houses in Harris and Lewis, FWL Thomas, PSAS Vol 3 (1859),
139 & Plates XIV, XV & XVI
Afoot in the Hebrides (1950), Seton Gordon, Chapter 19
The Past in the Present, Arthur Mitchell, 1880, Lecture III, 64–65
Hebrides: A Cultural backwater, EC Curwen, *Antiquity* (Sept 1938), 277, Figs. 6–9
A Swedish Field Trip to the Hebrides—1934, (2012), Fenton & Mulhern, Figs. 8a & 8b
A Study of the Beehive Structures in the Uig Area of the Isle of Lewis (1996), E Logan,
Sites 30–33

2.3.3 Màghannan
A Study of Beehive Structures in the Uig Area of the Isle of Lewis (1996), E Logan, Site 13

2.3.4 Loch Tana
A Study of Beehive Structures in the Uig Area of the Isle of Lewis (1996), E Logan, Site 12

2.4 Loch a' Sguair Loop
2.4.1 Tom Ni Bharabhais
Notes on certain Structures of Archaic Type in the Island of Lewis—Beehive Houses, Duns, and Stone Circles, WM Mackenzie, PSAS Vol. 38 (1904), 173–174
The Haunted Isles (1933), Alasdair Alpin Macgregor, Chapter 2 (*The Road to Uig*)

2.4.2 Airigh a' Sguair
Notes on certain Structures of Archaic Type in the Island of Lewis—Beehive Houses, Duns, and Stone Circles, WM Mackenzie, PSAS Vol. 38 (1904), 174–178, Figs. 2–4

2.4.3 Gearraidh Coire Geurad
Notes on certain Structures of Archaic Type in the Island of Lewis, WM Mackenzie, PSAS Vol. 38 (1904), 178 & Fig. 5
RCAHMS Ninth Report with Inventory of Monuments and Constructions in the Outer Hebrides (1928), Fig. 10 (p.xxxviii)

2.4.4 Gleann Marstaig
West Over Sea, DDC Pochin Mould, Chapter XIX, 262
Tales and Traditions of the Lews, Donald Macdonald, Chapter 85
Notes on certain Structures of Archaic Type in the Island of Lewis, WM Mackenzie, PSAS Vol. 38 (1904), 174 and Fig. 1

2.4.5 Airigh Creagan nam Beartan
No references found

2.5 Bo'h Hunting in Morsgail
2.5.1 Gearraidh Ascleit
No references found

2.5.2 Airigh a' Chlàir Mhòir
No references found

2.5.3 Both a' Chlàir Bhig
Poachers Pilgrimage (2016), Alastair McIntosh, Chapter 10

2.6 Beinn a' Bhoth
2.6.1 The Cell of Beinn a' Bhoth
Tales and Traditions of the Lews, Donald Macdonald, Chapter 85

2.6.2 Both Ghriosamul
No references found

3 Harris and North Uist
3.1 Bothan Sròn Smearasmal
Notice of Beehive Houses in Lewis and Harris, FWL Thomas, PSAS Vol. 3 (1859), 127–129, Plate X Figs. 1–6
The Hebrides: A Cultural backwater, EC Curwen, *Antiquity* (Sept 1938), Fig. 5
Someone Else's Story (2017), Michael Robson, 19

3.2 Dun Charaigearaidh
RCAHMS *Ninth Report with Inventory of Monuments and Constructions in the Outer Hebrides, Skye, and the Small Isles* (1928), Site 187
North Uist (1911), Erskine Beveridge, 163–165, photo p.163
West Over Sea (1953), DDC Pochin Mould, Chapter XIX

4 Inner Hebrides
4.1 Eileach an Naoimh - Garvellachs
RCAHMS *Inventory of the Monuments—Argyll, Vol 5* (1984), 174–175
Scotland in Early Christian Times (first series, 1881), Joseph Anderson, 95–101
Ecclesiological Notes on some of the Islands of Scotland (1885), TS Muir, 18–19
Characteristics of Old Church Architecture in the Mainland and Western Islands of Scotland (1861), TS Muir, 137–143
Argyll and the Western Isles (1985), G. Ritchie & M. Harmon, Site 38
Wanderings in the Western Highlands and Islands (1921), MEM Donaldson, Chapter 9
A visit to Eileach an Naoimh, WW Ireland, PSAS Vol. 37, 189 & Fig. 6

4.2 Allt nam Bà - Islay
RCAHMS *Inventory of Monuments Vol. 5, Argyll: Islay, Jura, Colonsay & Oronsay*, Site 131

4.3 Port nan Urrachann - Scarba
Netherlorn, Argyllshire and its Neighbourhood (1909), Patrick Gillies, Chapter VII

4.4 Gleann Chàràdail - Eigg
The Small Isles (2001), Denis Rixson, 37–41
The Small Isles (2016), John Hunter, 138
Wanderings in the Western Highlands and Islands (1921), MEM Donaldson, 249

4.5 Sgòrr nam Bàn-naomha - Canna
The Western Seaboard (2006), Mary Miers, 160–161
Canna: The Story of a Hebridean Island (1984), JL Campbell, 5–7
The Small Isles (2001), Denis Rixson, 31–33
The Small Isles (2016), John Hunter, 68–72

Notice of an ancient Structure called 'The Altar' in the Island of Canna, JE Somerville, PSAS Vol. 33 (1899), 133–140

RCAHMS Ninth Report with Inventory of Monuments and Constructions in the Outer Hebrides, Skye, and the Small Isles (1928), Site 679

5 Remote Outliers
5.1 Rona
Ronay (1933), Malcolm Stewart
Rona–The Distant Island (1991), Michael Robson
A Desert Place in the Sea: The Early Churches of Northern Lewis, M Robson, Chapter 3
Island Years (1940), Fraser Darling
A Naturalist on Rona: Essays of a Biologist in Isolation (1939), Fraser Darling
Island Going (1949), Robert Atkinson
A Survey of the Antiquities of North Rona (1960), HC Nisbet & RA Gailey
Island Memories (1923), JW Dougal, Chapter 8
Ecclesiological Notes on some of the Islands of Scotland (1885), TS Muir, 80–96
Characteristics of Old Church Architecture (1861), TS Muir, 189–200
Descriptions and Plans of Primitive Chapels in Rona and Sula Sgeir, FWL Thomas and TS Muir, Archeology Scotland, Vol. 5 (1890), 245–247

5.2 Sùlaisgeir
A Desert Place in the Sea: The Early Churches of Northern Lewis, M Robson, Chapter 4
Island Going (1949), Robert Atkinson, Chapters 23–26
Ronay (1933), Malcolm Stewart
Ecclesiological Notes on some of the Islands of Scotland (1885), TS Muir, 96–99
Descriptions and Plans of Primitive Chapels in Rona and Sula Sgeir, FWL Thomas and TS Muir, Archeology Scotland, Vol. 5 (1890), 247–248
Characteristics of Old Church Architecture in the Mainland and Western Islands of Scotland (1861), TS Muir, 205–206
Island Memories (1923), JW Dougal, Chapter 9

5.3 St Kilda
St Kilda and other Hebridean Outliers, Francis Thompson (1970), 101
With Nature and a Camera, Richard & Cherry Kearton (1897), 82–83
An Isle called Hirte: History and Culture of St Kilda to 1930, M Harmon (1997), 147–148, 233
The Antiquities of the St Kilda Group of Islands, J Mathieson, PSAS Vol. 62, 126–7 & Figs. 4,5
A Last Voyage to St Kilda, AA Macgregor (1931), 198
St Kilda Summer, Williamson and Boyd (1960), 59
St Kilda: The Last and Outmost Isle, Gannon and Geddes (2015), 58
Calum Mor's House–Conservation Statement (2011), National Trust for Scotland
Cruises to St Kilda from Oban: Northern Light Cruising Company (www.northernlight-uk.com)

5.4 Flannan Isles

Tales and Traditions of The Lews, Donald MacDonald (2000), Chapter 86
Ecclesiological Notes on some of the Islands of Scotland, TS Muir (1885), 59–60
Ronay, Malcolm Stewart (1933), 48–65
Irish Pilgrimages, DDC Pochin Mould (1955), 25
Pilgrimage in Ireland: The Monuments and People, Peter Harbison (1991), 82 (evolution of the beehive oratory)
RCAHMS Ninth Report with Inventory of Monuments and Constructions in the Outer Hebrides (1928), Items 105 & 106
On the Primitive Dwellings and Hypogea of the Outer Hebrides, FWL Thomas, PSAS Vol. 7 (1866), 163 & Fig. 13 of appendix

5.5 Eilean Fir Chrothair

Tales and Traditions of the Lews, Donald Macdonald, Chapter 85
Notes on certain Structures of Archaic Type in the Island of Lewis —Beehive Houses, Duns, and Stone Circles, WM Mackenzie, PSAS Vol. 38 (1904), 182–183 & Fig. 9

Index

Aird Bheag, 15, 22-24
Airigh a' Chlàir Mhòir, 151, 161-165
Airidh a' Loch Thaine, 125-127
Airigh a' Sguair, 130-139
Airigh Creagan nam Beartan, 149, 150
Airighean an Fhorsa, 16, 127
Allt nam Bà (Islay), 198-203
Beinn a' Bhoth, 161, 173-177
Beveridge, Erskine, 182, 187, 189, 190, 250-252
Both a' Chlàir Bhig, 7, 165-170
Both a' Ghriosamul, 63, 161, 177-179
Both Cleit na Crich, 2, 101-103
Both Ruadh, 22, 69, 83, 85-87, 120, 121
Bothan Aird, 39-47, 58, 95, 108, 119, 152, 175
Bothan Chlann 'ic Phail (Flannans), 234, 235, 237-243
Bothan Mileabhat, 97-100
Bothan Ruadha, 26, 27, 29, 31, 254
Bothan Sròn Smearasmal (Harris), 182-186
Bothan Ura, 47-51
Calum Mòr's House (St Kilda), 11, 232-234
Canna, 192, 204, 209, 212-216
Ceann Chùisil, 56, 57, 70
Clàr Beag, 6, 7, 166-170
Clàr Mòr, 7, 162-165
Cnoc Dubh, 8-12
Crolà, 105, 165, 170, 171
Dun Charaigearaidh (North Uist), 182, 187-191
Eigg, 192, 207-211
Eileach an Naoimh (Garvellachs), 6, 193-197, 218
Eilean Fir Chrothair, 244-247
Elizabeth G, 205
Fianais (Rona), 217, 225, 226
Fidigidh Iochdrach, 69, 70, 80-84, 120
Fidigidh Uachdrach, 69, 83, 87-95
Flannan Isles, 217, 220, 234-243

Gearraidh Aineabhal, 47, 58-68, 177
Gearraidh Ascleit, 150, 152-158, 173
Gearraidh Bheinn na Gile, 71-73, 171
Gearraidh Cleit Gruineabhat, 47, 51-55
Gearraidh Coire Geurad (Choirigerod), 139, 140-147, 152
Gearraidh Druim Lomhainn, 159, 160
Gearraidh na h-Àirde Mhòire, 104, 105, 107-118
Gearraidh Uidh Phàil, 75-79
Gleann Chàràdail (Eigg), 207-211
Gleann Marstaig, 147, 148
Harris, 2-4, 8, 183-186, 251
Hjalmar Bjørge, 190, 219, 232, 235
Islay, 2, 192, 198-203
Kinlochresort, 17, 71, 73, 104, 105, 170, 171
Little Bernera, 244-247
Loch an Ath Ruaidh, 25-39, 107, 108, 119, 140
Loch na h-Airigh, 106, 107
Loch nan Learga (meteorite), 180, 181
Mackenzie, William, 128, 129, 132, 135, 140, 142, 147, 148, 246
Màghannan, 22, 121-124
Mitchell, Arthur, 3, 4, 7, 17
Muir, TS, 196, 229, 238, 239
North Uist, 3, 182, 187-191, 251
Pochin Mould, DDC, 5, 6, 39, 48, 85, 96, 111, 114, 218
Port nan Urrachann (Scarba), 204-207
Postman's Stones (Lewis), 73, 74, 104, 105, 171, 181
Rona, 2-4, 217-228, 230
Scarba, 192, 194, 204-207
Sgòrr nam Bàn-naomha (Canna), 192, 209, 212-216
Skellig Michael, 2, 5, 220
St Kilda, 3, 11, 190, 217, 232-234, 251
St Ronan's Cell (Rona), 63, 177, 217-224, 227
Sùlaisgeir, 217, 224, 226-231
Teampull Beannachadh (Flannans), 235-237
Thomas, Captian FWL, 3, 4, 10, 11, 17, 18, 20, 22, 27, 34-36, 40, 46, 48, 49, 70, 83, 114, 117, 118, 127, 128, 182, 183, 185, 250
Tighe Dhubhastail, 4, 16-22, 127, 130
Tom Ni Bharabhais, 13, 128-130, 151